D0429169

RA

ALSO BY MARY BUFFETT AND DAVID CLARK

Buffettology

The Buffettology Workbook

THE NEW BUFFETTOLOGY

The Proven Techniques for Investing Successfully in Changing Markets That Have Made WARREN BUFFETT the World's Most Famous Investor

MARY BUFFETT AND DAVID CLARK

Rawson Associates

Rawson Associates
SCRIBNER
1230 Avenue of the Americas
New York, NY 10020

For information regarding special discounts for bulk purchases,
please contact Simon & Schuster Special Sales at 1-800-456-6798 or
business@simonandschuster.com

Set in New Baskerville

Manufactured in the United States of America

10

Library of Congress Cataloging-in-Publication Data
Buffett, Mary.
The new Buffettology : the proven techniques for investing
successfully in changing markets that have made Warren Buffett the
world's most famous investor / Mary Buffett and David Clark.
p. cm.
Includes index.
1. Investments. 2. Buffett, Warren. I. Clark, David, 1955– . II. Title.

HG4521.B7692 2002
332.6—dc21 2002068110

ISBN 0-684-87174-2

Pluralitas non est ponenda sine neccesitate.

This book is dedicated to Charlie Munger and Billy Occam, who gave, respectively, to investing and science the idea that the simplest explanation is usually the best.

ACKNOWLEDGMENTS

We wish to thank first and foremost Warren Buffett; although he did not participate in the writing of this book, we are forever indebted to him for his wisdom and generosity over the years. His genius as an investor will someday be overshadowed by his tremendous philanthropy. The Buffett Foundation, the final repository for the masterpiece he calls Berkshire Hathaway, will ultimately be the world's wealthiest charitable foundation, providing future generations with the benefits of his earthly passion for investing.

We also wish to thank our publisher, Eleanor Rawson, for her inspiration and guidance. She is the best of her breed and we would be lost without her. We also would like to thank our editor, Lisa Considine, whose pen kept ours straight and true. She is a credit to her craft. And a special thank you to our assistant editor, Anne Bartholomew, and our amazing copy editor, Steve Boldt. We would also like to thank Simon & Schuster attorneys Jennifer Weidman and Emily Remes for their skillful guidance. These people are solid proof that the staff at Simon & Schuster is the best in the business.

We owe an enormous debt of gratitude to: Sam, for being Mary's knight in shining armor. To Erica and Nicol, for being wise beyond their years and two of the best daughters a mother could ever ask for. To the girls' father, Peter Buffett, for the wonderful years that we had together. To the magical and mystical Sabrina Benson, who, with a simple wave of her wand and a phone call, makes the impossible happen. To Kitty O'Keefe and Shih'hua Liu, for their friendship and brilliance. To Patti, for her love and support. To Cindy Connolly Cates, who suffered through our earlier drafts and who remains always the silent third author. We could not and would not write without her. To Ben Platt, for helping us burn out the demons after a hard day's night. To Jessica Schemm, for playing the enchanting muse. To Eric Hoffman, for being the best poet and proofreader that any author could ask for.

To Gerry Spence, John Johnson, and Robert Rose, for their words of encouragement when they were much needed. To Tim Vick, the most intellectually honest man on Wall Street, for his insight and thoughts. To Pauline Macardican, for being an angel in disguise. To Fritz Perlberg and Rob Gritze, for their friendship and wisdom. To Valerie Schadt, for being everything that counts. To Roger Lowenstein, the best writer on Wall Street, for his reflections on Warren and Berkshire Hathaway. To Andy Kilpatrick, for being the consummate Berkshire historian and a charming Southern gentleman. To Andy Clark, for the historical research. To Vincent Waldman at Manatt, Phelps & Phillips, for making the deal happen. To Terry Rosenberg, for his creative spirit. To Robert E., for his constant friendship and support through the most trying of times. And most important, to the beautiful Kate Benecke for her love.

CONTENTS

DISCLAIMER

FOREWORD

A FEW PERSONAL THINGS ABOUT A VERY PRIVATE BILLIONAIRE

In the annals of investment history the name Warren Buffett towers above all others. He turned an initial stake of $105,000 into a $30 billion fortune, by investing in the stock market. This is an unparalleled feat. Who is this man and what is his obsession with getting and staying rich?

Warren was conceived during the stock market crash of 1929, which nearly bankrupted his father's investment firm. Like so many children who grew up in a family financially strapped by the Depression, Warren developed an early fixation on money. As a child his favorite toy was a money changer. He carried it everywhere. He was consumed by mathematical calculations about the compounding of dollars. At six, he entered into his first business operation by buying bottles of Coca-Cola, six for a quarter, and selling them for five cents apiece to fellow vacationers at Lake Okoboji, Iowa. He memorized the book *A Thousand Ways to Make $1,000* and began saving most of what he made delivering the *Washington Post* and running a pinball business. Warren was so desperate to make money that in 1938, in the sweltering summer heat of Nebraska, he walked miles to the racetrack where he spent hours on his hands and knees scouring the sawdust-covered floors for discarded racing stubs, hoping to find a winning ticket.

Warren made his first stock market investment at eleven (three shares of Cities Service), and by the time he had graduated from high school, at seventeen, he had amassed the princely sum of $6,000. He made it through college in three years and then applied to MBA programs at both Harvard and Columbia. Harvard said no. Columbia said yes.

Everyone has a defining moment in youth that sets the course for adulthood. For Warren this happened at Columbia during a class taught by the legendary dean of value investing, Benjamin Graham. Warren and Graham had an instant intellectual rapport. "Sparks were flying," recalls classmate Bill Ruane, now head of the Sequoia Fund. "You could tell then that Warren was someone who was unusual." As if Graham had lifted a shroud from his eyes, Warren suddenly saw a way to make the money he had dreamed of as a child. Graham would be his guiding light.

After graduating, Warren tried to talk his former teacher into hiring him as an entry-level investment analyst at his Wall Street investment firm. Graham said no. Warren, who had learned well the theory of value investing, responded by offering to work for free. Graham contended that even at that bargain price Warren had overvalued his talents. Warren, however, continued to pester the master and eventually Graham relented and hired him.

Warren worked for the firm until Graham's retirement in 1956. Then, homesick for his beloved Nebraska, Warren returned to Omaha, where he beat the pavement trying to raise money to form an investment partnership similar to Graham's. Hounding everyone he knew for money, he gave lectures to investment clubs and even knocked on neighbors' doors. He finally convinced eight people that he was worth gambling on. With $105,000 of their money, as well as his own, Warren founded Buffett Partnership. Over the next thirteen years, the partnership produced a 30% average annual compounding return. As Warren's reputation as an investor grew, so did his desire to raise even more money to manage. He would often give potential investors a copy of the partnership's tax return to show how much he was making his backers. With 100% of his own wealth invested in the partnership, Warren "ate his own cooking," as he said. He didn't do anything with his investors' money that he wasn't willing to do with his own.

By 1969, however, Warren discovered that the raging bull market of the late sixties had produced a vastly overbought, and thus overpriced, stock market. He also saw that in this environment it was impossible to practice the value-oriented investment style that was working so well for him and his partners. Perceiving this, he did something quite unorthodox. Warren informed his partners that because of the overpriced stock market he could not maintain the stellar results he had been providing, and instead of adopting a new investment strategy with which he was uncomfortable, he was closing down the partnership and returning their money. In liquidating the investment partnership Warren gave his investors the option of either cash or shares in the companies in which the partnership held an interest.

One business in which the partnership held a controlling interest was the publically traded textile company Berkshire Hathaway. The partnership had acquired a majority interest in Berkshire in 1967. Once the partnership had control, Warren commandeered Berkshire's working capital to buy the first of many insurance companies it was to acquire over the next thirty years. After liquidating the partnership in 1969, Warren slyly bought up his partners' shares in Berkshire, which totaled 27% of the company, then continued to buy more shares on the open market until he personally controlled the company.

Warren wanted this for two reasons. The first was that Berkshire was acquiring insurance companies, which Warren knew would provide him with a pool of money called an investment float—this pool of capital is created by insurance premiums paid into an insurance company. The second reason was taxes. At that time personal income tax rates were much higher than corporate tax rates. By using an insurance company as an investment vehicle, Warren could take advantage of lower corporate tax rates, thus making it easier to accumulate capital. The insurance company also provided him with a method to avoid the little known "accumulated earnings tax," which was designed to keep people like Warren from hiding from high personal income tax rates by using a corporation as an investment vehicle. Insurance companies are one of the few business operations that are exempt from this tax.

With control of Berkshire's investment float and protection from high personal income tax rates, Warren used his investment knowledge to grow Berkshire assets and his net worth unhindered by traditional constraints. Because of his stunning performance investing his company's assets, Berkshire has over the last thirty years seen its book value grow at an average annual rate of 23%, from $19 a share to more than $40,000, and its stock market price increase at an average annual growth rate of 29%, from $13 a share to approximately $70,000.

Warren Buffett's initial investment in Berkshire Hathaway has grown from approximately $7 million to more than $30 billion. He created this wealth solely through his superior ability to make investment decisions and with his clever use of an insurance company as an investment vehicle. In addition to making him one of the richest people in the world, this also makes him the single greatest investor of all time.

INTRODUCTION

HOW WARREN BUFFETT TURNED $105,000 INTO $30 BILLION

The New Buffettology is the first comprehensive, fully updated, in-depth guide to Warren Buffett's *selective contrarian investment strategy* for exploiting bear markets and down stocks, a strategy that has made him the second-richest person on earth. It is the first book to discuss the new direction that this philosophy has taken him, with investments in such companies as H&R Block, Bristol-Myers Squibb, Mueller Industries, Furniture Brands International, Justin Industries, Yum Brands, Johns Manville, Shaw Industries, Liz Claiborne, Nike Inc., Dun & Bradstreet Corp., USG Corp., First Data Corp., HRPT Properties Trust, First Realty Trust, Aegis Realty, and JDN Realty. *The New Buffettology* is also the first book to explain how Buffett became legendary for taking advantage of bad situations and down markets and how he learned to achieve unheard-of profits with almost zero risk of losing his capital. It is the only book to explain how Buffett uses a *selective contrarian* investment strategy to make billions, and it is the only book to show readers the mathematical equations that the master uses to determine what to invest in. It is the first book to point out that Warren is only interested in companies that have what he calls a *durable competitive advantage* working in their favor. Also the question of when and why Warren Buffett sells a stock, something that other writers have missed, will finally be addressed in full. We include a full discussion of how, at the height of the bull market, he engineered the tax-free sale of 17% of his interest in Coca-Cola, at the outlandish price of 167 times Coke's 1998 earnings. Last, but not least, it is the first book to fully integrate Buffett's investment methods with the powerful investment research tools that the Internet now offers to individual investors.

The days in which only the superrich had access to privileged financial knowledge has given way to the new Internet-empowered era, in which individual investors have access to unparalleled information resources that rival those of Wall Street's leading investment houses. The Internet has taken the arcane world of finance and made it accessible to virtually everyone, ushering in a new kind of investment democracy that opens the door for the average investor to produce the results formally available only to insiders. No one elite group now has a monopoly on financial information. The playing field has been leveled with just a few clicks of a mouse.

Though the medium for delivery, the Internet, may be new, the problem of interpreting the information remains. How does one go about turning newfound data access into bankable gold? *The New Buffettology* is designed to teach you *how to decipher and use financial information as if you yourself were Warren Buffett,* the world's greatest and richest investor. Think of this book as a software program for your mind. We will program you to think and invest like Buffett does. A rewarding prospect!

To facilitate the programming, we have developed a step-by-step approach for teaching you Buffett's methodology. These steps teach you specific aspects of his investment strategy and how you can use it to grow your wealth—even in a troubled market. We'll take you through the methodology and financial equations that Warren uses, not only to determine *what* companies in which to invest, but *when* to invest in them. Finally *we will teach you how Warren determines when to sell an investment.*

Simply understanding the types of companies that interest Warren is not enough. You also have to know how to determine the right price to pay. Pay too high a price and it doesn't matter how great an economic engine the company has working for you. Your investment return is forever moored to poor results. Pay a low enough price for the right business and the riches you earn could win you a coveted place on the cover of *Forbes.*

Warren likes to think of himself as a business analyst, not a securities analyst, so we'll show you how he distinguishes an excellent business from a mediocre one. The first part of this book focuses on the qualitative side of the equation. This is where you will learn how Warren identifies the power and quality of a company's long-term economics. This is also where you come to understand that Warren is only interested in a certain kind of company, and then only when its stock price has dropped to *the right* low point to make it a good acquisition. We will teach you how Warren determines the soundness of a company's economic machinery: Can it weather and emerge from the storm that sank the company's stock price in the first place? You will learn that Warren's genius lies in his ability to grasp the long-term economic worth of a handful of great businesses and perceive how and when they are sometimes oversold by the stock market—making them bargain buys. You will learn how he turns this knowledge into huge profits.

The second part of the book is quantitative. This is where you will learn the mathematical equations that Warren uses to determine whether a business that has suffered a downturn is selling at a sufficiently low price to make, as Warren calls it, "business sense" to buy in. We will teach you the calculations he uses and how he interprets the numbers. Warren will only invest in a company when he can get it at a low enough price—which he determines by projecting an annual compounding rate of return for the investment. This projected rate of return is determined with a series of calculations that we will teach you. In this part of the book we will show you where to find, and how to use, financial information off the Internet.

To facilitate the number crunching, we incorporate into the book the use of a Texas Instruments BA-35 Solar financial calculator. Thirty years ago these marvelous little wonders didn't exist, but thanks to the brilliance of Texas Instruments, a world that once belonged exclusively to Wall Street analysts is now accessible and understandable to anyone. So, if you are apprehensive about math, don't be—we've got you covered. In no time at all you'll be making financial projections like the man himself.

We have also included several case studies incorporating Buffett's most recent investments and have included a special investment template that you can use to follow his methodology. This will enable you to work through a set of specific questions and calculations to help you obtain Warren's unique perspective.

In Chapter 16, in addition to showing you Warren's most recent investments, we also give you the names of his historical investments that, over the last thirty years, have earned him billions. A list worth keeping an eye on.

Those of you who have read the original *Buffettology* will find *The New Buffettology* provides a very different, but equally enlightening, perspective on Warren Buffett's investment methods. We have included and updated the original *Buffettology* case studies to help you determine whether Warren's past analysis was on the money. (It was and still is.) We also explore in detail how Internet trading has made Warren's brand of stock arbitrage—a game once played only by giants—a lucrative venture for even the smallest of investors. While *Buffettology* focused on Warren's use of *business perspective investing, The New Buffettology* takes an in-depth look at how Warren uses the stock market's pessimistic shortsightedness as a catalyst for investing in some of the great businesses of our time at bargain prices relative to their long-term economic worth.

The foundation of this book is Warren's writings, lectures, interviews, and conversations. Though both of us have in the past had access to the master investor, he was not involved in the writing of this book. As such, we were free to open as many doors as we thought necessary to teach you his style of selective contrarian investing. We not only delve into stocks that have been reported as official Buffett holdings, but we also explore his rumored purchases that we feel fit his pattern of investing. We want you to have it all, even the bits others might have left out.

You should know that the buying and selling dates of his official stock purchases are approximations based on SEC documents. Warren is known to make quick buys of millions of shares in a couple of days and to instigate buying programs that take weeks to complete. Selling occurs in the same manner. Thus, the exact dates are impossible to pinpoint. All the stock prices reported are current through February 2002, unless we tell you otherwise.

We felt that in order to drive home the concepts behind Buffett's selective contrarian investment style, it would be advantageous to ignore the effects of taxation and inflation. In *Buffettology*, we explored the tremendous impact that taxation and inflation had on Warren's investment style. To repeat those concepts would be redundant and only cloud the important principles we are presenting here for the first time.

You should understand that though Warren's investment methods are fairly simple to grasp, many of them go against basic human intuition and Wall Street wisdom. They are easy to learn, but implementing them can be difficult when the rest of the world seems to be selling when you are about to buy. Those of you who do come to understand Warren's selective contrarian investment philosophy and develop the ability to implement it will discover an endless stream of wealth, the kind of wealth that can make *you* one of the richest people in the world.

So grab your calculator, sharpen up a pencil or two, find a clean piece of paper, and start downloading Warren Buffett's billionaire brilliance for making money in the stock market!

Mary Buffett and David Clark
March 2002

1

The Answer to Why Warren Doesn't Play the Stock Market—and How Not Doing So Has Made Him America's Number One Investor

A fool does not see the same tree that a wise man sees.
—William Blake

Before we bust out of the gate you need to know something important about Warren Buffett. He doesn't "play" the stock market—at least not in the conventional sense of the word. He is not interested in current investment trends, and he avoids the popular investments of the day. He doesn't chart stock prices, nor does he partake of the current Wall Street rage known as momentum investing, which dictates that a stock is attractive if its price is rising fast, and unattractive if it is quickly falling. This is the most unusual aspect of his investment philosophy, for throughout his investing life he has made it a point to sidestep every investment mania to sweep the financial world. He happily admits to missing the Internet revolution and the biotech bonanza, and he will tell you with a sly smile and a wily chuckle that he has probably missed all of the big Wall Street plays. Then again, he has managed to turn an initial investment of $105,000 into a fortune that now exceeds $30 billion, solely by investing in the stock market.

Here is the big secret: *Warren Buffett got superrich not by playing the stock market but by playing the people and institutions who play the stock market.* Warren is the ultimate exploiter of the foolishness that results from other investors' pessimism and shortsightedness.

You see, most people and financial institutions (like mutual funds) play the stock market in search of quick profits. They want the fast buck, the easy dollar, and as a result they have developed investment methods and philosophies that are controlled by shortsightedness. Warren believes that acts of shortsightedness have great potential to unfold into investment foolishness of huge proportions. When this happens, Warren is patiently waiting with Berkshire's billions, ready to buy into select companies that most people and mutual funds are desperately trying to sell. He can buy fearlessly because he knows which of today's corporate pariahs the stock market will covet tomorrow.

Warren is able to do this better than anyone else because he has discovered two things that few investors appreciate. The first is that approximately 95% of the people and investment institutions that make up the stock market are what he calls "short-term motivated." This means that these investors respond to short-term stimuli. On any given day they buy on good news and sell on bad, regardless of a company's long-term economics. It's classic herd mentality driven by the sort of reporting you'll find in the *Wall Street Journal* on any given morning. As goofy as it sounds, it is the way most people and mutual fund managers invest. The good news—the news that gets them to buy—can be a headline announcing a prospective buyout or a quarterly increase in earnings or a quickly rising stock price. (It may seem insane that people and mutual fund managers would be enthusiastic about a company's shares simply because they are rising in price, but remember, "momentum investing" is the current rage. As we have said, Warren is not a momentum investor. He considers the approach sheer insanity.)

The bad news that gets these investors to sell can be anything from a major industry recession to missing a quarterly earnings projection by a few cents or a war in the Middle East. Remember that the popular Wall Street investment fad of momentum investing dictates if a stock price is falling, the investor should sell. This means that if stock prices are falling, many mutual funds jump on the bandwagon and start selling just because everyone else is. Like we said, Warren thinks this is madness. On the other hand, it's the kind of madness that creates the best opportunities.

Warren has realized that an enthusiastic stock price—one that has recently been going up—when coupled with good news about a company, is often enough to push the price of a company's shares into the stratosphere. This is commonly referred to as the "good news phenomenon." He has also seen the opposite happen when the situation is reversed. A pessimistic stock price—one that has been going down—when coupled with negative news about a company, will send its stock into a tailspin. This is, of course, the "bad news phenomenon."

Warren has discovered that in both situations the underlying long-term economics of the company's business is often totally ignored. The short-term mentality of the stock market sometimes grossly *overvalues* a company, just as it sometimes grossly *undervalues* a company.

The second foundation of Warren's success lies in his understanding that, over time, it is the real long-term economic value of a business that ultimately levels the playing field and properly values a company. Warren has found that overvalued businesses are eventually revalued downward, thus making their shareholders poorer. This means that any popular investment of its day can often end up in the dumps, costing its shareholders their fortunes rather than earning them a bundle. The bursting of the dotcom bubble is the perfect example of this popular here-today, gone-tomorrow scenario.

Warren came to realize that undervalued businesses with strong long-term economics are eventually revalued upward, making their shareholders richer. This means that today's stock market undesirable can turn out to be tomorrow's shining star. A perfect example of this phenomenon is when the insurance industry suffered a recession in 2000 that halved insurance stock prices. During this recession Allstate, the auto insurance giant, was trading at $19 a share and Berkshire Hathaway, Warren's company, traded as low as $40,800 a share. One year later Allstate was trading close to $40 a share and Berkshire popped up to $70,000, giving investors who bought these stocks during the recession quick one-year returns of 75% or better.

What has made Warren superrich is his genius for seeing that the short-term market mentality that dominates the stock market periodically grossly undervalues *great businesses.* He has figured out that the stock market will sometimes overreact to bad news about a great business and oversell its stock, making it a bargain from a long-term economic point of view. (Remember, as we said earlier, the vast majority of people and institutions like mutual funds sell shares on bad news.) When this happens, Warren goes into the market and buys as many shares as he can, knowing that over time the long-term economics of the business will eventually correct the negative situation and return the stock's price to more profitable ground.

The stock market buys on good news and sells on bad. Warren buys on bad news. This is why he made sure to miss the good-news bull markets in such popular industries as the Internet, computers, biotechnology, cellular telephones, and dozens of others that have seduced investors through the years with promises of riches. He shops when the stocks are unpopular and the prices are cheap—when short-term gloom and doom fog Wall Street's eyes from seeing the real long-term economic value of great businesses.

Key Point ➢ Speculating in good-news bull markets is something that Warren leaves to the other guys. It's not his game. He never owned stock in Yahoo!, Priceline, Amazon.com, Lucent, CMGI, or any of the other high-tech companies of the Internet boom. Warren's game is to avoid the popular, to wait for short-term bad news to drive down the price of a fantastic business, then jump on it, buying as many shares as possible. As Warren once said, "The most common cause of low stock prices is pessimism—sometimes widespread, sometimes specific to a company or industry. . . . We [Berkshire Hathaway] like pessimism because of the stock prices it produces." Pessimism, not optimism, is the fountain that produced all of Warren's fantastic wealth.

WHAT YOU SHOULD HAVE LEARNED FROM THIS CHAPTER

- ✦ Warren is not interested in popular investments of the day.
- ✦ Warren has discovered that the vast majority of stock market investors, including mutual funds, are short-term oriented; they buy on good news and sell on bad.

- The short-term stock market mentality sometimes grossly undervalues the long- term prospects of a great business.
- Warren likes to buy on bad news.
- Warren's genius lies in his ability to grasp other people's ignorance about the long-term economic worth of certain businesses.

2

How Warren Makes Good Profits Out of Bad News About a Company

"You know Wall Street," Warren tried to reassure me. "People don't think in a long-term way there."
—*Personal History,* Katharine Graham

Warren practices a *selective contrarian investment strategy.* A contrarian investment strategy is one in which the investor is motivated to invest by a falling stock price. Contrarian investors invest in what other investors find unattractive, thereby ensuring a low price, which will hopefully equate to huge profits once the company's fortunes, and stock price, recover. Warren believes that just because a company's stock price is in the dumps is not in itself reason enough to invest in a company. He is interested *only* when the company has exceptional business economics working in its favor *and* a contrarian stock price. He has found that attractive pricing of these exceptional companies is the result of the stock market's pessimistic shortsightedness. His basic investment philosophy is contrarian in nature, with the caveat that the companies be exceptional businesses that possess what he calls a *durable competitive advantage,* a topic we shall explore in greater detail later on. Warren's philosophy requires the investor to go against the basic human instinct to make a quick buck. It also requires that the investor have loaded into his or her brain the software that will help determine what a company with great economics working in its favor looks like *and* when it is selling at an attractive price.

CONTRARIAN INVESTMENT STRATEGY VERSUS SELECTIVE CONTRARIAN INVESTMENT STRATEGY

In a *contrarian investment strategy,* the investor buys stocks that have recently performed poorly and have fallen out of favor with investors. This strategy is based on the stock research of Eugene Fama and Kenneth French, who figured out that buying companies that have had their stock prices beaten down in the two previous years are likely to give investors an above-average return over the next two years. This strategy focuses on falling stock prices and pays little mind to the underlying economics of the companies. With the traditional contrarian investment strategy investors don't discriminate between price-competitive-type businesses and companies that possess a durable competitive advantage. So long as the share price has recently fallen, the stock is a candidate for purchase.

A *selective contrarian investment strategy*—Warren's approach—dictates that investors buy shares only when a company has a durable competitive advantage, and only when its stock price has been beaten down by a shortsighted market, to the extent that it makes business sense to purchase the entire company. This strategy differs from the traditional contrarian investment strategy in that it targets specific companies that have an identifiable durable competitive advantage over their competitors and are selling at a price that a private business owner would find attractive. (Don't worry if this is cloudy. We'll fill in the blanks later on.)

Key Point ➢ To be like Warren one has to know what to buy and when to buy it. What to buy? An exceptional business with a *durable competitive advantage* working in its favor. When? When the stock market's pessimistic shortsightedness has driven the price of its shares into the dumps.

Pessimistic shortsightedness and the bad-news phenomenon are what create Warren's buying opportunities. If the vast majority of the stock market did not suffer from occasional pessimistic shortsightedness, Warren Buffett would never have had the opportunity to buy some of the world's greatest businesses at discount prices. He could never have made his 2000 purchase of 8% of H&R Block for approximately $28 a share or the much discussed 1974 purchase of 1.7 million shares of the Washington Post Company for approximately $6.14 a share. H&R Block now trades at approximately $60 a share and the Post now trades at approximately $500 a share. His pretax rate of return on his H&R Block purchase, after one year, was approximately 41%, and his total pretax return on the Post purchase, after twenty-seven years, is approximately 8,468%, which equates to a pretax annual compounding rate of return of approximately 17.8%. Not too shabby.

It was the stock market pessimism of 2000 and 2001 that allowed Warren to make investments in such companies as Justin Industries, Yum Brands, Johns Manville, Shaw Industries, Liz Claiborne, Nike Inc., Dun & Bradstreet Corp., USG Corp., First Data Corp., and as mentioned H&R Block—investments that we'll fully explore later.

Warren also discovered early on in his career that the vast majority of those who buy and sell stocks, from Internet day traders (who have the attention span of gnats—professional day traders make an average forty-four trades a day, about one trade every nine minutes) to mutual fund managers (who cater to a shortsighted public), are only interested in making a quick buck. Yes, many pay lip service to the importance of long-term investing, but in truth they are stuck on making fast money.

Warren found that no matter how intelligent most people are, the nature of the beast ultimately controls their investment decisions. Take mutual fund managers. If you talk to them, they will tell you that they are under great pressure to produce the highest yearly results possible. This is because mutual funds are marketed to a public that is only interested in investing in funds that earn top performance ratings in any given year. Imagine a mutual fund manager telling his or her marketing team that their fund ranked in the bottom 10% for performance out of all the mutual funds in America. Do you think the marketing team would jump up and down with joy and drop a few million bucks on advertising to let the world know that their fund ranked in the bottom 10%? No. More likely, our underperforming fund manager would be out of a job and some promising young hotshot would take over.

Don't believe it? Ask people you know why they chose to invest in a particular mutual fund and they'll more than likely tell you it was because the fund was ranked a top performer. The nature of the mutual fund beast influences a lot of smart people into playing a short-term game with billions in capital. No matter what a fund manager's personal convictions may be, producing the best short-term results possible is the way to keep the job.

THE SHORTSIGHTEDNESS OF THE MUTUAL FUND BEAST

A number of years ago the authors were having dinner with a middle-aged mutual fund manager who oversaw tens of billions of dollars for the money management division of a large West Coast bank. He brought along an enormous book that contained a brief analysis of over two thousand different companies that he and his fellow analysts followed. They called it their "investment universe." At his invitation we thumbed through the book and found a company that we knew Warren had been buying, Capital Cities Communications. Capital Cities was a television and radio broadcasting company run by Tom Murphy, a management genius with a keen eye for the bottom line. Warren loved this company and once said that if he were stranded on a deserted island for ten years and had to put all his money into just one investment, it would be Capital Cities. Definitely a strong vote of confidence.

Our friend also had a list of the stocks his fund had purchased. As we read through the list, we noticed that he didn't own any Capital Cities. We quickly pointed this out and told him that Warren had recently been buying it. He said that he knew it was a great company but he didn't own it because he didn't think the stock price would do much over the next six months. We told him that was insane. That it was a fantastic long-term investment selling at a great price. He told us that he was under great pressure to produce the highest quarterly results possible. If he couldn't beat his competitors' returns quarterly, his clients would take their money elsewhere, which meant that he would lose his job, his Porsche, and the income to send his son to Harvard. (Sounds grim, doesn't it?)

Our mutual fund manager felt he couldn't buy a single share of Capital Cities for his fund, even though he *knew* it was a great investment, because he wasn't sure that it was going to go up in price over the next six months. This is the nature of the mutual fund beast: it caters to the short-term-oriented mutual-fund-buying public. If it doesn't, money flows out the door and down the street to the fund that produces better short-term results.

(In case you are wondering, Capital Cities eventually merged with the ABC television network, which eventually merged with entertainment giant Disney, making Warren billions in the process. Good things do come to those who have patience and foresight.)

Warren also discovered that investors who get caught up playing a short-term game have a very human reaction when they hear bad news about a company in which they own shares—they sell them. To make the big bucks in the short-term game the investor has to be one of the first to get in on the stock before it moves up, and one of the first to get out before it moves down. Having access to the most up-to-date information available is of utmost importance. A good earnings report and the stock price moves up. A bad earnings report and it moves down. It doesn't matter if all indications are that earnings will improve in a year or two. All that anybody is interested in is what is going to happen today. If things look great this week, people will buy the stock, and if they look bad next week, they'll sell it. This is why mutual funds are notorious for having such high rates of investment turnover. They get in and out of a lot of different stocks in the hope of beating the other guys to earn the all-important Top Fund of the Year title.

This "bad-news phenomenon"—the selling of shares on bad news—goes on every day. Watch any nightly business report on television and you'll see that after any negative news on a company is announced, the price of its shares drop. If the news is truly terrible, the shares will drop like a rock. As we said, it's the nature of the beast.

Bad news means falling share prices, and bad news means that Warren's eyes light up. To Warren, the shortsightedness of the stock market, when combined with the bad-news phenomenon, is the gift that keeps on giving. This one-two punch has produced one great buying opportunity after another for him, year after year, decade after decade, to the happy tune of $30 billion.

Key Point ➢ In an investment world dictated by shortsighted investment goals, where the human emotions of optimism and pessimism control investors' buy and sell decisions, it is shortsighted pessimism that creates Warren's buying opportunity.

HOW MR. MARKET HELPED WARREN GET RICH

When Benjamin Graham (Warren's mentor) was teaching Warren about the shortsightedness of the stock market, he asked Warren to imagine that he owned and operated a wonderful and stable little business with an equal partner by the name of Mr. Market.

Mr. Market had an interesting personality trait that some days allowed him to see only the wonderful things about the business. This, of course, made him wildly enthusiastic about the world and the business's prospects. On other days he couldn't see past the negative aspects of the business, which, of course, made him overly pessimistic about the world and the immediate future of the business.

Mr. Market also had another quirk. Every morning he tried to sell you his interest in the business. On days he was wildly enthusiastic about the immediate future of the business, he asked for a high selling price. On doom-and-gloom days, when he was overly pessimistic about the immediate future of the business, he quoted you a low selling price hoping that you would be foolish enough to take the troubled company off his hands.

One other thing. Mr. Market doesn't mind if you don't pay any attention to him. He shows up to work every day—rain, sleet, or snow—ready and willing to sell you his half of the business, the price depending entirely on his mood. You are free to ignore him or take him up on his offer. Regardless of what you do, he will be back tomorrow with a new quote.

If you think that the long-term prospects for the business are good and would like to own the entire business, when do you take Mr. Market up on his offer? When he is wildly enthusiastic and quoting you a really high price? Or when he feels pessimistic and quotes you a very low price? Obviously you buy when Mr. Market is feeling pessimistic about the immediate future of the business, because that's when you would get the best price.

Graham added one more twist. He taught Warren that Mr. Market was there to benefit him, not to guide him. You should be interested only in the price that Mr. Market is quoting you, not in his thoughts on what the business is worth. In fact, listening to his erratic thinking could be financially disastrous to you. Either you will become overly enthusiastic about the business and pay too much for it, or you become overly pessimistic and miss taking advantage of Mr. Market's insanely low selling price.

Warren says that, to this day, he still likes to imagine himself being in business with Mr. Market. To his delight he has found that Mr. Market still has his eye on the short term and is still manic-depressive about what businesses are worth.

Is your appetite whetted? It should be. Before we jump to the next chapter we'll let you in on one of Warren's best-kept secrets. He figured out that some, but not all, companies have what he calls a "durable competitive advantage" that creates an economic engine powerful enough to pull these companies' stock price out of almost any kind of bad-news mud that the shortsighted stock market can get them stuck in. He has developed specific criteria to help him identify those businesses. When these businesses are hit with bad news and the pessimistic shortsighted bias of most investors hammers their stock price, he steps in and buys like crazy. This is where he implements his selective contrarian investment strategy. Warren made his big money by investing in these types of companies. They are the Holy Grail of his success, and we predict that they will be the next great love of your investment life as well.

WHAT YOU SHOULD HAVE LEARNED FROM THIS CHAPTER

- ✦ Warren practices a selective contrarian investment strategy.
- ✦ Warren recognizes that everyone from mutual fund managers to Internet day traders are stuck playing the short-term game. It is the nature of the stock market.
- ✦ The bad-news phenomenon goes on constantly—people sell on bad news.
- ✦ Companies that have a durable competitive advantage have the economic power to pull themselves out of most bad-news situations.
- ✦ Warren made all his big money investing in companies that possess a durable competitive advantage.

3

How Warren Exploits the Market's Shortsightedness

What are the characteristics of the kinds of businesses Warren wants to invest in? After more than forty-five years of actively investing in common stocks, Warren has discovered that to take advantage of the stock market's pessimistic shortsightedness, he must invest in companies whose economics will allow them to survive and prosper beyond the negative news that creates a great buying situation.

To do this Warren has to make sure that the company in which he is investing is not only an intrinsically sound enterprise, but also has the economic ability to excel and earn fantastic profits. Warren isn't interested in the traditional contrarian investor approach of bottom picking. He's interested in using the market's pessimistic shortsightedness to give him the opportunity to own some of America's greatest business enterprises at bargain prices. Only by selectively picking the cream of the crop is he able to ensure that over time the company's share price will not only fully recover, but continue upward. It is nothing for Warren to see a dramatic increase in the value of one of these great businesses after he buys in. In the case of Geico he saw a 5,230% increase in value. With the Washington Post he did even better, all told a 8,468% increase in value. He bought into these companies at a time when all of Wall Street was running from them as if they had the plague. Then he held on to them, because they were fantastic companies that had the type of business economics working in their favor that over time would make him tremendously wealthy.

Think of it this way. You have two racehorses. One, called Healthy, has a great track record with lots of wins. The other, called Sickly, has a less-than-average track record. Both catch the flu and are out of action for a year. The value on both shrinks because neither is going to win any money this season. Their owners, intending to cut their losses, offer them up for sale. Which would you want to invest your money in? Healthy or Sickly?

Healthy is clearly the best bet. First of all, you know that Healthy is usually a strong horse. Not only does Healthy have a better chance of recovering from the flu than Sickly does, he has a better shot at winning races (and making you tons of money) once he does!

Even if Sickly recovers, the horse will more than likely remain true to its name and get sick again and again. The return on your investment will be like Sickly's health—poor.

Warren separates the world of business into two categories. The first, the sickly, are the companies with poor economics. These businesses are in what he calls *price-competitive industries* that sell *commodity* type products or services. A price-competitive type of business manufactures or sells a product or service that many other businesses sell and competes for customers solely on the basis of price.

The second type of business is the healthy. It has terrific business economics working in its favor, made possible by the presence of what Warren calls a *durable competitive advantage.* A company with a durable competitive advantage typically sells a brand-name product or service that holds a privileged position in the stream of commerce that allows it to price its product or service as if it faces little or no competition, creating a kind of monopoly. If you want this particular product or service, you have to purchase it from one company and no one else. This gives the company the freedom to raise prices and produce higher earnings. These companies also have the greatest potential for long-term economic growth. They have fewer ups and downs and they possess the wherewithal to weather the storms that a shortsighted stock market will overreact to.

First things first. Warren believes that if you don't have the ability to recognize and identify these two different types of business, you will be unable to exploit the pricing mistakes of a shortsighted stock market. You have to be able to identify them. You have to know what a price-competitive, "sick" commodity-type business looks like and be able to identify its characteristics. If you don't, you just may end up owning one. You also have to be able to identify a "healthy" company with a durable competitive advantage working in its favor, because this is the type of business that will make you a pot of gold.

HOW WARREN GOT ONE OF HIS BEST INVESTMENT IDEAS FROM A SPORTS TECHNIQUE BASEBALL GREAT TED WILLIAMS USED TO WIN GAMES

Warren has long been a student and fan of baseball. After reading baseball superhitter Ted Williams's book *The Science of Hitting,* Warren followed Ted's lead to achieve greatness. Warren carved up his investment strike zone to help him hit investment home runs.

Williams explained in his book that he carved up the strike zone into seventy-seven different cells, each the size of a baseball. Ted would swing only at balls that were in his "best" cells for hitting home runs. Warren says he took Ted's hitting philosophy and applied it to investing. Warren carved up the investment world into "sick" price-competitive businesses and "healthy" durable-competitive-advantage businesses. Then he determined that the way to hit investment home runs is to swing only at healthy companies and only when they are being oversold by a pessimistic shortsighted stock market. Warren also realized that, unlike superhitter Williams, he could never be called out. He could stand at the home plate all day and let mediocre business after mediocre business fly by. Warren waits for the perfect pitch, a healthy, oversold company. Then, and only then, does he swing his billion-dollar investment bat. That's how investment and baseball greats are made.

In the following chapters we'll take a deeper look at both commodity businesses and those with durable competitive advantage, so you will able to determine exactly which is which.

WHAT YOU SHOULD HAVE LEARNED FROM THIS CHAPTER

- Warren has separated the world of businesses into two categories: healthy, durable-competitive-advantage businesses and sick, price-competitive-commodity businesses.
- A company with a durable competitive advantage usually produces a brand-name product or occupies a unique position in the marketplace that allows it to act like a monopoly.
- A price-competitive-commodity business manufactures a generic product or service that many companies produce and sell.
- Warren believes that if you can't identify these two types of businesses, you will be unable to exploit the pricing mistakes of a shortsighted stock market with any degree of certainty.

4

How Companies Make Investors Rich: The Interplay Between Profit Margins and Inventory Turnover and How Warren Uses It to His Advantage

Before we go any further we need to devote a few paragraphs to explaining how companies make money. This is something Warren understands well, and it is something you should understand before going business-hunting in the stock market.

Businesses make money in two ways: by having the highest profit margins possible and/or by having the highest inventory turnover possible. Think of it this way: You have a lemonade stand in the desert. The lemonade costs $2 a glass to make and you sell it for $3 a glass. The difference between your costs and selling price is your profit margin. The bigger the profit margin the better.

If you make $1 a glass selling lemonade, you are going to have to sell a lot of glasses to get rich. Say that you always keep one glass of lemonade in your inventory, ready to sell to a passing desert wanderer. If you sold ten glasses to ten passing wanderers in a year, you would have turned over your lemonade inventory ten times. This means that you had a profit of $10 for the year ($1 a glass profit x 10 glasses sold = $10).

If you want to get rich selling lemonade, one of two things must happen: either your profit margins and/or your inventory turnover will have to increase. Say this is a really big desert and you are the only game in town. With a monopoly like that, you can charge a million dollars a glass. If you can charge that much for a glass and it only cost you $2 to make, then you really only need to sell one glass to get rich. Turn over your inventory once and it's easy street for the rest of your life. This is a case of low inventory turnover, but superfantastic profit margins.

There's another way to get rich selling lemonade. Stick with your $3 price tag and $1 profit margin, but sell a million glasses a year. This is a case of low profit margins with superhigh inventory turnover. You won't make a fortune on each glass sold, but you can make a fortune if you sell a lot of glasses.

You may have the highest profit margins in the world, but you won't get rich if you don't sell any lemonade—a case of low inventory turnover. And you definitely don't get rich if your profit margins are low and your inventory turnover is low.

With that information in your mental bank, let's pretend you are thinking about going into the lemonade business and you have the choice of two desert towns in which you might open up a lemonade stand. The first has one hundred thousand thirsty tourists going through it a year, but it also has fifty lemonade stands. The second has one hundred thousand tourists go through it a year and not a single lemonade stand.

If you put your lemonade stand in the first town, you know you are going to face a lot of competition, which means that you can't charge high prices for your lemonade. This means that your profit margins are going to be low. The high level of competition will also keep your inventory turnover low. Things are looking grim on the profit front. If you lower your prices to attract more business, your competitors will probably do the same thing. Face it, you're selling the same product everyone else is, which means that you are going to have to compete solely on price. That's not good for business and it's no way to get you rich. This is a classic example of a *price-competitive business,* which Warren wants no part of.

If you put your lemonade stand in the second town, you are going to be able to charge high prices because you are the only game around. You are also going to have high inventory turnover because you are selling a lot of lemonade. Individually, both of these things are great for profits; combined, they can make you rich. This is known as a *local monopoly.*

Let's say you are making so much money selling your overpriced lemonade to the thirsty hoards of tourists in the second town that you decide to make a special effort to use only the finest ingredients in your lemonade. It's the best in all the land. You also call your product by the brand-name Jack's lemonade. (Jack's your cousin who loaned you the money to get started.) Soon thousands of tourists have tasted Jack's lemonade and are delighted by it. They like it so much that they often ask why you don't sell it in the first town. Since you have a brand name, Jack's lemonade, and since your customers catch on that you are selling a much better product than first town's lemonade stands, you might be able to open a lemonade stand in the first town and maintain your high profit margins. This is because the first town's customers don't want regular old lemonade anymore. They're looking for that special taste treat known as Jack's lemonade. Your inventory turnover in the first town may not be as great as in the second, but it is still a very profitable business. This is what Warren would call a *competitive advantage,* which gives Jack's lemonade a *consumer monopoly.* If consumers want to drink Jack's lemonade, they have to buy it from you. That is the power of the brand name. It's what H&R Block did to tax preparation, Nike to the running shoe, Coke to the soft drink, Hershey's to the chocolate bar, Wrigley's to gum, McDonald's to the hamburger, Taco Bell to the taco, KFC to fried chicken, Sara Lee to cheesecake, and Pizza Hut to pizza.

Warren wants to own businesses with high profit margins and high inventory turnover. If he can't get one of these superbusinesses, he will settle for one with low profit margins and really high inventory turnover or one with high profit margins and low inventory turnover. These are the kinds of businesses that he can be certain will survive any bad-news situation that creates a buying opportunity and will go on to earn him a bundle over the long term.

Warren is not interested in companies that have low profit margins and low inventory turnover. These kinds of companies find it difficult to recover from a bad-news situation and have little or no chance of making him rich over the long term.

Remember, the higher the profit margin the better, and the higher the inventory turnover the better. If you can't get both, get one. A high profit margin with low inventory turnover can work, just as high inventory turnover with low profit margins can work. But under no circumstances is Warren interested in investing in a company with low profit margins *and* low inventory turnover. This combination can prove disastrous.

CHECKPOINT!
WHAT YOU ABSOLUTELY NEED TO KNOW AT THIS POINT

Okay. Let's stop for a moment and check to see what you have downloaded into your brain. You should now know that Warren is a *contrarian investor* who is only interested in *selective* companies that have seen a *fall in their stock price* due to the *shortsightedness* of the stock market and the *bad-news phenomenon.*

You should also know that Warren has divided the world of businesses into two groups: The first is made up of companies that have some kind of *durable long-term competitive advantage* that allows them to set prices on their products like a monopoly, thus giving them *higher profit margins* and/or higher *inventory turnover.* The second is made up of companies that are in *price-competitive industries* in which businesses compete solely on the price of their products, thus reducing their products to a *commoditylike* status that creates *low profit margins* and *low inventory turnover.*

Of these two business types, Warren is interested only in companies with a *durable long-term competitive advantage.* This is because they are *certain* to recover from the bad-news situation that created the buying opportunity in the first place and are the most likely to continue to grow in value over the long term. He is not interested in owning companies in a *price-competitive industry* because they are the least likely to recover from a bad-news situation or to grow in value over the long term.

Key Point ➢ The key is developing the ability to distinguish a company with a *durable long-term competitive advantage* from one that is in a *price-competitive business.* This is where Warren excels. After we identify a company with a durable competitive advantage, we need only wait until the shortsighted market has oversold its shares to get in on a great investment.

In the following chapters we will spend considerable time teaching you how to separate a company with a *durable competitive advantage* from one in a *price-competitive industry.* Once that is done, we will teach you how Warren determines when to begin buying. Let's start by discovering how to identify a company in a price-competitive business, the kind of company that Warren wants to stay away from. Then we will explain how to identify a company with a *durable competitive advantage,* the type that is key to Warren's investment philosophy and his fantastic success in the stock market.

WHY THE EFFICIENT-MARKET THEORY IS BOTH RIGHT AND WRONG

Once upon a time a couple of enterprising university professors got together and proclaimed that the stock market was efficient, meaning that on any given day a stock was accurately priced given the information available to the public. They also concluded that because of this efficiency, it would be impossible to develop an investment strategy that could do better than the market did as a whole. Because of the market's efficiency, they concluded, the most profitable approach to investing would be through index funds that go up and down with the rest of the market. (This type of fund buys a basket of stocks, without regard to price, representing the stock market as a whole.)

Warren recognizes that because 95% of all investors are hell-bent on trying to beat each other out of the quick buck, the stock market is very efficient. He sees that it is impossible to beat these people at their short-term game. He also realizes that the shortsighted investment mind-set that dominates the stock market is completely devoid of any true long-term investment strategy. You only have to look to the options market to see hard evidence of this. Short-term options trading, up to six months out, is a fully developed market with multiple exchanges, writing tens of thousands of option contracts, on hundreds of different companies, each and every day the stock market is open. The so-called long-term options market, up to two years out, is tiny and deals in fewer than fifty stocks. From Warren's investment perspective, two years out is still short-term. No exchange has an active options market writing contracts five to ten years out. It simply doesn't exist.

Warren's great discovery is that, from a short-term perspective, the stock market is very efficient, but from a long-term perspective, it is grossly inefficient. He had only to develop an investment strategy to exploit the shortsighted market's inefficient long-term pricing mistakes. To this end he developed selective contrarian investing.

WHAT YOU SHOULD HAVE LEARNED FROM THIS CHAPTER

- Warren thinks that the best kind of business to own is one with high profit margins and high inventory turnover.
- Warren believes that the second-best kind of business to own is one with either high profit margins or a high enough inventory turnover to compensate for lower profit margins.
- Warren is not interested in owning a business with both low profit margins and low inventory turnover.

5

The Hidden Danger: The Type of Business Warren Fears and Avoids

Warren believes that if you are exploiting the pessimistic shortsightedness of the stock market, knowing what *not* to invest in is just as important as knowing what to invest in. Warren does not want to invest in a price-competitive, "sick," commodity-type business. These companies lack the economic might that will ensure that they survive the situations that got them into trouble in the first place. Nor do they have any real long-term economic earning power that will ensure the kind of long-term rewards that will make investors superrich.

These types of companies can best be described as mediocre and are inherently plagued by problems. They present their managements with one tough decision after another. When problems do arise, they can quickly become life threatening. Collectively they vastly outnumber durable-competitive-advantage businesses. Because they are so prevalent and because they suffer tremendous economic ups and downs, they have become the investment favorites of traditional contrarian investors. However, Warren has found that these types of companies lack a *durable competitive advantage* that will absolutely ensure that their stock prices will recover and continue to increase in value. The *selective contrarian* investment philosophy that Warren practices dictates that he give the price-competitive business a pass regardless of how great the buying opportunity looks. Warren has found that no matter how many times investors kiss these frogs, they walk away with nothing more than a bad taste in their mouth.

To avoid investing in a price-competitive company you have to know what it looks like. Think of the investment landscape as a kind of forest. You are a naturalist identifying and categorizing little creatures called price-competitive businesses. The more you know about these mediocre creatures of commerce the easier they are to identify and avoid.

IDENTIFYING THE PRICE-COMPETITIVE, "SICK" BUSINESS

The price-competitive, "sick" business is easy to identify because it usually sells a product or service whose price is the single most important motivating factor in the consumer's decision to buy. We deal with many of these businesses in our daily lives:

- Internet portal companies
- Internet service providers
- Memory-chip manufacturers
- Airlines
- Producers of raw foodstuffs such as corn and rice
- Steel producers
- Gas and oil companies
- The lumber industry
- Paper manufacturers
- Automobile manufacturers

All of these companies sell a product or service for which there is considerable competition in the marketplace. Price of the product or service is the single most important motivating factor when the consumer makes his or her buy decision.

People buy gasoline on the basis of price, not on brand. Even though oil companies would like us to believe that one brand is better than another, we know that there really isn't any difference. Price is the dictating factor. The same goes for such goods as concrete, lumber, memory and processing chips for your computer (although Intel is trying to change this by giving its processing chips brand-name recognition). Automobile manufacturers are also selling a price-competitive product, for within each segment of the auto market, manufacturers compete to sell the product with the most bells and whistles at the lowest possible price. Airlines are notorious for price competition. The airline with the lowest-priced seats attracts the most business.

Internet service providers (ISPs)—the companies that connect individuals to the Internet—face such low cost of entry to this business that a flood of providers compete for the same customers. No one needs more than one ISP. Lots of companies offering the same service means price competition. Prices for logging on to the Internet have gone from a high of $100 a month a few years ago to a low today of nothing! That's right, firms like NetZero actually give the service away for free. Who wants to be in a business where the competition is giving the product away for free!

The same can be said for Internet portal companies like Yahoo! and AltaVista. Both were big names back in the early days of the Internet. But the cost of getting into the portal business is so low that dozens of companies are now competing for your search requests. Again, lots of companies offering the same service or product can only mean one thing—lower profits. The business model of Yahoo! had it giving the service away for free to get readers, then charging businesses to advertise on its Web site. Yahoo!, like any business that deals in a price-competitive product or service, tries to enhance its merchandise by adding as many content bells and whistles as possible. The problem is that there's nothing to stop the competition down the street from upping the ante by doing the same thing. On-line service provider AOL so needed content that it merged with Time Warner, the owner of *People* magazine and Bugs Bunny, in a bid to add something unique to its Internet offerings.

Let's face it. It really doesn't matter which Internet service provider you use to log on to the Internet. Nor are people all that choosy about which Internet search engine they use as long as it gets the job done. Nor does it really matter which airline you fly from Los Angeles to San Francisco, as long as it gets you there. GM and Ford make almost identical trucks, but if the Ford truck is a lot cheaper, you will probably end up buying the Ford. This intense level of price competition leads to low profit margins. Which means it is harder to get rich if you own one of these companies.

In a price-competitive business the low-cost provider wins. This is because the low-cost provider has greater freedom to set prices. Costs are lower. Therefore its profit margins are potentially higher than that of its competitors. It's a simple statement with complicated implications. In most cases the low-cost producer must constantly make manufacturing improvements to keep the business competitive. This requires additional capital expenditures, which tend to eat up retained earnings, which could have been spent on new product development or acquiring new enterprises, which would have increased the underlying value of the company.

Let's look at an example: Company A makes improvements in its manufacturing process that lowers its cost of production while increasing its profit margins. Company A then lowers the price of its product in an attempt to take a greater market share from Companies B, C, and D.

Companies B, C, and D start to lose business to Company A and respond by making the same improvements to the manufacturing process as Company A. Companies B, C, and D then lower their prices to compete with company A, thus destroying any increase in A's profit margin that the improvements in the manufacturing process created. And then the vicious cycle repeats itself.

An increase in consumer demand should, in theory, allow the seller of a product or service to increase its price. But if there are many sellers of the same product or service, they end up undercutting each other in an attempt to take business away from the other. Next thing you know, they're in a price war. This is a far cry from Warren's favorite type of business: the kind with a durable competitive advantage. The company with a durable competitive advantage has the ability to increase prices along with an increase in demand. The lack of competition means that these types of companies don't have to compete on price.

Price-competitive businesses occasionally do well. In a boom economy, in which consumers' desire to spend outstrips the available supply, producers like the auto manufacturers earn a bundle. Responding to meet the increase in demand, they will take their bloated balance sheet and expand their operations, spending billions. Their shareholders, seeing all the new wealth, will want their cut and the company will consent to their demands by raising the dividend payout. The unions, seeing how well the company is doing, will stick their hands out as well, and the company will have to pay them. Then when the boom is over—and all booms do eventually end—the company will be stuck with excess production capacity, a fat dividend being paid out every three months, and an expensive union workforce that just isn't going to go away. Suddenly, what was a nice fat balance sheet starts to bleed substantial sums of money. Consider this: Between 1990 and 1993, during a mild recession, General Motors bled $9.6 billion. In a serious recession auto manufacturers bleed even more. Suddenly the $20 billion or so that they tucked away for a rainy day doesn't look like much. Before long, they are shutting down plants and cutting dividends, which means the stock price gets tanked. It's not a pretty sight.

The same kind of thing occurs in the market for computer memory chips. When things are hot, the makers of memory chips, such as Micron Technology, make a ton of money. But if demand slackens, for even a short time, the swarm of memory-chip manufacturers the world over start dropping prices. Consider this: In July of 2000 the price for a standard 64-megabit dynamic random-access memory chip peaked at $9. Six months later, because of a decrease in demand and dumping of chips by Asian manufacturers, the same chip was selling for $3.50. Anyone in the memory-chip business does well in boom years, but when things slow down, all the excess production that was created to meet the swelling demand of the boom years turns around and bites these manufacturers in the butt. Too many memory chips chasing too little demand means falling product prices, which means falling profits, followed by falling stock prices.

These kinds of companies can make lots of money. When demand is high for computer memory, companies like Micron Technology can really do well. The airlines do well in the summer when everyone wants to travel. At times of high demand all the producers and sellers make substantial profits. But any increase in demand is usually met with an increase in supply. Then, when demand slackens, the excess supply drives prices and profit margins down.

Additionally, a price-competitive business is entirely dependent upon the quality and intelligence of management to create a profitable enterprise. If management lacks foresight or wastes the company's precious assets by allocating resources unwisely, the business could lose its advantage as the low-cost producer, thus opening itself up to competitive attack and possible financial ruin.

From an investment standpoint, the price-competitive business offers little future growth in shareholder value. To begin with, these companies' profits are erratic because of price competition, so the money isn't always there to expand the business or to invest in new and more profitable business ventures. Even if they do manage to make some money, this capital is usually spent upgrading the plant and equipment or doing research and development to keep abreast of the competition. If you stand still for a moment, your competitors will destroy you. Many of these companies carry the added weight of enormous long-term debt. In 2000, GM carried approximately $136 billion in long-term debt, a sum considerably greater than the $34 billion it earned from 1990 to 2000. Imagine, if you took every dollar that GM made for the last ten years down to the bank, you still couldn't pay off the loan. Over the last ten years GM's rival Ford earned $37.5 billion against a long-term debt burden in 2000 of approximately $161 billion. If Ford continues with its historical financial performance, it will take the company approximately thirty-eight years to pay off its long-term debt. Doesn't sound like a great business, does it? Imagine that you own a company that carries this sort of long-term debt when the boom is over. Guess whose company is going to lose a ton of cash? All that long-term debt suddenly becomes a very short noose.

The airlines really aren't any different. In 2000, United Airlines, one of the best-run airlines in the world, carried a long-term debt burden of approximately $5 billion against $4 billion in total net income for the last ten years. Unions and high fixed costs ensure that any airline flying the friendly skies will never allow their shareholders' riches to soar for very long.

Price-competitive businesses sometimes try to create product distinction by bombarding the buyer with advertising to create a brand name. The idea is to fool buyers into believing that their product is better than the competition's. In some instances considerable product modifications allow one manufacturer to briefly sneak ahead of the pack. The problem is that no matter what is done to a commodity product or service, if the choice the consumer makes is motivated by price alone, the company that is the low-cost producer will be the winner and the others will end up struggling.

Warren loves to use Burlington Industries, a manufacturer of textiles, a commodity product, to illustrate this point. In 1964, Burlington had sales of $1.2 billion and the stock sold for an adjusted-for-splits price of around $30 a share. Between 1964 and 1985 the company made capital expenditures of about $3 billion, or about $100 a share, on improvements to become more efficient and therefore more profitable. The majority of the capital expenditures were for cost improvements and expansion of operations. Although the company reported sales of $2.8 billion in 1985, it had lost sales volume in inflation-adjusted dollars. It was also getting far lower returns on sales and equity than it did in 1964. In 1985 the stock sold for $34 a share, or a little better than it did in 1964. Twenty-one years of business operations and $3 billion in shareholder money spent, and still the stock had given its shareholders only a modest appreciation.

The managers at Burlington are some of the most able in the textile industry. It's the industry that is the problem. Poor economics, which go hand in hand with excess competition, resulted in a substantial production overcapacity for the entire textile industry. Substantial overcapacity means price competition, which means lower profit margins, which means lower profits, which means a poor-performing stock and disappointed shareholders.

Investing in Burlington in a market downturn or on bad news isn't a great move if long-term growth is the goal. It is the kind of investment that Warren steers away from because it lacks the durable competitive advantage other companies can offer.

Warren is fond of saying that when management with an excellent reputation meets a business with a poor reputation, it is usually the business's reputation that remains intact. In other words no matter who is running the show, there is no way to turn an inherently poor business into an excellent one. Ugly ducklings only grow up to be beautiful swans in fairy tales. In the business world they stay ugly ducklings no matter what managerial prince kisses them.

WHAT YOU SHOULD HAVE LEARNED FROM THIS CHAPTER

- The *selective contrarian* investment philosophy that Warren practices dictates that he give price-competitive businesses a pass regardless of how great the buying opportunity looks.
- Price-competitive businesses lack the economic might that will ensure that they can survive the bad-news situations that got them into trouble in the first place.
- Many price-competitive companies carry the added weight of huge amounts of long-term debt because they are constantly upgrading their plant and equipment to stay competitive.

6

The Kind of Business Warren Loves: How He Identifies and Isolates the Best Companies to Invest In

During the dotcom bubble, as the entire world waxed on about the virtues of the "new economy," Warren remarked that the key to investing was to focus on the *competitive advantage* of the business and the *durability* of that advantage rather than how much a business could change society or grow. It is the *competitive advantage* of a company that allows it to earn monopolylike profits. It is the *durability* of the competitive advantage—the company's ability to withstand competitive attacks—that determines whether it will be able to maintain its competitive advantage and earn monopoly-like profits well into the future.

The competitive advantage creates the earning power that ensures Warren of the company's ability to pull itself out of any trouble to which its stock price may fall prey. The durability of the competitive advantage absolutely guarantees that the company will add to his fortune over the long term.

Two types of businesses possess competitive advantage in the business world: those that produce a unique product and those that provide a unique service.

- *Competitive advantage created by producing a unique product.*
- *Competitive advantage created by providing a unique service.*

At the right price Warren is interested in owning either type of business as long as the competitive advantage—the product or service—is *durable.*

Durability of the competitive advantage is the key to understanding Warren's selective contrarian investment philosophy. This fundamental concept has confused would-be Buffettologists for years, so let's begin there. We'll first explain Warren's concept of the competitive advantage, then we will focus on how you determine whether the competitive advantage is durable. Then we will explain how a durable competitive advantage is created by selling a unique product or service. And last, we will teach you how to identify one of these superbusinesses and where you can look to find them.

THE DURABLE COMPETITIVE ADVANTAGE

When explaining the concept of the competitive advantage, Warren likes to use the castle-and-moat analogy. Pretend that the business in question is a castle and surrounding the castle is a protective moat we'll call its competitive advantage. The competitive-advantage moat protects the castle from attack by other businesses, such as attempts to lure customers away. It can be as simple as a brand name. If you want to eat a Taco Bell chalupa you have to go to Taco Bell. The same goes for that finger-lickin'-good fried chicken that KFC serves. You want expert tax advice, go to H&R Block. You want a Bud after work, you have to buy it from Budweiser. Wrigley's controls the gum game. Hershey's is America's favorite chocolate company. Coca-Cola makes America's best-selling soft drink. Philip Morris makes Marlboro, America's best-selling cigarette. If you want to buy any of these brand-name products or services, you have to buy them from the sole producer and no one else. The same can be said of a large town with only *one* newspaper. If you want to advertise in the paper, you have to pay the rate the paper is charging or you don't advertise. (The newspaper has what is called a regional monopoly.) These companies have a competitive advantage—a brand name or regional monopoly—that enables the business producing the product or service to earn monopolylike profits. Competitive advantage allows these businesses greater freedom to charge higher prices, which equates to higher profit margins, which means greater profits for shareholders. Competing with them head-on is financial insanity.

Yet for Warren, the presence of a competitive advantage and the resulting consumer monopoly are not enough. For Warren to be interested in a company, it must possess a competitive advantage that is *durable.* What he means by *durable* is that the business must be able to keep its competitive advantage well into the future *without having to expend great sums of capital to maintain it.* That last phrase is key, for there are companies that *do* have to spend great sums of capital to keep their competitive advantage, and Warren wants no part of them.

Having a low-cost durable competitive advantage is important to Warren for two reasons. The first is the predictability of the business's earning power. If the company can keep producing the same product year after year, then it is more likely to keep going and thus is more likely to recover from any short-term bad-news event that could send its stock into a tailspin. Remember that the certainty of the outcome is a cornerstone of Warren's philosophy. *To him, consistent products equate to consistent profits.*

The second reason why lost-cost durability is important is that it enhances the company's ability to use the superior earnings that a competitive advantage produces to expand shareholders' fortunes as opposed to simply maintaining them. If a company must constantly expend its capital to maintain its competitive advantage, then that money isn't finding its way to the shareholders' pockets.

Low-cost durability. To get a better grip on this concept, let's return to Hershey's. Here is a company that sells a product that has changed little in the past seventy years—chocolate. Do you think it will change much in the next seventy years? Very doubtful. Your grandfather craved it, your mother loved it, you ate it as a child, your children eat it, and your grandchildren will more than likely eat it as well. (As a child, Warren had such a strong craving for sweets that when he ran away at age thirteen, he headed straight for the Hershey's plant in Hershey, Pennsylvania.) The same goes for Yum's Taco Bell, Pizza Hut, and KFC. All have been making and selling the same products for more than thirty years. Dun & Bradstreet's Moody's Investor Services has provided information on securities to investors for more than fifty years. A company like Coca-Cola has made the same product for the past eighty years. Do you think any of these companies will ever have to spend billions on research and development? Or to retool their production plants to make a new product? Again, it's doubtful. Warren says that if the company in question has been making the same product for the past ten years, it is highly likely that it will be making the same product for the next ten years. (Note: We are talking about making the *same* product or providing the *same* service!)

The key for Warren is that the *product or service* has durability. Some *companies* themselves have a competitive advantage based on intellectual talent and a large capital base, but they manufacture products that have a short life span in the marketplace and therefore don't qualify in Warren's book as being durable. Intel, a leading manufacturer of integrated circuits, is a perfect example. All you have to do is read Tim Jackson's wonderful book *Inside Intel* to realize that Intel is an amazing company filled with extremely talented people in a very, very competitive industry. You will also see that at times in Intel's history, management had to literally bet the entire company to ensure its survival. Intel keeps creating new and innovative products in direct competition with such companies as Motorola and Advance Micro Devices. But each new generation of products costs them dearly. Consider this: In 2000, Intel spent over $3 billion on research and development alone. If it doesn't spend the money, its product line becomes completely outdated in a few years. How much money do you think Hershey's spends on research and development of new products?

Intel's competitive advantage is *dependent* on management's ability to create new and innovative products to beat the competition. If management misses a beat, Intel and its shareholders lose the game.

The same can be said of large investment banks like Merrill Lynch. These pillars of capitalism are filled with some of the most brilliant minds in America. But their profits are solely dependent upon the use of the intellectual power and personal contacts of the people who work there. If key people leave to work for other firms, the company loses very real assets because stockbrokers and investment bankers will always try to take their clients with them. Imagine that the plant and equipment can get up, walk away, and go into business right down the street! That is what you have with an investment bank. This unique power to get up and walk with the business gives great power to top-level investment bankers, brokers, and traders when bargaining with management for multimillion-dollar salaries. Management has to comply or watch the guts of the operation leave and go to work for the competition. Management must shell out huge salaries to appease them or else. Warren discovered this oddity when he invested in Salomon Brothers, the investment bank that later merged with Travelers Group, which then merged with Citicorp. During his tenure, Salomon got itself into some deep water with the Federal Reserve Bank for violating the Fed's rules on buying government debt. Warren rode to the rescue and stepped in as chairman. One of the first things he attempted was to put the multimillion-dollar salaries of its key employees more in line with their economic performance. To Warren's surprise, these key people responded to the pay cuts by jumping ship and going to work for the competition. He quickly realized that the economic concerns of the shareholder took a second chair to the compensation needs of Salomon's key investment bankers and traders. The competitive advantage was not vested in the products or services the company was selling, but rather in an elite group of employees within the company.

Contrast Salomon's and Merrill Lynch's brand name with Taco Bell's or H&R Block's. Can a group of employees walk off with Taco Bell's and H&R Block's competitive advantages? Not a chance. Both of these companies own the rights to their brand names. If the employees want to jump ship and start a new firm, they have to come up with a new brand name and try to sell it to the public—a difficult and extremely expensive proposition that more than likely will fail.

Compare Yum's Taco Bell or H&R Block to a company like Intel. Taco Bell's business is filling a repetitive need—hunger—

that will crop up three times a day from now to the end of time. As long as there are hungry people who don't have time to cook, Taco Bell is going to have a constant stream of repeat customers. H&R Block is the nation's largest and best-known tax preparer. The service that H&R Block provides is as old as the Bible. As long as the government taxes people, H&R Block will help them fill in all those blank lines on their ever-so-complicated tax forms. It has been selling the same service for fifty years. H&R Block caters to a repetitive consumer need that will be there until we abolish income taxes—something that won't happen anytime soon, even with George W. Bush in the White House. Do you think that either of these companies has to reinvent their product line as Intel does? No way. Tacos and taxes, as we know, are as old as the hills. They don't change, nor does the repetitive need that these companies satisfy.

That is not to say that a company like Intel hasn't proven itself as a moneymaking machine. But its competitive advantage lies within the corporate culture that the company has created. By constructing a work environment that nurtures and spurs creativity, it has developed a business culture that possesses a strong competitive advantage. From Warren's point of view the competitive advantage that it has lies in its ability to constantly come up with new products, not in the products themselves. If Intel fails to come up with new products, it quickly becomes yesterday's news.

In contrast, Warren wants to invest in businesses that produce a product or provide a service that is so entrenched in the consumer's mind that the product never has to change. So even an idiot could run the business and it would still be successful.

Key Point ➢ When you think of a durable competitive advantage, think durable product or service. If the company in question has been selling the same product or service for the past ten years, it will more than likely be around for the next ten. Predictable product equates to predictable profits, which gives Warren the certainty he needs to bet big when the market's shortsightedness overreacts to bad news and kills the stock price of one of these companies.

WHAT YOU SHOULD HAVE LEARNED FROM THIS CHAPTER

- Warren believes that the key to investing is not to focus on how much a business is going to change society, or on how much it will grow in the future. Instead, the investor should focus all his or her energy on determining the *competitive advantage* of any given company and the *durability* of that advantage.
- The two types of competitive advantage in the business world are created by producing a unique product and by providing a unique service.
- The key for Warren is that the *product or service* has durability.
- Some companies, such as Intel, have a competitive advantage based on intellectual talent and a large capital base, but manufacture products that have a short life span in the marketplace. These types of companies may have a competitive advantage, but they do not manufacture a product that has a *durable* competitive advantage.

7

Using Warren's Investment Methods to Avoid the Next High-Tech Massacre

Now that you have Warren's concept of durability in your head, let's diverge from our path for a moment and discuss why Warren doesn't invest in transforming industries like the Internet.

Warren believes that many investors get caught up in the visions of grandeur that accompany new industries that promise to reshape and transform society. Other transforming industries have caught investors' imaginations—the radio, automobile, airline, and biotech industries. All sparked investors' dreams of immediate wealth, which in turn caused a massive run-up in share prices as the investing public went wild pumping money into them. This of course created higher share prices, which vindicated the investors' decisions and serves as an enticement to invest even more. Many people see others getting rich and they too join the game, which sends stock prices soaring even higher. This process often continues until economic reality is left far behind. But it can't go on forever, for economic reality is like gravity. At some point the bubble bursts and stock prices fall.

From 1919 to 1939 alone, more than three hundred airline manufacturers came and went. Fewer than ten survive today. And what about their brethren the airlines? In the past twenty years, 129 carriers have filed for bankruptcy. In fact, until 1992, the total amount lost by airlines that went bankrupt was far greater than the total they made. The Internet carnage is equally sobering—hundreds of these companies, some that once commanded $100 or more a share, have become nothing but bitter memories in the minds of their shareholders.

For Warren, the problem with transforming industries is that they seldom, if ever, establish any kind of durable competitive advantage due to the intense competition that exists in the infancy of any industry. Intense competition equates of course to lower profits, which ultimately kills a soaring stock price. Also, in new industry sectors, businesses evolve through countless permutations before establishing any kind of durable competitive advantage. That new businesses by definition have no history of product durability—one of the cornerstones of Warren's selective contrarian investment philosophy—is another strike against them.

Lack of durability keeps Warren from investing in these emerging industries on principle, but he nevertheless likes to hypothetically consider purchasing such businesses whole. He believes that if the entire company isn't worth purchasing at the current stock market price, he shouldn't even buy one share. It is a unique way to look at a prospective investment and one that is shunned by most of Wall Street.

To understand Warren's whole business approach you need to know how to calculate what is called the company's stock market capitalization or, as it is commonly known, the company's market cap.

The market cap is computed by multiplying the number of shares outstanding by the current market price of one share of the company's stock. Let's say that Company X has 100 million shares outstanding and is trading at $50 a share. The market cap for Company X would be $5 billion (100 million shares x $50 a share = $5 billion). If the price of Company X's stock dropped the next day to, say, $45 a share, its market cap would drop to $4.5 billion (100 million shares x $45 a share = $4.5 billion). Conversely the market cap would increase if Company X's stock price went up.

When Warren considers whether to make an investment in Company X, he asks himself the following questions: If the company in question had a market cap of $5 billion and I had $5 billion sitting in my bank account, would I use it to buy the whole company? What kind of return would I get if I paid $5 billion for the company? If he finds the rate of return attractive, he will invest in the company. Notice that he is not asking whether the stock price of the company will go up. Rather, he asks how much will he likely earn given the price that he pays for the entire business.

Let's run through an example. Suppose you were thinking about investing in Yahoo! back on March 10, 2000. Its trading price at that time was $178 a share, and it had a market cap of approximately $97 billion. The question would have been this: If you had $97 billion, would you have been willing to spend it to buy the entire company?

Before you spent your $97 billion, you might just have looked over your other investment options before forking over all that cash for a big ride on Yahoo!. The first thing you discover is that you can invest your $97 billion in U.S. treasury bonds and get a 7% return, which means that you would be earning approximately $6.7 billion a year in interest. Not bad. Compare this to the $70.8 million that Yahoo! was expected to earn in 2000 and the treasury bonds look far more enticing and enriching.

But say that you are a true believer in the Internet and think Yahoo! has a great future! Warren would argue that this may be true, but if you buy all of Yahoo!, you are going to be giving up $6.7 billion in yearly interest income in exchange for the $70.8 million a year that Yahoo! is earning. You, in turn, argue that Yahoo! will earn great sums in the future. Warren would argue that this may also be true. But for each future year you give up the $6.7 billion in interest income, that's $6.7 billion more that Yahoo! is going to have to earn just to keep you even. After even a few years, a billion here and a billion there start to add up. (To keep this in perspective, in 2000, Coca-Cola earned approximately $2.1 billion and General Motors earned approximately $4.4 billion. It takes a hell of a business to generate $6.7 billion in earnings.) It doesn't take a genius to see that buying all of Yahoo! might not be the smartest thing to do with your $97 billion. In Warren's mind it's a short step from there to the conclusion that buying a single share is also a bad idea.

Compare our prospective investment in Yahoo! with an investment in insurance giant and Buffett favorite Allstate. On March 10, 2000, during an insurance recession, Warren was rumored to have been buying Allstate at approximately $18 a share. (As of this writing, this rumor has not been confirmed. We shall assume it is true for the purposes of the hypothetical.) Allstate in 2000 had 749 million shares outstanding, which gave it a market cap of $13.4 billion (749 million shares x $18 a share = $13.4 billion.) It earned approximately $2.2 billion a year. This means that if you spent $13.4 billion buying all of Allstate in 2000, so that you owned the entire company, you would have earned $2.2 billion in income, which equates to approximately 16.4% a year on your money. This is a much better deal than you would have gotten by paying $97 billion for Yahoo! to earn only $220 million, which equates to earning less than 1% a year on your money. In fact, an investment in Allstate is a much better investment than Uncle Sam's treasury bonds.

In truth it is doubtful that anyone other than Warren and a few financial titans are going to cough up $97 billion for a company. We small frys are stuck buying fractional interests in these companies. But remember, Warren believes that if it isn't worth buying the whole company, you shouldn't even buy one share. He also believes that if it is worth buying the entire company, one should buy as many shares as possible.

So suppose we invested $50,000 in Yahoo! on March 10, 2000. Let's also assume that on March 10, 2000, Warren invested $50,000 in Allstate when it was trading at $18 a share. By April of 2001, Yahoo! had dropped from $178 a share to $15 a share, giving us a loss of approximately 91%, reducing our $50,000 investment in Yahoo! to $4,215. The stock price dropped because investors got tired waiting for the $6.7 billion in earnings to arrive. Remember, grim economic reality can drag a stock price to the ground. If the earnings don't show up, investors don't either.

On the other hand, Warren's Allstate investment grew from $18 a share to $40, giving him a 122% return, increasing his $50,000 investment to approximately $111,111. Warren was in good hands with Allstate because he wasn't buying pie in the sky, but real earnings at a price that made business sense. (It is interesting to note that one of the reasons why Allstate was selling so cheap was that everyone else was out chasing the fast bucks being made in Internet stocks. Investors' money fled the old economy for the new economy. They didn't want to own a stodgy old insurance company. The price of its shares went down and created Warren's rumored buying opportunity.)

What keeps Warren from investing in transforming industries is a lack of a durable competitive advantage, plus astronomical selling prices that don't make business sense given the economic reality of the business. If doesn't make sense to buy the entire business, it doesn't make sense to buy a single share no matter how sweet the pie looks.

WHAT YOU SHOULD HAVE LEARNED FROM THIS CHAPTER

- Lack of a historical durable competitive advantage keeps Warren from investing in emerging industries.
- When Warren considers whether to make an investment in Company X, he asks himself the following question: If the company in question had a market cap of $5 billion and I had $5 billion sitting in my bank account, would it be a wise use of my money to buy the whole company?
- Warren likes to play a little game and pretend that he is going to buy the whole business. He believes that if the entire company isn't worth purchasing at the current stock market price, he shouldn't buy even one share.

Interest Rates and Stock Prices— How Warren Capitalizes on What Others Miss

Let's pause for a moment to explain how changes in interest rates affect stock prices.

Warren believes that all investment returns ultimately compete with one another—the returns of a business compete with, say, the returns to an investor from owning a bond. Warren knows that a business is worth only what it will earn. He also knows that sometimes stock prices get ahead of what the underlying businesses will earn, just as sometimes they fall below. But at the end of the day a business is worth only what it can earn over the time that the investor owns it. No more, no less.

What a business will earn and the competing returns on other investments determine its selling price. Let's look at an example: If a business earned $100,000 a year before taxes, year after year, like clockwork, what would you be willing to pay for it? You'd have to do some comparison shopping. This is where interest rates come into play. Let's say that AAA-rated corporate bonds are paying 10%. This would mean that you'd have to buy $1 million worth of bonds to produce $100,000 a year ($1 million x 10% = $100,000).

If you had to pay $1.5 million for the business and it was earning $100,000, your rate of return would drop to 6.7% ($100,000 ÷ $1.5 million = 6.7%). But if you bought $1.5 million worth of bonds that paid 10%, you would be earning $150,000 a year ($1.5 million x 10% = $150,000). Why would you pay $1.5 million for a business when you could get a far better rate of return by buying bonds? You wouldn't. You would buy the bonds. The business would only become attractive at or below a selling price of $1 million. If you paid more than $1 million, you'd be better off buying the bonds. In this situation, that bonds were earning 10% would create downward pressure on the selling price of the business.

Now let's drop the interest rate that bonds pay to 5%. If you bought $1.5 million worth of 5% bonds, you would only earn $75,000 a year ($1.5 million x 5% = $75,000). That isn't as good as the $100,000 a year you would be earning if you paid $1.5 million for the business. In this situation the drop in interest rates would have caused an upward pressure on the selling price of the business.

The same kind of thing happens when the Fed raises or lowers interest rates. When it lowers them, the value of businesses increase, and stock prices then rise reflecting this increase in value. When it raises interest rates, the value of businesses decreases and stock prices fall reflecting the decrease in value. This is usually a very calculated dance. Interest rates go down, stock prices go up and vice versa. But sometimes things go out of whack and the market needs to see that the Fed is making a serious effort to raise or drop interest rates before stock prices make their adjustment. This is especially true in a bubble situation in which the market has succumbed to momentum investing and is no longer concerned with earnings. In a situation like that, the market needs to see a slowing down of the economy before it makes its price adjustment—which can then be dramatic.

The Fed is not interested in whether stock prices go up or down. It is only interested in growing the economy through sound fiscal policy. Too heated an economy gives birth to inflation, which is bad for the economy, so the Fed raises interest rates to try to cool it down, as it did in 1999. If the country falls into a recession, the Fed will lower interest rates to try to spark the economy back to life, as it did in 2001. This type of interest-rate engineering works because businesses and individuals borrow money to finance purchases. Lower interest rates mean cheaper money, which means that business opportunities and financed purchases become more attractive, which creates a more active economy. Higher interest rates mean that business opportunities and financed purchases are more expensive, which means a decrease in economic activity. Think of financing your home or car. Are you more likely to buy a new house or car if interest rates have fallen? Of course you are. Cheaper house or car payments make the purchase more attractive.

From our standpoint, you need only remember that if the Fed *lowers* interest rates, the economy heats up, the value of businesses increases, and stock prices rise. If the Fed *raises* interest rates, the economy slows down, the value of businesses decreases, and stock prices fall. The stock market and the economy always dance to the Fed's tune.

WHAT YOU SHOULD HAVE LEARNED FROM THIS CHAPTER

- ✦ Higher interest rates make businesses' earnings worth less to an investor and will drive stock prices down.
- ✦ Lower interest rates make businesses' earnings worth more to an investor and will drive stock prices up.

9

Solving the Puzzle of the Bear/Bull Market Cycle and How Warren Uses It to His Advantage

The buy side of Warren's selective contrarian investment strategy is made up of two parts. The first is identifying a company with a durable competitive advantage, which we have just covered. The second is identifying a buying opportunity.

Warren's buying opportunity is *price dictated.* Just because he has recognized that a company possesses a durable competitive advantage doesn't mean he will pay any price for it. H&R Block at $60 a share is not a buy in his book, but at $30 it's the deal of a lifetime. Being able to identify the buying opportunity that will give him the biggest returns on his investment is one of the keys to his success. He will only buy into a situation when it makes "business sense." Business sense investing is a pricing philosophy that is intricately interwoven with Warren's selective contrarian investment philosophy. It dictates that he buy only when the stock is trading at or below a certain price. The second part of the book will show you how to identify what is and is not a business sense price.

Warren has found that certain *repetitive* types of market, industry, and business conditions provide him with situations that produce the best pricing for companies that have a durable competitive advantage. Note: The key word here is *repetition.* The repetition of these events makes them identifiable. We shall label them *bear/bull market cycle, industry recessions, individual calamities, structural changes,* and *war.* When you learn what these conditions are, you will know when and where to look for buying opportunities. In this chapter we'll discuss the various stages of the bear/bull market cycle, leaving the other market conditions for the following chapter.

Many aspects of the bear/bull market cycle offer Warren opportunities to practice his particular brand of selective contrarian investing. Let's start with the bear market and then progress through the bear/bull market cycle, identifying the individual buying opportunities that these different market segments offer us.

BEAR MARKETS

True bear markets devastate stock prices across the board and offer Warren the best opportunity for selective contrarian investing. They are the rarest of buying opportunities but the easiest to spot because the media has announced to the world that "we" are in a bear market. Once it is universally proclaimed, the financial world becomes overly pessimistic and access to capital is severely constrained—meaning that banks aren't making loans. Bear markets usually appear after protracted bull markets, which crescendo with astronomically high stock prices, commonly referred to as bubbles. The protracted bull market of the 1920s created the bubble of 1929, which burst and gave birth to the bear market of the early thirties. The bull market of the 1960s exploded stocks to a spectacular level that the investment world hadn't seen since the 1920s. This bubble didn't burst until 1973, causing the bear market of 1973–74. The bull market of the 1990s bubbled in 1999 and burst in 2000, causing the bear market of 2001.

During the bull market of the 1960s Warren sold out near the top of the market three years before the crash of 1973–74. And during the bull market of the 1990s he sold huge positions in 1999, a year before the crash of 2000 and the bear market of 2001. He used the 1973–74 bear market as a buying opportunity, likening himself to a sex-starved man who suddenly awakens to find himself in a harem, buying huge positions in several companies including the Washington Post, American Broadcasting Companies, Knight-Ridder Newspapers, and Ogilvy & Mather. During the bear market of 2000–2002, Berkshire invested in such companies as Yum and H&R Block. For Warren, the secret is to be fearful when others are greedy and greedy when others are fearful. Bear markets offer the buying opportunity, while bull markets vindicate his bear market investments with big profits.

Warren's power to foresee impending disaster is based on a thorough understanding of the life cycle of a bull-to-bear market and the buying and selling opportunities that it offers the selective contrarian investor.

Key Point ➢ During a bear market it is possible to find some spectacular buys. Companies with durable competitive advantages are selling for a fraction of their long-term worth. It's easy pickings, so pick the very best.

TRANSFORMATION OF A BEAR MARKET INTO A BULL MARKET

A bull market comes into being after an economic recession and a resulting bear market have devastated stock prices. During a bear market it is nothing to find stocks like Coca-Cola, Intel, and GE trading with P/E ratios in the single digits or low teens (contrast that situation with a bull market P/E of 30 or better for those same companies). In 2001 the Federal Reserve Bank repeatedly dropped interest rates to help stimulate the economy, thus making stocks more attractive. Since the bear market has brought down stock prices, there is plenty of selective contrarian investment opportunity. A bear market also brings back into vogue general contrarian and value-oriented investing, and money managers who follow these strategies are hired by mutual funds to replace the momentum investors who got killed when stock prices sank. These new fund managers invest in "value plays," often paying below book value for companies. Warren calls this kind of investing "buying a dollar for fifty cents." In a bear market environment, many companies see their stock price suffer from nothing more than a downturn in the economy and stock market. No corporate cancer is eating away at their earnings. Their durable competitive advantage is solid and still generating an abundance of wealth. It's just that the shortsighted stock market, to Warren's delight, has oversold their shares.

A BULL MARKET

The lowering of interest rates by the Federal Reserve Bank stimulates the economy and makes corporate earnings more valuable, which causes a corresponding increase in stock prices. This is what causes the start of a bull market. Investors see stock prices rise and jump in on the action, which causes the market to heat up a little more, which attracts more investors. The rise in stock prices vindicates the value-oriented fund managers' investment decisions, which the mutual fund industry advertises to the world to attract more investors' money. Seeing the spectacular results, usually in the neighborhood of 20% to 30%, investors respond by taking their money out of low-interest money-market accounts and start buying mutual funds. Also, about this time, the momentum investor/mutual-fund manager, a creature who plays a big role in this financial drama, reappears on the scene and begins to hit a few home runs.

STOCK MARKET CORRECTIONS AND PANIC SELLING DURING A BULL MARKET

Then comes the month of October and the stock market suffers a correction or goes through a short period of panic selling. The big crash of 1929 occurred in October. This makes investors nervous, and nervous investors sell their shares and wait on the sidelines until things look good again. The number of stock market corrections that have occurred in September and October are too many to name. Occasionally this October correction turns into panic selling, an example being the crash of October 1987. People panic because they believe on some primal level that the crash of 1929 is once again knocking on their doors, so they sell like crazy, trying to avoid financial ruin.

Key Point ➢ Warren knows very well that if the bull market has not yet "bubbled," these corrections and panics will be short-lived and present great buying opportunities.

Stock market corrections and panics are easy to spot and usually offer the safest investment opportunities because they don't change the earnings of the underlying businesses—that is, unless a company is somehow tied to the investment business, in which case a market downturn tends to reduce general market trading activity, which means brokerage and investment banks lose money. Otherwise the underlying economics of most businesses stay the same. During stock market corrections and panics, stock prices drop for reasons having nothing to do with the underlying economics of their respective companies.

This, like a bear market, is the easiest kind of situation to invest in because there is no real business problem for the company to overcome, nor is there any real problem with the economy. There is only the perceived specter of doom, not the reality of a drop in corporate earnings. To get a bear market going you need a drop in corporate earnings.

Key Point ➢Warren believes that corrections and panics are perfect buying opportunities for the selective contrarian investor. Their brevity means that you must act quickly and with great conviction to take advantage of them. Warren made his first purchase of Coca-Cola during the crash of 1987. While others were in panic, Warren jumped into the pit of fear and began to buy Coke's stock like a man possessed, with a deep thirst for value.

A market correction or panic will more than likely drive all stock prices down, but it will really hammer those that have recently announced bad news, such as a decline in earnings. Remember, a market panic amplifies the effect that bad news has on stock price. *Warren believes that the perfect selective contrarian buying situation can be created when a stock market panic is coupled with bad news about the company.*

After a market correction or panic, stock prices of companies with a durable competitive advantage will usually rebound within a year. This bounce effect often allows an investor who picked up an exceptional business at a great price to see a dramatic profit within a relatively short time.

One correction or panic, however, puts fear in the hearts of every investor. That is one that comes at the top of the market, after stock prices have bubbled.

THE TOP OF THE BULL MARKET

Bull markets can run on for years, suffering minor corrections and panic sell-offs as stock prices ratchet higher and higher. Since nothing is wrong with the economy and stock prices are not too terribly high, there is always a recovery. Think of it this way: The bottom line of how low a stock will go is its intrinsic value as a business. When momentum fund managers decide to flee a stock en masse and oversell past the point of its intrinsic value, then the value-oriented fund managers step in and buy the stock. This buying entices momentum investors to jump back in on the action. They want to get rich overnight, and the quick money is always in the momentum game, a game that no one player can win year after year.

During a bull market P/E ratios that were single digits during the bear market start going up, from the teens to the twenties, then thirties, forties, and fifties. During this mass reevaluation, some value-oriented mutual fund managers begin to change their valuation criteria, ultimately shifting over to a relative form of value that dictates that a stock is cheap if it's selling for a lower P/E than the market's average P/E. This lets value-oriented managers stay in the game, and since the market as a whole is headed upward, their investment choices are usually vindicated. However, after stocks begin to trade at P/Es of fifty or better, a funny thing happens: The investment community announces that earnings no longer matter. Instead, valuations are based on total sales and revenues. The result is that even businesses that don't have earnings see their share prices soar. It happened in the late 1920s, the late 1960s, and the late 1990s.

Investment banks, which during the bear market and the early and middle stages of the bull market had priced public offerings on the basis of net earnings, then follow suit and stop using earnings as a method of valuing the businesses, switching over to total sales and revenues. At the top of the bull market in 1998 and 1999, investment bankers priced some initial public offerings at twenty times total sales and revenues. That's precisely how venture capital funds got so rich during the late nineties. They would fund a start-up company that would generate revenues, but no earnings, then take it public. The stock market would value it at twenty times total sales and revenues, making the venture capitalists instantly rich. Consider this: During this period Jim Clark, one of the founders of Netscape, sold his interest in the company for a billion dollars, even though it had never made a dime.

Key Point ➢ *When stock market analysts and media pundits proclaim that earnings are no longer important in valuation, the bull market is in its final phase. This is where it begins to bubble.*

At this point the vast majority of fund managers have been pushed into playing a momentum game. It is not uncommon during this period for mutual funds to post annual returns of 70% or better. Fund managers who use a value approach can't even begin to post 70% returns, so they either embrace momentum investing or they are driven out of the business as their clients leave for the riches momentum-fund managers are producing.

Key Point ➢ *The bubble is about to burst when you read that value-oriented fund managers are quitting the business because they can't compete with momentum-fund managers.*

WHEN VALUE INVESTORS LEAVE THE GAME

In 1999, at the top of the bull market, Charles Clough, Merrill Lynch & Co.'s top value-oriented stock picker, realized that he could no longer make a rational argument to buy stocks. They simply weren't worth the inflated prices. Instead, he became sanely bearish in the midst of madcap investors willing to pay anything for a piece of the action. Yet Merrill Lynch's stockbrokers were making a fortune selling shares to a public that was pumped up on making a fast buck. To them Clough had lost touch with what investors wanted to hear: buy, buy, buy. Rather than change his tone and cater to the demands of Merrill's brokers and the madness of the crowd, Clough kept his integrity and quit. Today his bearish predictions look amazingly prophetic.

Warren knows that when value-oriented investors like Clough quit the game, it is a sign that the bull market has bubbled and it's time to get out. It also tells him that some great buys are right around the corner and he'd better have lots of cash to take advantage of them. If you had sold out when Clough quit, you would've been cash rich when the stock market crashed—a nice position to be in. However, if you had ignored this sign, you would've lost your shirt and wouldn't have been able to take advantage of all those great bear-market prices that showed up in 2000, 2001, and 2002. In a bear market cash is king, and Warren had it—$28 billion to be exact.

In a bull market more and more money gets pumped into the stock market as more and more people, enticed by easy riches, jump into the game. This mass speculation sends stock prices up across the board, making the public feel rich and prosperous. A public that feels rich acts like it, spending money like crazy, which heats up the economy. A heated economy means inflation. This cues the Federal Reserve Bank to raise interest rates. If the Fed raises rates enough, it will eventually burst the bubble. But this won't happen overnight. Initially the market will ignore the Fed's interest rate hikes. This happens because momentum investors don't care about earnings, nor are they concerned with changes in interest rates.

As interest rates begin to rise, certain stodgier industries will see their stock prices collapse as momentum investors sell out to generate more cash to throw at the hotter stocks. This happened in 1999 when investment fund managers, who were chasing high-tech stocks, sold out of the insurance industry during a recession, dropping insurance giants Allstate and Berkshire to half their bull market highs. Stocks in these newly unpopular industries hit insane lows as shortsighted momentum-oriented investors completely abandoned them. Remember that at this stage the value-type fund manager left the game long ago, which means that no one is left to invest in these companies when their stocks become buys. No one, that is, except Warren and a few other selective contrarian investors. At the same time, share prices in the hot segments—such as high-tech stocks were in 1999—are sent even higher. In the momentum game you have to go where the action is. When you see this kind of market bifurcation happening, you should be aware that the hot segment's bubble is about to burst. Buying into a correction or panic selling at this point could spell disaster if you are chasing after hot stocks.

Key Point ➢ When you see this splitting of the market, you should begin to look at investing in stocks that are being rejected by momentum investors. The lows that these stocks hit will be completely irrational, and the value-oriented fund managers who would once have been their buyers will have long since vanished. Warren knows that a lot of sellers and very few buyers means that stock prices can hit some enticing lows.

THE POPPING OF THE BUBBLE

Rising interest rates, a shift from earnings to revenue in valuations, value-oriented fund managers being driven from the game, and a bifurcated market in which some industries get creamed and others soar spell impending disaster. If you are in the hot segment, you should call it quits, sell out, and go shopping in the unpopular segments. When the bubble pops, it will destroy stock prices in the hot segment and send unpopular stocks suddenly upward. This is caused by a flight of capital from the overvalued hot segments of the market to the undervalued ones. As the undervalued segments pick up a little steam, momentum investors will jump in to send them even higher. It is nothing to see stock prices in the unpopular segments double in a few months as once-hot-segment stocks completely crumble. After the bubble has burst, put on your selective contrarian investment hat and go shopping for durable-competitive-advantage businesses. Many of these businesses will have had their stock prices hammered to the point that it makes business sense for you to buy them.

Any company with a durable competitive advantage will eventually recover after a market correction or panic during a bull market. *But beware:* In a bubble-bursting situation, during which stock prices trade in excess of forty times earnings and then fall to single-digit P/Es, it may take years for them to fully recover. After the crash of 1973–74, it took Capital Cities and Philip Morris until 1977 to match their 1972 bull market highs. It took Coca-Cola until 1985 to match its 1972 bull market high of $25 a share. On the other hand, if you bought during the crash, as Warren did, it didn't take you long to make a fortune. *Be warned:* Companies of the price-competitive type may never again see their bull market highs, which means that investors can suffer real and permanent losses of capital if they buy them during a bubble.

AFTER THE BUBBLE BURSTS

After the bubble bursts, a couple of things can happen. The first is that the country will slip into a recession. You will see reports of layoffs and falling corporate profits. The Fed will actively drop interest rates, which will, in a year or so, respark the economy. The immediate impact of lower interest rates will be an increase in car and house sales. Seeing this, investors will anticipate the revival of the economy and jump back into the market. This time, though, they will be investing in the big names—like GE and Hewlett-Packard—that have earnings. They won't chase after the once-hot bubble stocks. Those stocks are dead until they begin earning money. There's an ugly trick though: If the Fed's dropping of interest rates doesn't revive the economy, the country will slip into a depression and stock prices will really go to hell. It happened in the early 1930s, and the ensuing crash made 1929 pale in comparison. If that happens, you are in a major recession/depression and the stock market will be giving companies away. Warren dreams of such an opportunity, while the rest of the world dreads it. That's because Warren is a selective contrarian investor with a ton of cash and a long-term perspective.

Warning: *Warren Buffett does not* buy *or* sell *based on what he thinks the market will do. He is price-motivated.* This means that he will only invest when the price of a company makes business sense. This is the subject of the second part of the book.

WHAT YOU SHOULD HAVE LEARNED FROM THIS CHAPTER

- The bull/bear market cycle offers many buying opportunities for the selective contrarian investor.
- The most important aspect of these buying opportunities is that they offer the investor the chance to buy into durable-competitive-advantage companies that have nothing wrong with them other than sinking stock prices.
- The herd mentality of the shortsighted stock market creates buying opportunities for both you and Warren.

10

How Warren Discerns Buying Opportunities Others Miss

In this chapter we'll discuss other buying opportunities, namely those precipitated by industry recessions, individual calamities, changes in corporate structure, and war.

INDUSTRY RECESSIONS

Warren often utilizes industry-wide recessions to buy into great companies. In this case, an entire industry suffers a financial setback. These situations vary in their intensity and depth. An industry recession can lead to serious losses or can mean nothing more than a mild reduction in per share earnings. Recovery time from this situation can be considerable—generally one to four years—but it does present excellent buying opportunities. In extreme cases, a business may even end up in bankruptcy. Don't be fooled by a selling price that appears too cheap. Stay with a well-capitalized leader, one that was very profitable before the recession.

Capital Cities/ABC Inc. fell victim to this weird manic-depressive stock market behavior in 1990. Because of a business recession, advertising revenues began to drop, and Capital Cities reported that its net profit for 1990 would be approximately the same as in 1989. The stock market, used to Capital Cities growing its per share earnings at approximately 27% a year, reacted violently to this news and in six months drove the price of its stock from $63.30 down to $38 a share. Thus, Capital Cities lost 40% of its per share price, all because it projected that things were going to be the same as they had been the previously year. (In 1995, Capital Cities and the Walt

Disney Company agreed to merge. This caused the market to revalue Capital Cities upward to $125 a share. If you bought it in 1990 for $38 a share and sold it in 1995 for $125, your pretax annual compounding rate of return would be approximately 26%, with a per share profit of $87.)

Warren used the 1990 banking industry recession as the impetus for investing in Wells Fargo, an investment that brought him enormous rewards. *Remember, in an industry-wide recession, everyone gets hurt. The strong survive while the weak are removed from the economic landscape.* At that time Wells Fargo was one of the most conservative, well-run, and financially strong of the key money-center banks on the West Coast, as well as the seventh-largest bank in the nation. (For the sake of clarity we have not adjusted Wells Fargo's historical numbers for splits up to 2000. If you're a stickler for that sort of thing, you can adjust them by dividing all per share figures by six.)

In 1990 and 1991, Wells Fargo, responding to a nationwide recession in the real estate market and an increase in defaults in its real estate loan portfolio, set aside for future loan losses a little more than $1.3 billion, or approximately $25 a share of its $55 per share net worth. When a bank sets aside funds for potential losses, it is merely designating part of its net worth as a reserve for *potential* future losses. It doesn't mean that those losses *have* happened nor that they *will* happen. It means the losses may occur and that the bank is prepared to meet them.

This means that if Wells Fargo lost every penny it had set aside for potential losses—$25 a share—it would still have $30 a share left in net worth. Losses did eventually occur, but they weren't as bad as Wells Fargo had prepared for. In 1991, the losses wiped out most of Wells Fargo's earnings, but the bank was still very solvent and reported a small net profit of $21 million or $0.04 a share.

Wall Street reacted as though Wells Fargo were a regional savings and loan on the brink of insolvency and in four months hammered its stock price from $86 down to $41.30 a share. Wells Fargo lost 52% of its per share market price because essentially it was not going to make any money in 1991. Warren responded by buying 10% of the company—or 5 million shares—at an average price of $57.80 a share.

Warren saw Wells Fargo as one of the best managed and most profitable money-center banks in the country, selling for considerably less than what comparable banks were sold for in the private market. Although all banks compete with one another, money-center banks like Wells Fargo have a kind of toll-bridge monopoly on financial transactions. If you are going to function in society, be it as an individual, a mom-and-pop business, or a billion-dollar corporation, you need one or more of the following: a bank account, a business loan, a car loan, or a mortgage. And with every bank account, business loan, car loan, or mortgage comes fees charged by the bank for the myriad services it provides. California, by the way, has a large population, thousands of businesses, and a lot of small and medium-size banks. Wells Fargo is there to serve them all—for a fee.

Wells Fargo's loan losses never reached the magnitude expected, and ten years later, in 2001, if you wanted to buy a share in Wells Fargo, you would have to pay the equivalent price of approximately $270. Warren ended up with a pretax annual compounding rate of return of approximately 16.8% on his 1990 investment. To Warren, there is no business like the banking business.

In both cases, Capital Cities and Wells Fargo saw a dramatic drop in their share prices because of an industry-wide recession, which created the opportunity for Warren to make serious investments in both of these companies at bargain prices.

INDIVIDUAL CALAMITY

Sometimes brilliant companies do stupid things, and when they do, they lose some big money. Nine out of ten times the stock market, upon seeing this, will slam the stock price. Your job is to figure out whether this situation is a passing calamity or irreversibly damaging. A company that has the financial power of a durable competitive advantage behind it has the strength to survive almost any calamity. Warren first invested in Geico and American Express when they made business blunders that literally cost them their entire net worth. In the early 1980s he was investing in Philip Morris and R. J. Reynolds after tobacco-related lawsuits hammered their stock price. He was rumored to have invested in Mattel after it made a costly and unprofitable acquisition that nearly destroyed its bottom line.

Occasionally, a company with a great durable competitive advantage in its favor does something stupid and correctable. From 1936 to the mid-1970s Geico made a fortune insuring preferred drivers by operating at low cost and bypassing agents with direct-mail marketing. But by the early 1970s, new management had decided that it would try to grow the company further by selling insurance to just about anyone who knocked on its door.

This new philosophy of insuring any and all brought Geico a large number of drivers who were accident-prone. Anyone could have predicted that more accidents would mean that Geico would lose more money—and it did. In 1975 it reported a net loss of $126 million, placing it on the brink of insolvency. In response to this crisis, Geico's board of directors hired Jack Byrne as the new chairman and president. Once on board, he approached Warren about investing in the company. Warren had only one concern, and that was whether Geico would drop the unprofitable practice of insuring all comers and return to the time-tested formula of insuring only preferred drivers at low cost via direct mail. Byrne said that was the plan and Warren made his investment. Warren initially invested in 1976 and continued to buy shares until 1980. His total investment cost him $45.7 million, and in 1996, right before he bought the rest of the company, his investment had grown to be worth $2.393 billion. This equates to an annual compounding rate of return of approximately 28% for the sixteen-year period.

American Express faced a different sort of disaster in the mid-1960s. The company, through a warehousing subsidiary, verified the existence of about $60 million worth of tanks filled with salad oil, owned by a commodities dealer, Anthony De Angelis. De Angelis in turn put up the salad oil as collateral for $60 million in loans. When De Angelis failed to pay back the loans, his creditors moved to foreclose on the salad oil. But to the surprise of his creditors, the collateral they had loaned money against didn't exist. Since American Express had inadvertently verified the existence of the nonexistent oil, it was held ultimately responsible to the creditors for their losses. American Express ended up having to pay them off to the tune of approximately $60 million.

This loss essentially sucked out the majority of American Express's equity base, and Wall Street responded by slamming its stock into the ground. Warren watched it all unfold and reasoned that even if the company lost the majority of its equity base, the inherent consumer monopolies of the credit card operations and traveler's check business remained intact. This loss of capital, he reasoned, would not cause any *long-term* damage to American Express. Seeing this, Warren invested 40% of Buffett Partnership Ltd.'s investment capital to acquire approximately 5% of American Express's outstanding stock. Two years later the market reappraised the stock upward. Warren sold it and pocketed a cool $20 million profit.

A more recent example of this type of individual calamity is Mattel's 1999 acquisition of the Learning Company. Mattel consistently bled cash to the point that it sent the stock price from a high of $46 a share in 1998 to a low of $9 in 2000. This created a perfect selective contrarian buying opportunity since Mattel's main product line, Barbie, continued to do an excellent business. (Warren was *rumored* to have been buying Mattel in the $9-to-$10 range.) Mattel's solution to the problem was to sell off the Learning Company and take its lumps. By the spring of 2001, Mattel's stock had recovered to a healthy $18 a share, giving Warren nearly a 100% return on a one-year investment. This is a perfect example of a company suffering a onetime calamity with one division of its business, while another part with a durable competitive advantage saves the company and its stock price, giving selective contrarian investors like Warren a huge profit.

Think of it this way. Say you sued fast-food giant Yum and in *2001* won a judgment of $456 million or roughly a little more than what the company is expected to report in net earnings for that year. The stock market, hearing the news of your judgment, would kill Yum's stock price. In truth, however, this loss would have little or no effect on the amount of money that Yum would earn in *2002*. The durable competitive advantage that Yum possesses would still be intact. Effectively, your $456 million judgment would be the same as if Yum had paid out a dividend of $456 million in 2001. Instead of paying out the dividend to its shareholders, Yum would have paid it out to you. In the next year, 2002, Yum will more than likely show a net profit of $456 million or better. By the time 2005 rolls around, no one will remember what happened in 2001 and the price of the stock will have returned to its prejudgment price. How soon they forget!

STRUCTURAL CHANGES

Structural changes in a company can often produce special charges against earnings that have a negative impact on share price. Mergers, restructuring, and reorganizing costs can have a very negative impact on net earnings, which translates into a lower share price, which might mean a buying opportunity. Warren invested in Costco after it had suffered negative earnings due to merger and restructuring costs.

Structural changes like a conversion from corporate form to partnership form, or the spinning off of a business, can also have a positive impact on a company's stock price. Warren's investments in Tennaco Offshore and Service Master were based on these companies' converting from corporate form to a master partnership. His investment in Sears was based on the announcement that it would spin off its insurance division, Allstate.

THE WAR PHENOMENON

The threat of war will send stock prices downward regardless of the time of year. The uncertainty and great potential for disaster presented by any major armed conflict will kill the entire market. The sell-off is motivated by outright fear, which results in people selling stocks and hoarding cash, which, in turn, disrupts the economy. The most recent examples of this kind of sell-off were the 1990 war against Iraq and the 2001 war against Afghanistan. Both sent stock prices tumbling and both created fantastic buying opportunities for Warren. A perfect example of this phenomenon was the mass sell-off that occurred after September 11, 2001. Airlines, car rental agencies, hotels, travel companies, and cruise lines all saw their stock prices decimated as a result of a massive disruption of the travel industry. People simply stopped traveling, and overnight these businesses started to lose money. Will people eventually resume traveling? Of course they will. And when they do, these companies will see their stock prices recover. Yes, there may be a few permanent casualties, but the selective contrarian investor, using Warren's methods, should be able to pick out the ones that will recover from the ones that won't.

To recap, five major types of bad-news situations give rise to a prospective investment situation: a stock market correction or panic, an industry recession, an individual calamity, structural changes, and war. All can have a negative impact on a company's stock price, and any combination of the five can really slam prices into the floor, creating the perfect buying situation.

WHAT YOU SHOULD HAVE LEARNED FROM THIS CHAPTER

- ✦ Bad-news situations come in five basic flavors: stock market correction or panic, industry recession, individual business calamity, structural changes, and war.
- ✦ The perfect buying situation is created when a stock market correction or panic is coupled with an industry recession or an individual business calamity or structural changes or a war.

11

Where Warren Discovers Companies with Hidden Wealth

A durable competitive advantage is a kind of hidden wealth that a company can develop through pure competitive struggle. It can have such an advantage granted to it via a patent or copyright. It is also possible for a price-competitive business to develop a durable competitive advantage. This metamorphosis most commonly occurs when a price-competitive business develops into a regional monopoly by becoming the low-cost producer of a product or the sole provider of a sought-after service. Because of price competition, neither of the two newspapers that operate in the same town may do well. However, if one of the newspapers, through poor management, loses its competitive edge and goes out of business or is bought out by the other newspaper, the remaining newspaper ends up with a regional monopoly. This allows it to earn monopoly-like profits. Because of the monopoly position, the economics of the one newspaper, if properly managed, will continue to improve. The result is an operating plant that is fully paid for and a balance sheet that is debt free. This puts the regional monopoly newspaper in an excellent position to be a formidable foe if it has to defend its position. Any competition is faced with superhigh start-up costs, which equate to higher fixed costs, which equate to much lower profit margins. Thus, the once price-competitive business ends up as a durable competitive advantage business.

You will also find that through product specialization a manufacturer in a price-competitive industry, such as the automobile business, can develop a brand-name niche that gives it a durable competitive advantage. This equates to superior business economics compared to the rest of the industry. It's something that

German sports car manufacturer Porsche did brilliantly. They created a luxury product that consumers *want* to be expensive. Porsche has discovered that its more expensive models sell out long before its cheaper models. This of course means higher profit margins and happier Porsche shareholders.

Once the domain of a durable competitive advantage business is established, it is nearly impossible for it to lose its advantage unless a major change in the business environment occurs. At one time only three television networks were competing for the viewer's eye. Now there are literally hundreds of channels, and they in turn compete with the Internet. The durability of the networks' competitive advantage has been damaged. Even so, it is still difficult to destroy a durable competitive advantage overnight. One has only to look at how Philip Morris, a company with a very durable competitive advantage, survived both the lawsuits filed against it by fifty states and the federal government's regulatory attacks. What saved it was the most popular-selling cigarette in the world—Marlboro—a product that over the last forty years has made Philip Morris the economic powerhouse it is today.

Certain areas of commerce have a greater propensity to spawn companies with a durable competitive advantage. For instance:

1. Businesses that fulfill a repetitive consumer need with products that wear out fast or are used up quickly, that have brand-name appeal, and that merchants have to carry or use to stay in business. This category includes everything from cookies to panty hose.
2. The advertising business, which provides a service that manufacturers must continuously use to persuade the public to buy their products. This is a necessary and profitable segment of the business world. Whether you are selling brand-name products or basic services, you need to advertise. It's a fact of business life.
3. Businesses that provide repetitive consumer services that people and businesses are consistently in need of. This is the world of tax preparers, cleaning services, security services, and pest control.

4. Low-cost producers and sellers of common products that most people have to buy at some time in their life. This encompasses many different kinds of businesses, from jewelry to furniture to carpet to insurance.

Let's examine each of these categories:

1.

BUSINESSES THAT FULFILL A REPETITIVE NEED WITH A CONSUMER PRODUCT WITH BRAND-NAME APPEAL.

BRAND-NAME FAST-FOOD RESTAURANTS

Warren likes to eat in fast-food restaurants and he likes to invest in them. These companies have taken generic food—such as the hamburger—and branded it. Warren has owned shares in McDonald's, Burger King (then owned by Pillsbury), and Yum Brands—which owns Taco Bell, KFC, and Pizza Hut. He knows from experience that nothing gets used up faster than fast food. The hungry consumer associates the taste pleasure of these particular foods with these companies' brand names, which equates to many repeat customer visits. Their durable competitive advantage is locked up in their brand name and supported by a vast chain of restaurants and a sophisticated distribution network. All the above-mentioned companies have been serving up the same products for the last thirty years, have high returns on total capital and equity, and have a history of superior earnings growth. These companies are essentially recession-proof, which means that your best buying opportunities are a bear market, a correction, or a panic sell-off during a bull market. Sometimes a single tainted hamburger or pizza can send their stock price downward.

PATENTED PRESCRIPTION DRUGS

The next time you go to the doctor and he or she gives you a prescription that costs a small fortune to get filled, think about the pharmaceutical company that the medicine came from. Our overcrowded planet is interconnected by thousands of daily international flights, which make it possible for new diseases to jump from one country to another in a matter of hours. Throw in that viruses can mutate into new diseases almost overnight and it doesn't take a genius to see that these modern elixir salesmen, the pharmaceutical companies, are going to have an ever-increasing demand for their lifesaving products. These are products that people desperately need, and they are *protected by patents.* This means that if you want to get well, you have to pay the toll. The gatekeeper, the doctor, has to prescribe the products or else you remain ill. All the leading manufacturers of prescription drugs, such as Bristol-Myers Squibb, Merck & Company, Marion Merrell Dow, Inc., Mylan Labs, and Eli Lilly and Company, earn high returns on capital and equity and have a history of fantastic earnings growth. They are very profitable enterprises that stand with their hands out each time you get sick. The last real great buying opportunity in this category occurred in 1993 when Hillary Clinton tried to do something about health care and the high cost of prescription drugs—the threat of government intervention caused the shortsighted stock market to run from these stocks. Warren used this buying opportunity to purchase 957,200 shares of Bristol-Myers Squibb for approximately $13 a share against earnings of $1.10 a share, which equates to an initial rate of return of 8.5%. By 2001 investors were paying $70 a share for Bristol-Myers Squibb, which gives Warren an average annual rate of return of approximately 23% on his initial investment.

Short of a Democrat with a health care agenda as first lady, your only great buying opportunities come with a bear market or a correction or panic sell-off during a bull market. These companies are essentially recession-proof, but occasionally something odd will happen, such as the threat of government intervention, that hammers their shares.

BRAND-NAME FOODS

This is the world of companies like Kellogg's (cereal), Campbell's (soup), Hershey Foods (chocolate), Wm. Wrigley Jr. Company (chewing gum), Pepsi-Cola Company (maker of Doritos),

Sara Lee (cheesecake and hot dogs), Kraft/General Foods (you name it, they make it), and ConAgra (the nation's second-largest food processor). Warren made big money investing in Pillsbury (bought out by Grand Met) and General Foods (bought out Philip Morris). All these companies produce multiple brand-name products, and many have been making the same products for more than fifty years. Their durable competitive advantage is that they manufacture products that own a piece of the consumer's mind. When we think of chocolate, we think of Hershey's; when we think of gum, we think of Wrigley's; and when we think of soup, we think of Campbell's. These companies have been making money for a long, long time. For a buying opportunity, look for bear markets, corrections, or panic selling during a bull market. These are also the kinds of stocks that get hit in a bifurcated market. They offer long-term growth but not the quick buck. If they get oversold, they can be fantastic buys.

BRAND-NAME BEVERAGES

Coca-Cola (Coke), Pepsico (Pepsi), and Anheuser-Busch (beer) are companies that Warren owns, has owned, and is interested in owning. All have proven durable competitive advantages that produce strong earnings and high returns on total capital and shareholders' equity. All have served up the exact same product for more than seventy years. Talk about durable! Coca-Cola alone produces 30% of the liquids consumed by Americans on any given day. That is one mean feat if you think about it. Anheuser-Busch is the world's largest brewer. Warren used a bull-market panic sell-off to make his first investments in Coke. Bear markets and bull-market corrections and panic sell-offs offer your best opportunities to buy these companies.

BRAND-NAME TOILETRIES/HOUSE PRODUCTS

In the world of brand-name products there is nothing we consume more of than toiletries and household items. Every morning, without fail, toothpaste, soap, shampoo, detergent, tampons, and razor blades are consumed by hundreds of millions of Americans, and Colgate-Palmolive, Procter & Gamble, and Gillette are ever so happy to sell them to us. (Warren owns shares in Procter & Gamble and Gillette.) All three companies have superstrong earnings, high returns on capital and equity, and low debt-to-net-earnings ratios. Their products have virtually bombproof durability. True, they make slight modifications—a little more mint flavor in the toothpaste, a better design on the razor—but in truth they're still peddling the same products they did twenty-five years ago. They'll probably keep peddling them for another fifty. Warren loves these businesses and will certainly buy more whenever he can get them at low enough prices. When will that be? In a real bear market, a correction, or panic sell-off during a bull market. These businesses aren't given to industry recessions. However, recessions in the economy will affect their sales. And these companies are doing major business worldwide, so if the economy gets hit in Europe, the bottom line gets hit in America. This is a problem Gillette recently experienced when a recession struck Western Europe, where it generates approximately 30% of its overall sales.

BRAND-NAME CLOTHING BUSINESS

Brand-name clothing is one of the oldest and most profitable games in town. Think about Levi's jeans for a moment. During the California gold rush Levi Strauss took heavy denim that was being used to make sails and sewed together pants that even a hardworking gold miner couldn't wear out. They came to be known as the blue jean or simply Levi's. Levi Strauss made a fortune selling his jeans, as did his sons, and his grandsons and great-grandsons. Until recently, when the company began to have problems due to more competition and costs, the blue jean business has been very good to the Levi's family.

The durable competitive advantage that Levi had was perceived quality and durability, which customers were willing to pay more for. Later on Levi's became a fashion statement. Fashion is where the money is. People are willing to pay a lot of money for an item of clothing made for just a few dollars. The coolest part of the business is that actual manufacturing is contracted out to the lowest bidder. Your Nike shoes could be made in Korea one year and in Indonesia the next, wherever labor is cheaper. The actual manufacturing is price competitive, but the finished product is a brand-name product that commands a brand-name price. The durable competitive advantage belongs to the brand owner—the company that contracts manufacturers to actually produce the goods.

Do these companies make money? They make a lot of money. In 2000, Nike made $579 million and Liz Claiborne made $183 million, and Berkshire owns an interest in both.

2.

THE ADVERTISING BUSINESS PROVIDES A SERVICE THAT MANUFACTURERS MUST CONTINUOUSLY USE TO PERSUADE THE PUBLIC TO BUY THEIR PRODUCTS.

ADVERTISING

The best and oldest advertising is word of mouth. When that doesn't work, we have advertising agencies to design ads to get the message to the consumer. We have radio, television, newspapers, billboards, direct mail, Internet banners, and a huge number of highly specialized magazines. What interests Warren about advertising is that it has become the battleground on which manufacturers compete with one another. Huge consumer corporations spend hundreds of millions of dollars a year to get their "buy our product" message to potential customers. There is no turning back. Manufacturers have to advertise or they run the risk that their competitors will sweep in and take over their coveted niche in the marketplace.

Warren found that advertising creates a conceptual toll bridge between the potential consumer and the manufacturer. For a manufacturer to create a demand for its product, it must advertise. Call it an advertising toll bridge. This advertising toll bridge is owned by the agencies, radio stations, television networks, newspapers, billboards, direct-mail and e-mail companies, and a huge number of highly specialized magazines. Warren found that once businesses begin to advertise, it is almost impossible for them to stop. Competition creates a repetitive need. If a company stops advertising, its competitors will step in and fill the void.

ADVERTISING AGENCIES

When a huge multinational company wants to sell its products all over the world, it calls on a handful of international advertising agencies. These ad agencies are unique in the world of business in that they create, write, produce, and test-market ads that appear in print, on billboards, and on radio and TV. They develop entire ad campaigns that companies use to sell their products to the masses. One thing that General Motors and Philip Morris have in common is that both have an ad agency to help them sell their wares. If one of these multinationals wants to launch an advertising campaign, it will more than likely contract an advertising agency like Interpublic, the second largest in the world, servicing more than three thousand clients through offices in fifty-two countries. Interpublic is part of the advertising toll bridge to the consumer that the multinational manufacturers must cross. Warren used the 1973–74 recession to buy 17% of Interpublic, which at the time was selling for $3 a share and earning $0.81 a share, or 3.7 times earnings. At about the same time he bought 31% of the Ogilvy Group, the fifth-largest ad agency in America for approximately $4 a share against earnings of $0.76 a share. Today you should check out Omnicom Group, the largest advertising company in terms of worldwide billing, and a stock that Warren has in his investment sights, should its price ever drop.

TELEVISION

Once an ad has been written, recorded, photographed, or shot for TV, it has to be pitched to potential customers. Television, newspaper, magazine, and direct-mail companies all have the power to reach millions of potential customers. These companies are the last part of the advertising toll bridge to the consumer. Because they reach the most people, they also make the most money.

Televison is king in this part of the game because of its vast reach. For this privilege companies will spend a fortune. It costs millions to advertise during the Super Bowl. The economics of the business are incredible. You buy a transmitter, build an antenna, plug it into the wall, and you're in business for a long time. Television companies buy programming based on how much money it earns them in advertising. In the early days, ABC, NBC, CBS, and the independently owned affiliates basically had licenses to print money. In 1978, after the 1973–74 stock market crash had devastated stock prices, Warren invested heavily in the ABC television network for $24 a share against earnings of $4.89 a share, which equates to a P/E of 4.9. (Note the very low P/E. During the 1972 bull-market bubble, ABC traded at a P/E of 20. In the bull-market bubble of 1999, Disney, after it acquired ABC, traded at a P/E of 42.) Warren also invested in Capital Cities when it was trading with a P/E of 8.

NEWSPAPERS

A lone newspaper has a monopoly on reaching consumers in its area. Think about it. If you so much as want to sell your car, you have to advertise in the newspaper. In a good-size town a newspaper can make excellent returns, but add a competitor and neither will do very well. This is what Warren experienced with the *Buffalo Evening News.* With a competitor in town the paper was, at best, an average business. Since the competitor went out of business, the *Buffalo Evening News* has been getting spectacular results. Warren has found that if there is only one newspaper "toll bridge" in town, it can jack its advertising rates to the moon and still not lose customers. Where else are the manufacturers and merchants going to cross the river to reach consumers? Warren used this rationale when he bought into Knight-Ridder Newspapers in 1977 for $8.25 a share on earnings of $0.94 a share, which equates to a P/E of almost 9. During the 1972 bull-market bubble, this same company was trading at a P/E of 24, and during the bull-market bubble of 1999 it traded at a P/E of 20. Warren actually bought shares of the Washington Post Company during the 1973–74 crash for $5.69 a share against earnings of $0.76 a share, which equates to a P/E of 7.5. During the 1972 bubble it traded at a P/E of 24. His 1980 purchase of Times Mirror, the owner of the *Los Angeles Times,* was for $14 a share against per share earnings of $2.04 a share, which equates to a P/E of 6.9. During the 1999 bubble it traded at 21 times earnings. His 1994 purchase of shares in Gannett, which publishes 134 newspapers, was made during an advertising recession for 15 times earnings. During the 1999 bubble it traded at 24 times earnings. Newspapers can still be great investments if you pay a low enough price. Recessions and bear markets are the times to look for the best buys.

MAGAZINES

Established magazines have a lockdown on certain segments of the market, which allows them to earn tremendous amounts of money. That's why Warren invested in Time Inc., the publisher of *Time, People,* and *Sports Illustrated* magazines, in the early eighties during a recession triggered by the Fed's raising interest rates. (Remember, if interest rates go up, stocks go down.) Time merged with Warner Brothers to form Time Warner, which then merged with AOL to form AOL Time Warner. Warren could be interested in purchasing shares again if it ever got its long-term debt down. (At one time Warren actually owned shares in AOL, which he saw as a cross between a magazine and cable TV.) He is also a big fan of Reader's Digest, a company that has been in business since 1922, carries no debt, and has returns on equity and total capital of 20% and better.

DIRECT-MAIL AND BILLBOARD COMPANIES

One of the most effective means of advertising is direct mail, and Advo is king in that game. It's a very profitable business. The same can be said for billboard companies. (Ted Turner made his original money in the billboard business.) Outdoors Systems has 112,000 outdoor display faces nationwide, 125,000 subway signs in New York City, and has recently gotten into broadcasting. It would make a great buy at the right price.

3.

BUSINESSES THAT PROVIDE REPETITIVE CONSUMER SERVICES THAT PEOPLE AND BUSINESSES ARE CONSISTENTLY IN NEED OF.

These companies provide services that can be performed by nonunion workers, often with limited skills, who are hired on an as-needed basis. This odd segment of the business world includes such companies as Service Master, which provides pest control, professional cleaning, maid service, and lawn care; and Rollins, which runs Orkin, the world's largest pest and termite control service and also provides security services to homes and businesses. Think about the home-security business for a moment. You wire it up and the customers send you a monthly check, sometimes for the rest of their life. We all know that at tax time H&R Block is there to save our neck by filling in all those lines on our tax forms. All these companies earn high rates of return on equity and total capital.

This segment of Warren's toll bridge world also include the credit card companies that he has invested in, such as American Express. This is an interesting kind of business. American Express charges the merchant a fee every time you use one of this company's cards, they also charge you a fee for having it, and if you have one of their credit cards, they get to charge you almost usurious amounts of interest on any unpaid balance you keep with them. Little tolls on millions of transactions add up. Toss in the interest charges and you will soon see why Warren finds these companies so attractive. These strange credit card toll bridges don't need capital-depleting plants and research-and-development budgets, either. The company that helps them operate this lucrative business model is First Data Corp., which processes millions of credit card transactions for businesses like American Express (Warren was buying it in 1998 during a fall contraction/panic sell-off).

Cintas Corp. rents uniforms, dust mops, entrance mats, and

wiping cloths to businesses and makes a fortune doing so. The rental business is very profitable because in essence it sells the sames wares over and over. Companies are constantly in need of uniforms. It's a demand that will never go away. The same goes with Warren's purchase of Dun & Bradstreet, which provides businesses with information about other businesses. It gets to sell the same information over and over. InfoUSA is another company that makes great money providing businesses with information about other businesses.

The key to these companies is that they provide necessary services but require little in the way of capital expenditures or a highly paid, educated workforce. Additionally, there is no such thing as product obsolescence. Once the management and infrastructure are in place, the company can hire and fire employees as demand dictates. You hire people to process data for $10 an hour, give them a few hours of training, and then turn them loose. When there is no work, you fire them.

Also, no one has to spend billions upgrading or developing a new production plant. The money these companies make goes directly into their pockets and can be spent on expanding operations, paying out dividends, or buying back stock.

4.

LOW-COST PRODUCERS AND SELLERS OF COMMON PRODUCTS THAT MOST PEOPLE HAVE TO BUY AT SOME TIME IN THEIR LIFE.

Sellers and producers of price-competitive products can become the low-cost seller or producer. If they can maintain this position long enough, they can establish a niche and after a number of years can acquire the capital and infrastructure to dominate their game. Warren's first discovery of the earning power of the low-cost producer was with his investment in Geico. Geico is the low-cost seller of auto insurance—a high-ticket item that every car owner must purchase. You buy car insurance on the basis of price, and it makes sense to buy from the cheapest seller in town. That's its competitive advantage.

Large retailers earn quasi-monopoly profits by selling cheap and moving a lot of inventory. It's the game Wal-Mart plays. When a store's name comes to mean quality, good service, and cheap prices, it also acquires a great deal of economic goodwill. Warren found this to be particularly true with large furniture stores that dominate their marketplace, such as the Nebraska Furniture Mart, owned by Berkshire Hathaway. Its buying power allows it to purchase large quantities of inventory deeply discounted from manufacturers. This in turn allows it to sell furniture for less than the competition can. This is known as monopoly buying power. The purchaser is so large that it can dictate lower prices for large quantities of goods. The manufacturer makes up for the lower profit margin on each item by selling greater quantities. This is where economies of scale come into play and into pay, for the manufacturer can earn a bundle on just one huge order. The Nebraska Furniture Mart can then pass part of the savings on to the customer, thus undercutting the prices of its competitors.

These merchants, as a rule, own their stores and the property they sit on. The cost of their large retail space was paid for years ago. Cheap retail space means lower prices and happier customers, which means that they keep coming back, which means that the store sells more products and makes more money. This is a classic situation in which low profit margins are okay as long as there is high inventory turnover (you sell a lot of goods).

These companies create an enormous barrier to entry by being the low-cost operator, carrying large inventories, and selling so cheap. Any company trying to muscle in on their market would face huge expenses just opening its doors. It would have to finance the acquisition of a large retail space, acquire a huge inventory, and advertise like crazy just to get started. If profit margins were a little higher, a competitor might be able to make a beachhead and start to challenge the monopoly-positioned retailer, but since profit margins are so low, the economic barrier to entry for would-be competitors is almost insurmountable.

Warren's 2000 purchase of Furniture Brands International at $14 a share against earnings of $1.92 a share is exactly this kind of business. FBI is the number one manufacturer of residential furniture in America. Everyone buys furniture at some time or another, and FBI is there to sell it to them. It has been in business since 1921 and has strong earnings and great returns on equity and total capital. Over the years it has come to dominate its field. Warren bought in after the 1999 bubble burst and its stock price fell. It didn't stay down for long. By February 2001 it was trading at $25 a share, giving Warren a speedy 78% return on his money.

He bought Mueller Industries, the leading low-cost producer of plumbing fittings, tubes, and related products, during the October 2000 sell-off that knocked Mueller down from $32 a share to $21 against solid earnings of $2.16 a share. The company has been in business since 1917 and has a low-cost infrastructure that allows it to stomp the competition.

The same can be said of large jewelry-store chains, which have an enormous buying power to acquire jewelry at the lowest possible price. They then sell it at a price lower than the local mom-and-pop jewelry store can. They too can create monopoly situations that make it hard to compete against them. In Warren's hometown of Omaha, one store called Borsheim's competed by doing business out of a cheap downtown location and by selling expensive jewelry cheaper than it could be purchased from a high-profile retailer such as Tiffany. Local chain stores didn't even try for the top-end business, so this store managed to acquire it all. Word eventually got around that the owner, Ike Friedman, was honest and would always make you a great deal. Soon people were flying in from out of town just to do business with him. This is an example of a high-end jewelry store working on the theory that you can do great business with lower profit margins and higher volume. Business became so good at Ike's store that Borsheim's became the largest single high-end jewelry store in the world. Warren loved the business so much that he bought the company from Ike in 1986 and has been profiting from the sale of gold, silver, diamonds, and rubies ever since.

As long as people need beds to sleep in and couches to sit on, insurance for their cars and help completing their tax forms, these companies will make money. Lots of money, for a very, very, very long time to come.

WHAT YOU SHOULD HAVE LEARNED FROM THIS CHAPTER

✦ Warren has discovered four basic types of businesses with durable competitive advantages:

1. Businesses that fulfill a repetitive consumer need with products that wear out fast or are used up quickly, that have brand-name appeal, and that merchants have to carry or use to stay in business. This is a huge world that includes every thing from cookies to panty hose.
2. Advertising businesses, which provide a service that manufacturers must continuously use to persuade the public to buy their products. This is a necessary and profitable segment of the business world. Whether you are selling brand-name products or basic services, you need to advertise. It's a fact of life.
3. Businesses that provide repetitive consumer services that people and businesses are consistently in need of. This is the world of tax preparers, cleaning services, security services, and pest control.
4. Low-cost producers and sellers of common products that most people have to buy at some time in their life. This encompasses many different kinds of businesses from jewelry to furniture to carpets to insurance.

12

Financial Information: Warren's Secrets for Using the Internet to Beat Wall Street

Warren is obsessed with numbers. He loves them. As a child he memorized license-plate numbers on cars and the statistics on baseball cards. At nine he filled entire notebooks with page after page of number progressions. He often spent the entire evening counting the number of times a certain letter appeared in the newspaper. He memorized the populations of every major city in the United States. In church he spent his time calculating the life spans of ecclesiastics. Warren counted everything from bottle caps to the number of cars that passed his house.

That childhood fixation with numbers has been transformed into an obsession with financial statistics. Now Warren reads hundreds of annual reports. He is notorious for bringing a stack of financial reports on family vacations and to social events to read when things get dull. He loves to do his own income taxes and still has a copy of the first tax return he ever filed. His favorite thing in the world to do is sit in his office, the "temple" as he calls it, and read financial reports.

He has made it a daily habit to read the *Wall Street Journal, New York Times,* and *Washington Post,* as well as the business sections of several leading regional newspapers, including the *Los Angeles Times* and *Chicago Tribune. Fortune, Forbes,* and *Business Week* are also a regular part of his reading diet. He samples industry trade publications such as *American Banker.* When he worked out of his home, in a side room off the upstairs master bedroom, he filled it with old *Value Line Investment Surveys*, and *Moody's Stock Guides*. In the basement Warren also kept a row of large, green filing cabinets stuffed with the annual reports of companies that interested him. These were later moved to Berkshire's corporate offices. Even today, though he loves the Internet, Warren is irritated if his newspapers aren't laid out for his evening reading.

The Internet has made retrieving information infinitely easier, and Warren has taken full advantage of all it has to offer. The on-line services that he regularly uses are Bloomberg's Professional Service at www.bloomberg.com, which covers everything including bond prices, and *Value Line Investment Survey,* www.valueline.com. The survey was created by Arnold Bernhard, a contemporary of Warren's mentor, Benjamin Graham, who began to compile and publish stock figures in 1937. Bernhard sought a standard of value for stocks. He subscribed to the Grahamian concept of intrinsic value but had reservations about the methods Graham used to calculate it for a specific business. *Value Line* covers thirty-five hundred companies and lists key financial figures dating back fifteen years. It's a key tool in the game that Warren uses *regularly. Value Line* is full of important figures such as the earnings per share and return-on-equity computations. Warren also subscribes to *Moody's,* www.moodys.com, and *Standard and Poor's Stock Reports,* www.standardpoor.com, which follow six thousand stocks.

Warren also makes prodigious use of the PRNewswire, www.prnewswire.com, a world leader in the electronic delivery of business news and provider of a complete, up-to-the-minute database of news from the past thirty days, as well as annual reports for more than two thousand companies. He also makes prodigious use of the SEC EDGAR Database, www.sec.gov/edgar.html, to retrieve 10-Ks and 10-Qs—annual and quarterly financial statements filed with the SEC—along with other juicy SEC information involving every publicly traded company in the United States.

On-line investment services such as www.msn.com (your authors' favorite free service) offer the ten-year financial histories of thousands of companies that would normally be difficult to obtain. That's a lot of information and it's all free. We like free information.

When Warren decides to research a company, he gathers together its most recent 10-K and 10-Qs, the annual report, and any news and financial information that he can gather from Bloomberg, *Value Line,* and *Moody's.* He likes to have the most recent news stories and at least ten years' worth of financial numbers. From these he will carefully examine the company's historical annual return on capital and equity; earnings; the company's debt load; whether it has been repurchasing its shares; and how well management has done allocating capital.

IF YOU DON'T HAVE ACCESS TO A COMPUTER

If you don't have a computer and an Internet connection, you can gather this information the way Warren did before his friend Bill Gates gave him a computer and hooked him up. Begin by going to the periodical desk at the local library and asking to see their copies of *Value Line, Moody's,* and/or *Standard and Poor's,* where you will find ten to fifteen years of financial information on the company in question. You will also find the company's home office phone number. Call it. Ask the receptionist to connect you with somebody in shareholder relations. Once you are connected, ask for a copy of the company's annual report and its most recent 10-K and 10-Q. The person at the other end of the line will take your address and send you a copy free of charge. That's right, free of charge.

Also at your local library you will find a set of books called the *Guide to Business Periodicals.* This amazing resource will refer you to every magazine article published on the companies you're researching. The guide dates back about thirty years, so you should start with the most recent stories in major business periodicals such as *Fortune, Business Week, Forbes,* and *Smart Money.* Though there may be countless other listings, these will more than likely give you a good overview of the company and the industry it is in.

This is amazing when you think about it. Some hotshot reporter has done your research for you—talked to the company's competitors, interviewed its head, and gleaned the opinions of all the big-name analysts who cover its stock. And you don't pay a thing for this service. After you get the listing, you simply go to the periodical desk in the library and ask the librarian how to retrieve the story. More than likely, the library will either have the magazine itself or a copy of it on microfilm. All for free. (University libraries are often a better source of information than city libraries, especially if the university has a business school.)

As you are reading these stories, remember to take notes. List the names of the competitors and anybody quoted. Do this because at some future date you may want to contact these sources yourself and ask a few questions. Now, I know you're thinking, "How can I call these people and ask them questions!" Just pick up the phone and dial! Tell them you are thinking about investing in the company. Nine times out of ten they will be happy to talk to you about it.

After you have read the stories you found in the *Guide to Business Periodicals* and have assembled the financial figures for the company over at least the last ten years, you are ready to answer the key questions about the nature of the business, chief among them, does it have a durable competitive advantage or is it a price-competitive business? You can also answer a few things about the management: Does it have shareholders' interests at heart or is it out to foolishly spend the shareholders' money on low-return projects?

If things look enticing, you will want to run figures for the return on equity and earnings growth over the last eight to ten years. You will also want to calculate the company's value to you as an investor using the equations discussed in our section on mathematical tools. But remember, the earnings of a company have to have some strength and the company's products have to be of a nature that will allow you to project the company's future earnings with a fair degree of comfort.

CIRCLE OF CONFIDENCE

Warren often refers to a "circle of confidence," using Bill Gates and the incredible Microsoft as an example. Warren says that Microsoft is probably one of the best run and most profitable companies in the world. However, he admits to being unable to determine whether Microsoft has a durable competitive advantage, because he readily confesses that he doesn't understand the business. Warren feels that to determine durability of a company's competitive advantage you have to understand the nature of the business and the products that it makes. Determining whether the company's product has been around for a long time is easy, but determining whether it will be around ten years from now is far more difficult. It requires an understanding of a product and the needs it fulfills. For Warren, certain fields of business—high tech, for example—are evolving so fast that it is impossible to make any sort of determination of future product durability. If Warren can't evaluate it, he's not going to invest in it.

Let's say that all things considered, the company looks as if it might be what we are looking for. At this point you'll want to go on to the next step.

SCUTTLEBUTT

The next step is an adaptation of something that Philip Fisher explained in his *Common Stocks and Uncommon Profits,* a process of investigation he calls the scuttlebutt approach. This is an investigative technique in which the prospective investor calls the competition and customers of a business and asks them about the company in question. It's not unlike checking references provided by a prospective employee.

Warren actually gets on the phone, calls the competition, and asks what it thinks of a particular company. Or he may question someone he knows who has knowledge about a particular area of business. He is famous for asking CEOs what competitor they are most afraid of. When Warren met Bill Gates at a party in 1993, just after IBM's shares had sunk from $30 a share to $10, he peppered him with questions about IBM and the durability of its competitive advantage. Gates, who had initially written Warren off as a stock speculator, fell into an intense conversation with him about the computer business. Gates found Warren's line of questioning to be an interesting new way of thinking. Soon afterward, the two billionaire buddies started taking family vacations together and giving lectures to college students on the secrets of their success.

Another great Warren scuttlebutt story is about Geico, a company that has made him a fortune. As a student in Columbia's MBA program, Warren learned that his favorite professor, Benjamin Graham, was the chairman of an insurance concern called Government Employees Insurance Company (Geico). Upon learning this, Warren took the train down to Washington, D.C., where Geico had its home office. He got to Geico's headquarters at around 11 A.M., where he found the doors locked. Frustrated and mad at himself that he hadn't thought it might be closed on Saturday, he banged on the front door until a janitor answered. A wide-eyed and desperate Warren beseeched the janitor to find someone in the building with whom he could talk about the company. The janitor, taking pity, told him a guy on the sixth floor might be able to help him. So he let Warren in and escorted him up to the sixth floor to none other than Lorimar Davidson, then Geico's chief investment officer, who would later become CEO. Davidson, flattered and impressed with Warren's desire to know about the company, spent four hours explaining the insurance business and how Geico worked. Warren became totally enamored of the company. As we have noted, he later added Geico to his circle of confidence and over the next forty years earned more than $1.6 billion on a $45 million investment in the company. (You could argue that the janitor, by opening the door, was responsible for making Warren so rich.) If you haven't danced the scuttlebutt yet, give it a try.

In the old days these investigative techniques were costly and not easy to implement. It could take you weeks to get all the data you needed. The average working person didn't stand a chance. But today the tables have turned. Financial information on a company can be assembled by the average person, on the Internet, in less than an hour.

It's a brave new world, and for the average investor the sky's the limit.

WHAT YOU SHOULD HAVE LEARNED FROM THIS CHAPTER

- The Internet gives everyone with a connection access to all the information they need to employ Warren Buffett's selective contrarian investment strategies.
- Start with the services Warren uses:

    www.bloomberg.com
    www.valueline.com
    www.standardpoor.com
    www.moodys.com
    www.prnewswire.com
    www.sec.gov/edgar.html

13

Warren's Checklist for Potential Investments: His Ten Points of Light

If you're looking for buried treasure, you'd better have a good idea where it's hidden before you start digging. Warren has discovered certain identifiable characteristics that help determine if the business in question has a durable competitive advantage and is resilient enough to weather the vicissitudes of a shortsighted stock market.

If you truly want to invest like Warren, prior to the moment when the shortsighted players in the market present you with a buying opportunity, you'll need a working knowledge of several hundred companies that have a durable competitive advantage. When the action gets hot, you want a game plan in place. Then you will act intelligently and with confidence when everyone else is panicking. And when Mr. Market offers an insanely high price for one of your companies, you'll have the business sense to take him up on his offer. To get you up to Warren's speed, we have assembled his screening criteria and will explain each component in detail. Along with showing you how to determine what kinds of companies to buy—the ones with a durable competitive advantage—we will also show you how to determine what kinds of companies you shouldn't buy, the price-competitive type. We will conclude by bringing it all together in a special template for you to use as you compile your wish list of acquisitions.

NO. 1

THE RIGHT RATE OF RETURN ON SHAREHOLDERS' EQUITY

There are several places you can begin to screen for the presence of a durable competitive advantage. You can hunt for a brand-name product, for example, or an announcement that a particular company is having problems to which the shortsighted market has overreacted. We have found through experience that a good way for beginner Buffettologists to start is to familiarize themselves with American companies that produce consistently high rates of return on "shareholders' equity" or what is commonly referred to as book value.

You can start this exploration from several places. We suggest that you use *Value Line,* because it is the best service for gathering historical financial information. We also suggest *Fortune* magazine's list of the top five hundred companies in America and/or an on-line stock-screening service, such as that offered by Wells Fargo's on-line brokerage, which will allow you to screen for companies with high rates of return on shareholders' equity. Not too many companies fit this criterion, so you should be able to easily identify most of them and learn a little about each. This is something that Warren did long ago, and it is where he points promising young investors when they ask where to begin.

Warren realizes that a company with a durable competitive advantage almost always shows a *consistent* high rate of return on shareholders' equity. The key word is *consistent,* for consistency is indicative of *durability.*

We define shareholders' equity as a company's total assets minus its total liabilities, the same way you determine the equity you have in your house. Let's say that you bought a house as a rental property for $200,000. To close the deal you invested $50,000 of your own money and borrowed $150,000 from a bank. The $50,000 you invested in the house is your equity in the property. A balance sheet of your one-property rental business would look like this:

One-Rental-Property Balance Sheet: June 1, 2001			
ASSETS		LIABILITIES	
Rental Property	*$200,000*	Bank Loan	*$150,000*
Total Assets	$200,000	Total Liabilities	$150,000
	Your down payment →	Shareholders' Equity	*$50,000*
		Total Shareholders' Equity & Liabilities	$200,000

Balance-sheet statements keep track of a business's assets, liabilities, and shareholders' equity. They are like snapshots showing the financial condition of the company on a particular day and are usually presented to the investing public quarterly and at the end of the year. This means that every three months the financial department of a company gathers all its numbers and publishes a balance sheet. A balance sheet doesn't tell you whether the business is making money. It only tells you the value of the business's assets, the value of the liabilities, and whether the business is worth anything when liabilities are subtracted from assets. In your personal life you would call the difference between your assets and liabilities your net worth. In the business world it's called shareholders' equity or book value.

When you rent your house out, the amount of money that you earn from the rent, after paying your expenses, mortgage, and taxes, would be your net profit. If you rented your house out for $15,000 a year and had $10,000 in total expenditures, then you would be earning $5,000 a year. An income statement for your rental-property business would look like this:

One-Rental-Property Income Statement for the Year 2001	
Income	$15,000
Expenses	*$10,000*
Net Income	$5,000

An income statement lists all income and expenses and tells you how much money a business has earned over a period of time. In the business world these statements are traditionally issued every three months and at the end of the year. An income statement for the first quarter would include income and expenses for the months of January, February, and March. An income statement for the year would include income and expenses for all twelve months.

When calculating the return on your equity, you would take your $5,000 in profit and divide it by your $50,000 in shareholders' equity. This equates to a 10% return on equity ($5,000 ÷ $50,000 = 10%).

Likewise, if you owned a business (Company A) that had $10 million in assets and $4 million in liabilities, the business would have shareholders' equity of $6 million. If the company earned, after taxes, $1.5 million, the business's return on shareholders' equity would be 25% ($1,500,000 ÷ $6,000,000 = 25%).

The average return on shareholders' equity for an American corporation over the last fifty years has been approximately 12%. This means that, as a whole, year after year, American business earns only 12% on its shareholders' equity base.

Anything above 12% is *above* average. Anything below 12% is *below* average. *And below average is not what we are looking for.* Price-competitive commodity-type businesses historically have returns on shareholders' equity under 12%. Companies that benefit from some kind of durable competitive advantage have returns on shareholders' equity above 12%.

Key Point ➢ *Companies that benefit from some kind of durable competitive advantage have high returns on shareholders' equity—typically* above *12%.*

Key Point ➢ *Price-competitive commodity-type businesses historically have low returns on shareholders' equity—typically* under *12%.*

What Warren looks for in a business are consistently higher-than-average returns on shareholders' equity. The higher the better.

Look at some of the companies that have caught Warren's interest in the past and consider their returns on shareholders' equity. H&R Block was averaging a 25% return on shareholders' equity when Warren took his position; Nike about 14% with a historical average around 20%; Johns Manville was in the 20% to 30% range; Knight-Ridder Newspapers, 14% to 20%; super ad agency Ogilvy Group, 15% to 22%; General Foods Corporation was averaging an annual 16% return on equity during the time Warren was buying it; Coca-Cola's return on shareholders' equity was approximately 33% when Warren first jumped in; Interpublic was in the 15% to 22% range; American Broadcasting, 13% to 21%; Geico, 20% to 30%; R. J. Reynolds Inds., 14% to 18%; Philip Morris, 20% plus; Times Mirror had a historical average of approximately 16%; Hershey Foods has long fascinated Warren, with a historical return in the neighborhood of 16%; Capital Cities had a return of 18% when it first caught Warren's eye; Walt Disney Company was in the 15% to 21% range; Service Master's return on equity was in excess of 40% and UST's was more than 30%; Gannett Company had a return of 25%; Washington Post clocked in at 19%; McDonald's was 18%.

Key Point ➢ *Consistency is everything. Warren is not after a company that occasionally has high returns on shareholders' equity, but one that consistently earns high returns. Understand that consistency equates to durability, and in Warren's world* durability *of the competitive advantage is the name of the game.*

ANALYZING THE COMPANY'S RETURN ON EQUITY

Does the *return on shareholders' equity* of a company you're researching look like Company I or Company II?

Company I		Company II	
YEAR	RETURN ON EQUITY	YEAR	RETURN ON EQUITY
92	28.4%	92	0%→Year that it lost money
93	31.2	93	3.8
94	34.2	94	7.0
95	35.9	95	14.5
96	36.6	96	7.6
97	48.8	97	23.8
98	47.7	98	10.0
99	48.8	99	0
00	55.4	00	24.3
01	56.0	01	6.9

Warren would be interested in Company I and not Company II. Company II's return on shareholders' equity, even with its occasional high years, is on average way too low and way too erratic. Company I shows a high rate of return on shareholders' equity, indicating that it benefits from having a strong competitive advantage, which is a good indication of the presence of the elusive durability that Warren so covets. Company II's low and erratic return on shareholders' equity is a good indication that it is in a *price-competitive commodity-type* business, which Warren is not interested in owning.

When a company with a competitive advantage suffers a severe decline in earnings due either to an industry recession or a one-time problem, the returns on equity will drop substantially. This will create a return-on-equity picture that looks like this:

Company I	
YEAR	RETURN ON EQUITY
92	28.4%
93	31.2
94	34.2
95	35.9
96	36.6
97	48.8
98	47.7
99	48.8
00	55.4
01	6.0→Problem year

This type of situation may cause an overreaction by the shortsighted stock market. If you determine that the market has overreacted, you may have a buying opportunity.

The gist of all this is that Warren has learned that a consistently high return on shareholders' equity is indicative of a strong and possibly durable competitive advantage, which will allow the company to recover quickly from almost any business misfortune that a shortsighted stock market might overreact to.

NO. 2

THE SAFETY NET: THE RIGHT RATE OF RETURN ON TOTAL CAPITAL

The problem with looking at high rates of return on shareholders' equity is that some businesses have purposely shrunk their equity base with large dividend payments or share repurchase programs.

They do this because increasing the return on shareholders' equity makes the company's stock more enticing to investors. Thus, you will find companies in a price-competitive business, like General Motors, reporting high rates of return on shareholders' equity. To solve this problem, Warren looks at the return on total capital to help him screen out these types of companies.

Return on total capital is defined as the net earnings of the business divided by the total capital in the business. In our one-property-rental business, discussed in the last lesson, the total capital would be $200,000—the amount of the bank loan, $150,000, plus your $50,000 equity. The return on total capital is calculated by dividing our one-property-rental business's net earnings, $5,000, by the $200,000 in total capital, for a return of 2.5% ($5,000 ÷ $200,000 = 2.5%).

Warren is looking for a consistently high rate of return on total capital *and* a consistently high rate of return on equity. Let's compare the returns on equity and total capital for General Motors, a price-competitive business, and H&R Block, a company selling a specialty service with a durable competitive advantage.

General Motors' return on equity for the ten-year period clocks

General Motors			H&R Block		
YEAR	*ROE*	*ROTC*	*YEAR*	*ROE*	*ROTC*
92	0%	0%	92	27.8%	27.8%
93	44.1	9.7	93	26.7	26.7
94	44.1	14.0	94	27.8	27.8
95	29.7	13.0	95	12.0	12.0
96	19.9	9.9	96	30.1	30.1
97	34.1	13.0	97	13.0	11.2
98	24.4	7.8	98	22.4	18.8
99	30.0	10.0	99	23.0	15.0
00	24.5	9.0	00	24.0	17.0
01	22.0	9.0	01	29.7	16.0

in at an average annual rate of 27.2%, which is very respectable but suspect because of the 0% return in 1992. Its total return on capital for the ten-year period shows a different story. Its 9.5% average is not what we are looking for. Compare this to H&R Block, which logged in an average annual rate on shareholders' equity of 21.5% and an average annual total return on capital of 20.7%.

Key Point ➢ Companies with a durable competitive advantage will consistently earn both a high rate of return on equity and a high rate of return on total capital. Again, the key word is *consistent.*

Key Point ➢ Companies in a price-competitive business, the type of business Warren's selective contrarian strategy won't work, will typically earn a low rate of return on total capital.

Let's look at the return on total capital of some of the companies in which Warren has invested. As we said, H&R Block was averaging a 20.7% return on total capital; Nike was in the neighborhood of 23% with a historical average around 21%; Johns Manville was in the 18% to 19% range; Yum Brands, averaged 30%; Knight-Ridder Newspapers, 13% to 15%; the super ad agency Ogilvy Group, 15% to 22%; General Foods Corporation averaged an annual 13% to 15% return on total capital during the time Warren was buying it. Coca-Cola's return on total capital the year Warren started buying it was approximately 18%. Interpublic was in the 15% to 22% range; American Broadcasting, 13% to 17%; R. J. Reynolds Inds., 12% to 15%; Philip Morris, 20% plus; publishing giant Times Mirror, 13%; Hershey Foods, 13% to 20%; Capital Cities, approximately 17%; Gillette, 14% to 19%; Walt Disney Company, 13% to 19%; Service Master, in excess of 19%; UST, 30%; Gannett Company, 12% to 18%; Washington Post, 17%; McDonald's, 13%.

Key Point ➢ Warren is looking for a consistent return on total capital of 12% or better.

BANKS, INVESTMENT BANKS, AND FINANCIAL COMPANIES

Banks, investment banks, and financial companies rely on borrowing large amounts of money that they hope to loan out at higher interest rates to businesses and consumers. A company like Freddie Mac, which deals in residential mortgages, carries $175 billion in short-term debt and $185 billion in long-term debt. If your business is borrowing money at 6% and loaning it out at 7%, there is no way your return on total capital is going to even approach 12%. In these instances, Warren likes to look at what the bank or finance company earned in relation to the total assets under its control. The rule here is, the higher the better. Anything over 1% is good and anything over 1.5% is fantastic.

Key Point ➢ With banks, investment banks, and financial companies, look for a consistent return on assets in excess of 1% and a consistent return on shareholders' equity in excess of 12%.

WHERE THE ENTIRE NET WORTH OF THE COMPANY HAS BEEN TAKEN OUT

On occasion, a company has such a strong durable competitive advantage that its earning power allows it to pay out a portion or all of its entire net worth to shareholders. In this situation shareholders' equity decreases, which in turn causes the *return* on shareholders' equity to increase dramatically—often to 50% or better. When the entire net worth is paid out, it creates a negative net worth, which means that the company will not report a return on shareholders' equity even if it is earning a fortune.

This is rare and can only happen if the earning power of the company is exceptionally strong. Advo, Inc., a business in which Warren has owned stock, is just such a company. Advo is the nation's largest direct-mail marketing company. Think of it as an advertising company. When a business wants to reach potential customers via direct mail, it goes to Advo. Its competitive advantage is that it is the biggest, the best, and the most cost effective at the direct-mail game. Advo was originally founded in 1929. Talk about durable! Until 1996 it had seen a long and steady growth of its per share earnings and had produced consistent returns on shareholders' equity in the 18% to 20% range. From 1986 to 1996 it carried zero long-term debt. That's right, zero debt. Then in 1996 it added $161 million in debt and paid it out to shareholders via a $10-per-share dividend. This effectively wiped out the $130 million in shareholders' equity that it carried on its books and replaced it with debt. Advo can do this because the earning power of the business is so strong and consistent. Few companies can do this, and those that can, almost without exception, benefit from some kind of durable competitive advantage.

The same situation applies to Warren's 2000 purchase of shares in Yum Brands. Yum owns Taco Bell, Pizza Hut, and KFC. It was once part of the Pepsi Company but was spun off to shareholders in 1996. Pepsi, realizing the phenomenal earning power of these three restaurant chains, loaded it up with $4.5 billion in long-term debt before the spin-off. This effectively wiped out all of Yum's net worth. For most companies this would be devastating, but not for Yum. Its earnings are so strong that it managed to pay off $2 billion of the debt within the first three years. (We'll go through a case study on Yum later in the book, so if you're curious about this company, stay tuned.)

In situations like these in which there is no net worth, you need to look at the return on total capital. In 2000, Advo posted a 35% return on total capital, and Yum also posted a 35% return. Historically, in these situations Warren has only made investments in companies that show a *consistent return on total capital* of 20% or better.

To recap, Warren has learned that a consistently high return on total capital is indicative of a durable competitive advantage. With banks and finance companies he looks at the return on total assets to determine if the company is benefiting from some kind of durable competitive advantage.

NO. 3

THE RIGHT HISTORICAL EARNINGS

A durable competitive advantage has the power to consistently produce phenomenal earnings. Thus a screen to determine the consistent earning power of the business is in order. Consistency is an indication of durability. Additionally, a company may have a durable competitive advantage but management may have done such a poor job running the company that annual per share earnings fluctuate wildly. Warren is looking for annual per share earnings that historically show a strong and upward trend. Per share earnings is defined as the company's total net earnings divided by the number of shares outstanding. Historical per share earnings figures are available through *Value Line,* yahoo.com, and msn.com.

Does the per share earnings picture of the company in question look like Company A or Company B?

Company A's historic per share earnings are strong and show

Company A		Company B	
PROBABLE DURABLE-COMPETITIVE-ADVANTAGE BUSINESS		PROBABLE PRICE-COMPETITIVE BUSINESS	
Year	*Per Share Earnings*	*Year*	*Per Share Earnings*
92	$1.07	92	$(1.57) loss
93	1.16	93	.06
94	1.28	94	.28
95	1.42	95	.42
96	1.64	96	(.23) loss
97	1.60	97	.60
98	1.90	98	(1.90) loss
99	2.39	99	2.39
00	2.43	00	(1.25) loss
01	2.60	01	.99

an upward trend. This is a sign that Company A probably has some type of durable competitive advantage.

Company B's earnings are way too erratic to predict. This kind of earnings pattern indicates a company in a price-competitive business.

Key Point ➢ Historical per share earnings that are both strong and show an upward trend indicate a durable competitive advantage.

Key Point ➢ Historical per share earnings that are wildly erratic indicate a price-competitive business.

Understand that the big buying opportunities for companies with durable competitive advantages are going to happen either when the entire stock market suffers a setback, as was the case when Warren started buying H&R Block, Justin Industries, Yum Brands, Johns Manville, Shaw Industries, Liz Claiborne, Dun & Bradstreet Corp., USG Corp., First Data Corp., Washington Post, and Coca-Cola, or when a company experiences a business setback that depresses its current earnings, as when Warren bought Nike and Geico and in his original purchase of stock in American Express.

Stock market downturns and panics are easy to spot and understand, but a calamity that causes a reduction in a company's net earnings must be thoroughly understood before an investment is made. It may be that an entire industry is suffering from a cyclical business recession or that a company has a single division that is giving it problems. *Warren believes that a wonderful investment opportunity exists when a company suffers a onetime solvable problem to which the stock market has overreacted.*

When a business with a durable competitive advantage suffers a setback, the per share earnings might look like those of Company C or Company D:

Company C		Company D	
Year	*Per Share Earnings*	*Year*	*Per Share Earnings*
92	$1.07	92	$1.07
93	1.16	93	1.16
94	1.28	94	1.28
95	1.42	95	1.42
96	1.64	96	1.64
97	1.60	97	1.70
98	1.90	98	1.90
99	2.39	99	2.39
00	1.75	00	2.43
01	0.52→Shows a sharp decline	01	(1.22)→Shows a sudden loss

Company C has an excellent history of long-term earnings growth, but shows a sharp earnings decline starting in 2000. This kind of thing is immediately suspect and should be thoroughly investigated to determine the nature of the decline. Is it an anomaly or a sign of things to come? Is it something that can be corrected?

Company D, on the other hand, has a strong earnings history, but shows a sudden loss in 2001. This too is a suspect situation, but a thorough investigation might reveal that it is suffering from a onetime, solvable problem and that it has a huge potential for long-term profit. Beware of situations like that of the auto industry, which makes lots of money for seven or eight straight years, then produces two to four years of heavy losses. When you look at a suspect situation, Warren says that the attractiveness of the investment should hit you over the head. Because of the pessimistic shortsightedness of the majority of investors, the stock market is like a stream in which you occasionally find hunks of gold so huge you'd have to be blind to miss them.

Remember, when looking for a company with a durable competitive advantage, look for a company with per share earnings that are both strong and show an upward trend. Price-competitive businesses typically show per share earnings that are wildly erratic. Treat as suspect any company that shows a loss, and proceed only after careful analysis and only if the quality of the investment is clearly apparent. When in doubt, go out to a movie and wait for the market to pitch you another ball.

NO. 4

WHEN DEBT MAKES BUFFETT NERVOUS

A good indication that a company has a durable competitive advantage is that it will be relatively free of long-term debt. Warren has found that a company with durable competitive advantage spins off a lot of cash and has little or no need for debt. Companies in a price-competitive business often need to upgrade their plant and equipment or to develop new products to stay ahead of the competition and thus require lots of long-term debt to fund product enhancement or diversification.

Large long-term debt makes Warren nervous because it

impedes a company's ability to survive a business recession or calamity. Because these events often decrease a business's profitability, leaving the company strapped for cash, they can be life threatening if the company is also carrying a large debt (and hence equally large interest payments). Think of it this way—if you lost your job, what are the chances you could continue to pay off a mortgage many times the base salary you just lost? Warren invests in companies that he is *certain* will survive the bad-news situation that got them into trouble in the first place. If the company has a lot of long-term debt, it may not survive. Warren's selective contrarian philosophy dictates that his potential investment candidates have a durable competitive advantage that makes them financially powerful enough to survive almost any disruption of their business.

Warren has found the traditional debt-to-equity ratio for ascertaining the financial strength of a company to be a poor measure of the financial power of a business. This is because a company's assets are never a source of funds for retiring long-term debt unless the company is in bankruptcy. Banks loan money to businesses based on their ability to pay the interest on the debt. Any equity in the company is merely a safety net securing the loan. The same is true of getting a home mortgage. When the bank loans you money to buy a house, it does so based on your ability to pay off the loan. The value of your home is merely security for the bank in case you default on the loan. Your income ensures that you will be able to make the interest payments, and the value of the home ensures the bank that it will get its money back if you fail to pay off the loan. Likewise the ability of a company to use its cash flow to service and pay off the loan is far more important than the assets backing up the loan.

Warren has found that most capital equipment is so unique to the business that, in truth, it is worthless to anyone else, even though it might be carried on the books at considerable value. He has discovered that the wealth of a company is in its ability to earn a profit, not what it could sell its assets for.

The best test, then, of a company's financial power is its ability to service and pay off debt out of its earnings. Companies with a durable competitive advantage have strong enough earnings that they can easily pay off their long-term debt within just a few years. H&R Block carries a long-term debt of $872 million versus net earnings of $251 million per year. It could easily pay off its long-term debt within 3.5 years. Wrigley's carries a long-term debt of less than one year's current net earnings. Think about it. The earnings for a single year can wipe Wrigley's balance sheet squeaky-clean. In 2000, Gannett Co. had $800 million in long-term debt and $1 billion in net earnings, so it would take Gannett a little under one year's net earnings to pay off all of its long-term debt. In the same year Gillette had long-term debt of $2.4 billion and net earnings of $1.2 billion, so it would take approximately two years of net earnings to pay off the debt. Even Yum, with its $2.2 billion in long-term debt and $520 million in net profits, would need little more than four years to pay off the debt.

In contrast, General Motors, a price-competitive business, carried approximately $136 billion in long-term debt in 2000, a sum considerably greater than its total net earnings of $34 billion for the ten-year period of 1991 to 2000. If you took every dollar that GM earned in the last ten years, you still couldn't pay off all its long-term debt. Ford Motor Company isn't in any better shape. It managed over the last ten years to earn a total of $37.5 billion against a long-term debt burden in 2000 of $161 billion. If Ford continues its historic financial performance, it would take the company approximately thirty-eight years to pay off its debt. Doesn't sound like a great business, does it? Imagine that you bought such a company and a recession hit. Guess whose company would bleed to death.

Key Point ➢ *Companies with a durable competitive advantage typically have long-term debt burdens of fewer than five times current net earnings.*

When a company has a durable competitive advantage, there is usually a lot of money in the bank and little or no debt, which means that the company has the financial firepower to solve almost any problem the business might suffer. A company with a ton of debt relative to what it can earn may not have the financial power to get itself out of trouble, which is certainly not good for the stock's price or for your pocketbook.

AN EXCEPTION: BANKS, INVESTMENT BANKS, AND FINANCIAL COMPANIES

As we said earlier, banks, investment banks, and financial companies rely on being able to borrow huge amounts of long-term debt. The five-times-current-net-earnings rule doesn't apply to them. This kind of large-scale borrowing usually poses no problem for the financial institutions in question because the debt is offset by an equally large diversified loan portfolio. An institution gets into trouble when businesses, governments, and individuals default en masse on the loans. If enough loans fall into default, the institution faces the specter of insolvency. This negative news would naturally cause the shortsighted stock market to oversell the institution's stock, creating a potential buying opportunity. Warren used this rationale when he made his investment in Wells Fargo, which at the time was suffering through a real estate recession. Again, a consistently high return on assets is a good indication that the financial institution is making good use of all that debt. Quality use of the money is usually a good indication of the soundness of the enterprise. Besides Wells Fargo, Warren has also used the threat of insolvency to make bargain purchases of Geico, American Express, and Fannie Mae. It also sparked his interest in acquiring 20th Century Insurance and Long-Term Capital, neither of which he bought because they would not meet his price.

LONG-TERM DEBT USED TO ACQUIRE ANOTHER BUSINESS

Sometimes an excellent business with a durable competitive advantage will add a large amount of debt to finance the acquisition of another business. Warren has discovered that adding large amounts of debt to acquire another company may or may not be a good idea. It depends on two variables. The first is whether the company being acquired also has a durable competitive advantage. Often a company with a durable competitive advantage will mistakenly venture into a price-competitive business. This usually proves disastrous as it dilutes the earning power of the side of the company that has a durable competitive advantage. You want a company with a durable competitive advantage to be acquiring other companies that also possess a durable competitive advantage.

The same can be said of a price-competitive business. You want it to be acquiring businesses that have a durable competitive advantage, not another price-competitive business.

When long-term debt is used to acquire another company, the rule is:

- ✦ When two companies with durable competitive advantages join together, it will more than likely be a fantastic marriage. Two durable-competitive-advantage businesses will spin off lots of excess cash, and it won't take long for the combined companies to pay down even a mountain of debt. You can buy into a situation like this on bad news and expect the financial wealth of the two durable competitive advantages to turn the situation around even if the company is burdened with a large debt.
- ✦ When a durable-competitive-advantage business marries a price-competitive business, the results are usually mediocre. This is because the commodity business will eat into the profits of the durable-competitive-advantage business to support its poor economics, thus leaving little to pay down the newly acquired debt. Exploiting a bad-news situation in this case has a great deal more risk to it and should only be undertaken after careful analysis. When in doubt, Warren likes to sit and wait for another pitch. You should too.

THE FOLLY OF PAYING TOO MUCH FOR A COMPANY

The second, and most important, variable that determines whether an acquisition is a good idea is the amount the company is paying to acquire the other company. If it pays too much, then even acquiring another business with a durable competitive advantage can be a bad idea. This sort of thing happens all the time and is the cause of many a disaster, especially when a company with a durable competitive advantage pays too much for a price-competitive business. The disaster can compound itself if the company finances the transaction with a huge amount of stock, which causes dilution of ownership, or with debt, which causes severe financial strain.

A recent example of this type of folly came in 1999 when toy giant Mattel, which manufactures a line of products that each possess a durable competitive advantage, acquired the Learning Company in exchange for Mattel stock, diluting ownership in Mattel by approximately a third. The Learning Company proved not to have a durable competitive advantage in its marketplace and in no time caused once-powerful Mattel to bleed cash.

So when you're looking to take advantage of a bad-news situation, try to determine whether the company has a durable competitive advantage and is conservatively financed. Warren has found that this type of business is the safest bet when playing on the stock market's shortsightedness.

NO. 5

THE RIGHT KIND OF COMPETITIVE PRODUCT OR SERVICE

Once you have identified a company that earns a consistently high return on shareholders' equity and total capital, shows a consistent upward trend in earnings, and is conservatively financed, you need to find out whether it is selling a product or service that has a *durable* competitive advantage. Does it sell a brand-name product or a key service that people or businesses are dependent on? Products are much easier to identify than services, so let's start with them.

Ask yourself these questions: Is the product the kind that stores have to carry to be in business? Would the businesses that carry this kind of product be losing sales if they didn't carry this particular brand-name product?

If the company has the economics of a business with a durable competitive advantage but you don't understand the business itself, get on the Internet and see if you can find any information on the company or the industry that it is in. Often you can find a magazine article or a book on the company. These are excellent sources of information, which Warren constantly makes use of. (It is nothing for him to sit down and read an entire book on a company he is thinking about investing in. When he was thinking about investing in food giant ConAgra, he sought out an obscure self-published history of the company.)

Thumb through a copy of *Value Line* and list all the companies that show consistently high returns on equity and on total capital, and that have strong earnings that show an upward trend. Then make a list of the products they sell and visit retailers where they are sold. Talk to a salesclerk who sells the product every day and find out whether it is number one or two in its field. You don't want to throw your money behind number three or four. What you are looking for is a brand-name product that has been on the market for years and hasn't changed at all. If you remember your parents using it, eating it, drinking it, smoking it, or doing something else with it, it is usually a good sign. Brand-name product longevity equates to durability, and durability is the name of the game. If you don't understand the product, ask someone who does. Go ask a pharmacist about drugs and the companies that manufacture them—a car mechanic about automobile products, a computer salesman about computers, a salesclerk in a grocery store about food products. These are the people who can tell you the history of the product and whether it sold well in the past and continues to sell well today.

You're looking for a product that consumers are continuously in need of, not one they buy once in their lifetime. The easiest to identify are things that we buy and use up immediately, such as fast food: hamburgers (McDonald's, Wendy's, Burger King); pizzas (Pizza Hut); fried chicken (KFC); and of course tacos (Taco Bell). Then there are products that we buy and consume over a short period, such as magazines (Times Mirror), coffee and cigarettes (Philip Morris); candy (Hershey's); gum (Wrigley's); soda (Coke and Pepsi); panty hose (L'eggs, owned by Sara Lee); tampons (Playtex); toothpaste (Procter & Gable); household products (Colgate-Palmolive); drug (Merck & Co.). Then there are things that are consumed over time but wear out within a year or two: jeans (Levi's and Lee); athletic shoes (Nike); underwear (Sara Lee); clothes (Liz Claiborne); and car insurance (Geico, Allstate).

The key here is that a consumer ends up buying the same product many times in a year. This repetitive buying makes a competitive advantage profitable. A strong indication of durability would be if the company can keep producing and selling the same product, without modifying it, with the same manufacturing facility, year after year.

YOU WANT TO INVEST IN A COMPANY THAT SELLS SOMETHING PEOPLE USE EVERY DAY BUT WEARS OUT QUICKLY

In 1895, while working at the Crown Cork factory, a coworker told King Camp Gillette that he should invent something that is used up quickly and that customers keep coming back for more of—like a cork. While shaving one day, he realized that men might need a disposable razor. He then spent the next eight years developing and setting up production for the world's first disposable razor blade. During World War I, Gillette supplied the U.S. military with 3.5 million razors and 36 million disposable blades. When the soldiers returned from Europe, not only were they clean shaven, but they were also in need of blades for their Gillette razors. This gave Gillette an instant 3.5-million-man-strong customer base on which he built his shaving empire.

Another good exercise is to stand outside a convenience store, supermarket, pharmacy, bar, gas station, or bookstore and ask yourself what brand-name products such a business needs to sell to be in business. What products would a manager be insane not to carry? Make a list.

Now go into the establishment and examine the product, which is usually hard to miss if its producer advertises wisely. Brand-name products that we immediately recognize usually have some kind of durable competitive advantage.

Companies providing *services* that have durable competitive advantages are much harder to identify. Again, look to the economics of the business to determine whether the results are indicative of a business with a durable competitive advantage or of one that is price-competitive. Ask whether the company's service is necessary for businesses that use it to stay in business. If the service is aimed at individual consumers, ask whether consumers are constantly in need of it. As in the world of products, the frequency of the consumer's need differentiates the quality of the competitive advantage. Key areas that have caught Warren's eye in the past have been the fields of advertising—television networks (Capital Cities), advertising agencies (Ogilvy), newspapers (Washington Post, Gannett, Knight-Ridder), which are consumed daily and provide businesses everyday access to consumers; key financial-service providers—such as banks (Wells Fargo) that provide businesses and individuals with everyday banking services; and cleaning services for businesses (Service Master). (Don't worry. An entire chapter just ahead tells you exactly where to look for companies that have durable competitive advantages.)

Just because the business has a brand-name product or service that gives it a competitive advantage in the marketplace does not mean that it is an excellent business. Management can fail in dozens of ways to maximize the magic of a durable competitive advantage product or service. You must employ quantitative/qualitative screens to determine whether the company truly has a durable competitive advantage.

NO. 6

HOW ORGANIZED LABOR CAN HURT YOUR INVESTMENT

The inherent financial weakness of the price-competitive business has given organized labor enormous power to demand a higher cut of a company's profits. This is especially true whenever you find a heavy investment in capital equipment, accompanied by high fixed costs. When airplane pilots strike, they can cripple an airline overnight and cause it to hemorrhage money, because a fleet of airplanes is enormously expensive to own and maintain, especially if none of them are flying. Management has to give in to the pilots' demands or risk doing irreparable harm to the business. As soon as the auto manufacturers start showing an increase in profits, labor unions start demanding higher salaries for their workers. If management refuses to meet union demands, its members cripple the company by going on strike, and those fat profits can become fat losses overnight. In situations like these, unions become demanding quasi-owners with whom shareholders must constantly share their wealth or risk a strike that could lead to the financial destruction of their business. Warren doesn't like to own businesses that have organized labor.

Seldom will you find a durable-competitive-advantage company with an organized labor force. These businesses have the economic might to make it through any strike that labor could throw at them. Also, since these businesses are typically more profitable, they can afford to pay their employees more to keep them happy. If you find a company that you think has a durable competitive advantage, but it has an organized labor force powerful enough to demand an ever-increasing piece of the pie, you should proceed with caution. The company may be strong enough to make it through any kind of bad-news event that kills its stock, but it may not be the type of company that you want tucked away in your portfolio for the next twenty years.

NO. 7

FIGURING OUT WHETHER THE PRODUCT OR SERVICE CAN BE PRICED TO KEEP ABREAST OF INFLATION

Inflation causes prices to rise. In a price-competitive business, when prices for labor and raw materials increase, overproduction may force the company to drop the prices of its products to stimulate demand. In that case, the cost of production sometimes exceeds the price the product will fetch in the marketplace, and that's no way to run a business. The company responds by cutting back production until the excess supply dries up. But that takes time. The laws of supply and demand work, but not overnight. In the meantime, the losses pile up and viability of the business diminishes. (Ranchers are constantly faced with this dilemma. The price of live cattle is dropping, but the costs of feed, fuel, labor, insurance, veterinarians, and grazing land continue to increase. Miscalculate next fall's cattle price and the family ranch may end up in foreclosure.)

This situation occurs periodically in the airline business. Airlines commit themselves to all kinds of heavy fixed costs. Airplanes, fuel, union contracts for pilots, ground crews, mechanics, and attendants all cost a lot of money and all increase in cost with inflation. Then along comes a price war or a catastrophic event that makes people afraid to fly and the airlines have to cut ticket prices to fill seats. Want to fly from New York to Los Angeles? A half dozen or more airlines will compete for your business. If one drops prices significantly, they all end up losing. In the 1960s a round-trip airplane ticket from Omaha to Paris cost $1,000 or more. Recently, you could get one on United for $439. Even though the cost of airplanes, fuel, pilots, ground crews, mechanics, and those terrible airline meals have more than quadrupled in the last thirty years, my ticket, thanks to price competition, got cheaper. The airline that sold me that bargain ticket sure didn't get any richer. Now you know why airlines sometime miss the runway and land in bankruptcy court.

With a price-competitive business the cost of production may increase with inflation while the price it can charge for its product decreases—a miserable situation to be in.

THE DURABLE COMPETITIVE ADVANTAGE AND INFLATION

For Warren, a business with a durable competitive advantage is free to increase the prices of its products right along with inflation, without experiencing a decline in demand. That way its profits remain fat, no matter how inflated the economy gets. H&R Block, Nike, Coca-Cola, Hershey's, Mattel, and Allstate all have increased the prices of their products with inflation without experiencing a decline in demand. Yet the most interesting aspect of the durable competitive advantage and inflation is that this increase in product price has also caused an increase in earnings, which has led to an increase in the underlying value of the business. Let me explain.

Say that every year, like clockwork, Hershey's sells ten million chocolate bars. In 1980 it cost Hershey's twenty cents to manufacture each chocolate bar, which it then sold for forty cents. This gives Hershey's a twenty-cent profit on each chocolate bar. To calculate what Hershey's earned selling chocolate bars in 1980, all you have to do is multiply the number sold, 10 million, by the twenty-cent profit that each bar produced, which equals \$2 million (10 million x \$0.20 = \$2 million).

So in 1980, Hershey's made \$2 million selling chocolate bars. If Hershey's had 4 million shares outstanding in 1980, then you could calculate that it had earnings of \$0.50 a share (\$2 million ÷ 4 million = \$0.50). If, in 1980, Hershey's stock was trading at a multiple of 15, it would have been trading at \$7.50 a share (15 x \$0.50 = \$7.50).

Jump ahead to 2000, when everything has doubled in price since 1980 because of inflation. This means that Hershey's chocolate bars now cost forty cents apiece to manufacture. The company is in turn charging double what it charged in 1980—eighty cents a bar. This equates to a profit of forty cents per chocolate bar. If Hershey's sells ten million chocolate bars in 2000 (the same amount of chocolate it sold in 1980), we can calculate that Hershey's will earn \$4 million in 2000 or double what it earned in 1980.

(Now you are about to see a really interesting thing happen.) If Hershey's still has 4 million shares outstanding in 2000, the same amount that it had in 1980, it will post a profit of \$1 a share (\$4 million ÷ 4 million = \$1). So in 2000 Hershey's sells the same number of chocolate bars as it did in 1980, yet it earns \$1 a share or \$.50 more per share than it did in 1980. If you multiply the Hershey's per share earnings of \$1 by 15, the P/E ratio that it had in 1980, you come up with a stock price of \$15 a share or \$7.50 more than you paid for it back in 1980.

Hershey didn't have to manufacture any more chocolate bars in 2000 than it did in 1980. It didn't have to hire any more employees, nor did it have to increase the size of its manufacturing plant. All it had to do was raise prices to stay level with the costs of inflation. As it raised prices, it also increased the amount of money it was earning, causing a corresponding rise in the company's stock price.

Don't get all excited and start thinking inflation is a great wealth-building tool. It's not. If prices double, you need to double the amount of money you started with just to keep your purchasing power the same. What the company with the durable competitive advantage offers you is an investment vehicle that will increase in value right along with inflation.

Again, with a *price-competitive* business, it is possible to have increasing costs with declining prices, which can spell disaster for the company's stock. With a *durable-competitive-advantage business,* however, you have a company that can increase the prices of its products right along with any increases in its costs of production, which means that the underlying value of the company and its stock price will at least keep pace with inflation. What Warren has discovered is that a durable-competitive-advantage business is basically inflation-proof.

NO. 8

PERCEIVING THE RIGHT OPERATIONAL COSTS

Companies that have a durable competitive advantage usually don't have to spend a high percentage of their retained earnings to maintain their operations. The key word here is *maintain.* In theory, the more durable a competitive advantage, the less a business has to spend to maintain it. Warren's perfect business would be one that spends zero on maintaining its competitive advantage. That would free every dollar it earns to be paid out as a dividend or reinvested in the business, which should, in theory, make its shareholders even wealthier.

A simple mathematical formula measures the capital requirements of maintaining a company's competitive advantage and management's ability to utilize retained earnings to improve shareholders' wealth. In essence this calculation takes the *amount of earnings retained by a business for a certain period and measures its effect on the earning capacity of the company.* With a durable competitive advantage the company will be able to use its retained earnings either to expand its operations, invest in new businesses, and/or repurchase its shares. All three should have a positive effect on per share earnings. On the other hand, a price-competitive business would need to spend its retained earnings to maintain its business in the face of fierce competition from other companies in the same line of business, leaving little or nothing to invest in new operations and/or buying back its shares.

Let's look at several examples to give you a better idea of how this works.

H&R BLOCK

In 1989, H&R Block, a company with a durable competitive advantage, earned $1.16 a share. This meant that all the capital the business had accumulated until the end of 1989 produced for its owners $1.16 a share. Between the end of 1989 and the end of 1999, H&R Block's total earnings were $17.14 a share. Of that $17.14, H&R Block paid out in dividends a total of $9.34 a share. So for that ten-year period, H&R Block had retained earnings of $7.80 a share ($17.14 – $9.34 = $7.80) to add to its equity base.

The company's per share earnings increased during this time from $1.16 a share to $2.56 a share. We can attribute the 1989 earnings of $1.16 a share to all the capital invested and retained in H&R Block up to the end of 1989. We can also argue that the increase in earnings from $1.16 a share in 1989 to $2.56 a share in 2000 was due to H&R Block's durable competitive advantage and management's doing an excellent job of investing the $7.80 a share in earnings that the company retained between 1989 and 1999.

If we subtract the 1989 per share earnings of $1.16 from the 1999 per share earnings of $2.56, the difference is $1.40 a share. Thus we can argue that the $7.80 a share retained between 1989 and 1999 produced $1.40 a share in additional income for 1999, for a total return of 17.9% ($1.40 ÷ $7.80 = 17.9%).

WM. WRIGLEY JR. COMPANY

In 1990 the Wm. Wrigley Jr. Company, a durable-competitive-advantage business, earned $1 a share. This means that all the capital that the business had accumulated until the end of 1990 produced that year for its owners $1 a share. Between the end of 1990 and the end of 2000, Wrigley had total earnings of $20.12 per share. Of that $20.12, Wrigley paid out in dividends a total of

$10.57 a share. So for this period, Wrigley had retained earnings, added to its capital base, of $9.55 a share ($20.12 – $10.57 = $9.55).

Between 1990 and 2000, Wrigley's per share earnings increased from $1 a share to $2.90 a share. We can attribute the 1990 earnings of $1 a share to all the capital invested and retained by Wrigley up to the beginning of 1990. We can also argue that the increase in earnings from $1 a share in 1990 to $2.90 a share in 2000 was caused by Wrigley's durable competitive advantage and management's doing an excellent job of investing the $9.55 a share in earnings that the company retained.

If we subtract the 1990 per share earnings of $1 from the 2000 per share earnings of $2.90, the difference is $1.90 a share. This means that the $9.55 in retained earnings earned $1.90 in 2000 for a total return of 19.9% ($1.90 ÷ $9.55 = 18.9%).

GENERAL MOTORS

Let's compare these returns to those of General Motors, a price-competitive business, which had total per share earnings of $42.96 between the end of 1990 and the end of 2000, of which $10.30 was paid out in dividends and $32.66 was retained by the company. Per share earnings for General Motors increased from $6.33 in 1990 to $8.50 in 2000. General Motors' management kept $32.66 per share of shareholders' earnings and allocated it so that per share earnings increased by $2.17. This equates to a return on retained capital of 6.6% ($2.17 ÷ $32.66 = 6.6%). This is about what you would have earned had you left it in the bank.

BETHLEHEM STEEL

In 1990, Bethlehem Steel, also a price-competitive business, earned $.82 a share. This means that all the capital the business had accumulated up to the end of 1990 produced for its owners $.82 a share that year. Between the end of 1990 and the end of 2000, Bethlehem Steel had total earnings of $4.93 a share. Of that $4.93, Bethlehem Steel paid out in dividends a total of $.80 a share. This means that for this period, Bethlehem Steel had retained earnings of $4.13 a share ($4.93 – $.80 = $4.13).

Between the end of 1990 and the end of 2000, Bethlehem Steel had total losses of $7.48 a share. This means that management had to spend $7.48 a share in additional sums that they either borrowed or took from earnings retained during prior years. Since this $7.48 in shareholder capital was depleted, rather than paid out as a dividend, we'll add it with the $4.13 in retained earnings, giving us a total of $11.61 a share that was kept from shareholders.

Between 1990 and 2000, Bethlehem Steel's per share earnings decreased from $.82 a share to $.25 a share. We can argue that the decrease in earnings was caused by Bethlehem Steel's being a price-competitive business that sucks up capital but does nothing to increase shareholders' wealth.

If we subtract the 1990 per share earnings of $.82 from the 2000 per share earnings of $.25, the difference is a negative $.57 a share. Thus we can argue that the $4.13 a share retained between 1990 and 2000 and the $7.48 depleted during this period produced zero additional income. Steel is a tough business in which to develop a competitive advantage.

COMPANIES THAT CAN'T PROFITABLY DEPLOY RETAINED EARNINGS MAKE LOUSY INVESTMENTS

Even if we have no idea what business these four companies are in, we can tell that H&R Block and Wrigley do an infinitely better job of allocating retained earnings than General Motors or Bethlehem Steel does. In fact, if you had invested $100,000 in General Motors stock in 1990 and sold it at its high in 2000, you would have had a net profit of $141,025, which equates to an annual compounding return of approximately 9.1%. If you had done the same with Bethlehem Steel, you would have had a loss of approximately $40,000.

If you had invested $100,000 in Wrigley's in 1990 and sold out at its high in 2000, you would have had a net profit of $566,666, which equates to an annual compounding return of approximately 20%. With H&R Block you would have earned a net profit of $299,960, which equates to an annual compounding return of 14.8%.

So which stocks would you rather have owned from 1990 to 2000? The price-competitive businesses General Motors and Bethlehem Steel, or the durable-competitive-advantage businesses Wrigley's and H&R Block? It's not a tough choice.

This test is not perfect. Be careful that the per share earnings figures you employ for this test are not aberrations, but rather are indicative of the company's earning power. The advantage to this test is that it gives you, the investor, a fast method of determining whether it is a durable-competitive-advantage business that lets its management utilize retained earnings to increase shareholders' riches or whether it's a price-competitive business that is stuck allocating its retained earnings to maintain its current business. Remember, this is just one of nine screens that you have at your disposal, so if you find yourself in a gray area, make certain to use the other screens to help you make a clear-cut judgment.

In sum, durable-competitive-advantage companies wield a one-two punch when it comes to allocating resources. They can better take advantage of retained earnings than price-competitive businesses, which over the long term will make their shareholders a lot richer than those who own stock in price-competitive businesses. Price-competitive businesses are able to retain earnings, but because of the high costs of maintaining their businesses, they are unable to utilize them in a manner that will cause a significant increase in future earnings. This means that their stock prices end up doing little or nothing.

NO. 9

CAN THE COMPANY REPURCHASE SHARES TO THE INVESTORS' ADVANTAGE?

A good sign that the company you are investigating has a durable competitive advantage is that it will have a long history of buying back its shares. To buy back shares over a number of years a company needs an abundance of free cash. Companies with a durable competitive advantage have the economic power to earn the money they need to implement long-term share-repurchase programs. Consider this: H&R Block bought back approximately 9 million shares between 1990 and 2000.

Price-competitive businesses seldom have the excess capital necessary to buy back shares. Instead the reverse happens: They issue more shares to raise new money to support their cash-hungry businesses. Bethlehem Steel increased its outstanding shares from 75 million in 1990 to 132 million in 2000. General Motors increased the number of shares that it had outstanding by 30 million during the same period.

THE DYNAMICS OF SHARE REPURCHASES

When a company spends its capital to buy back its shares, it is in effect buying its own property and increasing future per share earnings of the owners who didn't sell. For instance, if you have a partnership with three partners, you each in effect own one-third of the partnership. If it makes any money, then each partner will take home one-third of the total. If the partnership, using partnership funds, buys one of the partners out, then the two remaining partners would each own 50% of the company and split the partnership's future earnings fifty-fifty. The pie remains the same size, but instead of being cut into three pieces, it is now cut into just two—two bigger slices.

In the case of publicly traded companies, share repurchases will cause per share earnings to increase, which results in an increase in the market price of the stock, which means richer shareholders. Here's how this works.

H&R Block had approximately 106 million shares outstanding in 1990 and 97 million in 2000. The decrease in the number of shares was the result of its active share-repurchase program during this period. To determine per share earnings you divide net earnings by the number of shares outstanding. In 2000, H&R Block reported net earnings of approximately $370 million, which, divided by the 97 million outstanding shares, equals per share earnings of $3.81 ($370 million ÷ 97 million = $3.81). Multiply $3.81 by a P/E ratio of 15 and you get a stock price of $57.15.

If H&R Block had not implemented a share repurchase program, it would still have had as many shares outstanding in 2000 as it did in 1990, which was 106 million, which would equate to per share earnings of $3.49 ($370 million ÷ 106 million = $3.49). Multiply $3.49 by a P/E ratio of 15 and you get a stock price of $52.35.

The bottom line here is that H&R Block's stock repurchase program increased per share earnings by $.32 a share ($3.81 – $3.49 = $.32), which caused a corresponding increase in its stock price from $52.35 a share to $57.15. H&R Block shareholders who didn't sell their stock during this period ended up the beneficiaries of the decrease of shares outstanding; their slices of H&R Block net earnings just got bigger.

Of course none of this would be possible if H&R Block didn't have a durable competitive advantage creating an abundance of excess cash.

HOW WARREN USES SHARE REPURCHASES TO INCREASE HIS WEALTH

Once Warren has invested in a company with a durable competitive advantage, he encourages the company's board of directors to increase spending on their share-repurchase program. He does this because when a business in which he owns an interest repurchases its own shares, it reduces the number of shares outstanding, which effectively increases Warren's ownership in the company without Warren having to invest another penny.

The logic goes like this: Let's say that a company has 100 million shares outstanding and Warren owns 10 million of those shares, which equates to 10% of the entire business (10 ÷ 100 = 10%). If over the next year the company goes into the stock market and buys back 40 million of its shares, it will have only 60 million shares outstanding. Warren's ownership in the business would have increased from 10% to 16.7% without his having to invest any more money. The company's capital increased his ownership.

Now consider this: If the company had paid out the money that it spent on buying back its shares, Warren would have had to pay income tax on his portion of the dividend, which means that he would've had about 30% less money to invest. By having the company repurchase its shares, Warren avoids the tax man and increases his ownership in the business. Let's take a closer look at a real example.

When Berkshire Hathaway bought into the Washington Post, it acquired approximately 10% of the Post for $10.2 million. Today Berkshire owns approximately 17.2% of the company. Berkshire's increase in ownership from 10% to 17.2% occurred because of the Washington Post's stock repurchase program, which Warren helped instigate shortly after he joined the Post's board of directors. Today the Washington Post has a market capitalization of approximately $5.02 billion. If the Washington Post hadn't repurchased its shares, then Berkshire's interest in the company would still be 10%, which would today be worth approximately $502 million ($5.02 billion x .10 = $502 million). But since the Washington Post did repurchase its shares, Berkshire now owns 17.2% of the company, which today is worth approximately $863.4 million ($5.02 billion x 0.172 = $863.4 million). Thus, because of the Washington Post's share repurchase program, Berkshire saw a $361.4 million increase in its net worth ($863.4 million – $502 million = $361.4 million).

Warren did the same kind of thing with Berkshire's 1980 initial investment in Geico. He acquired 33% of all its outstanding shares for $45.7 million. By the time 1995 had rolled around, Geico's share repurchase program, instigated by its board of directors, had increased Berkshire's stake in Geico to approximately 50%. In 1995, Geico had a total market capitalization of approximately $4.7 billion. If Berkshire had still owned only 33% of Geico in 1995, then the total value of this 33% stake would have been worth approximately $1.55 billion. But because of Geico's stock repurchase program, Berkshire's stake in Geico increased to 50%, which in 1995 was worth $2.35 billion. This means that Geico's share repurchase program added approximately $800 million in value to Berkshire's net worth. (In 1996, Berkshire acquired the other 50% of Geico, to take 100% control of the business.)

With share repurchases Warren has figured out how to acquire a larger ownership interest in a company with a durable competitive advantage without having to invest any more money in it. It's another of his neat tricks to get rich and one that he uses all the time.

Let's review. Companies that benefit from some kind of durable competitive advantage have a surplus of cash, which lets them implement share repurchase programs. On the other hand, price-competitive businesses are so strapped for cash that they have great difficulty implementing share repurchase programs. The magic of share repurchase programs are that they increase shareholders' ownership in the business with the company's capital, not their own.

NO. 10

DOES THE VALUE ADDED BY RETAINED EARNINGS INCREASE THE MARKET VALUE OF THE COMPANY?

Warren believes that if you can purchase a company with a durable competitive advantage at the right price, the retained earnings of the business will continuously increase the underlying value of the business and the market will continuously ratchet up the price of the company's stock. The key lies in the company's ability to properly allocate capital and keep adding to the company's net worth. A perfect example of this is his own Berkshire Hathaway, which in 1983 had a book value of $975 a share and was trading at around $1,000 a share. (Note: Book value is equal to assets minus liabilities. Trading value is whatever the shares are selling for on the stock exchange.) Eighteen years later, in 2001, it has a book value of approximately $40,000 a share and is trading at approximately $68,000. This means that Berkshire's book value has increased approximately 4,002% and the price of its shares by 6,874%. Warren grew the company's net worth by using the company's retained earnings to purchase whole or partial interests of other businesses with durable competitive advantages. As the net worth of the company grew, so did the market's valuation of the company, thus the rise in the price of the stock.

This is not true with a price-competitive business. It can retain earnings for years and still never show a real increase in the value of the company's stock. In 1983, General Motors had a book value of $32.44 a share and was trading at approximately $34. In 2001, General Motors' book value stood at approximately $36 a share and the price of its shares at around $55. All General Motors has to show for those eighteen years in business is a 10% increase in its book value and a 52% increase in the price of its stock.

I'd rather be driving a Berkshire. Wouldn't you?

Using this screen is easy. All you have to do is review a company's historical increase or decrease in the price of its shares and the historical increase or decrease in the company's per share book value. Use at least a ten-year spread. A company with a durable competitive advantage will have an increasing share price and an increasing book value.

Remember, the ultimate goal is to buy one of these businesses at a time that it is suffering from some bad-news situation that has caused the shortsighted stock market to send its stock price down. You are looking for a *recent* downturn in the price of a company's stock, not for a company whose stock price has done nothing over ten years.

WHAT YOU SHOULD HAVE LEARNED FROM THIS CHAPTER

The ten screens we've just discussed give you the ability to ascertain whether a company has a durable competitive advantage. Warren wants to own this type of company because it will experience a real increase in its long-term economic value, which absolutely ensures that it will recover from any shortsighted market sell-off of the company's stock. We've encapsulated those screening questions below.

1. *Does the company show a consistently high return on shareholders' equity (above 12%)?* This is indicative of a strong and possibly durable competitive advantage, which will allow the company to recover quickly from almost any business misfortune that a shortsighted stock market might overreact to. Consistently high returns are everything.

2. *Does the company show a consistently high return on total capital (12% or better)?* With banks and finance companies Warren looks at the return on total assets (in excess of 1%, and a consistent return on shareholders' equity in excess of 12%) to determine if the company is benefiting from some kind of durable competitive advantage.
3. *Do earnings show a strong upward trend?* The company with a durable competitive advantage can boast per share earnings that are both strong and on the rise.
4. *Is the company conservatively financed?* Companies with durable competitive advantages generally carry long-term debt of less than five times net earnings.
5. *Does the company have a brand-name product or service that gives it a competitive advantage in the marketplace?* That is not the same thing as a durable competitive advantage, but it's a good place to start. Employ quantitative/qualitative screens to determine whether the company truly has a durable competitive advantage.
6. *Does the company rely on an organized labor force?* Companies with organized labor forces seldom have durable competitive advantages.
7. *Can the company increase prices along with inflation?* A durable-competitive-advantage business can increase the prices of its products right along with any increases in its costs of production, which means that the underlying value of the company and its stock price will at least keep pace with inflation.
8. *How does the company allocate retained earnings?* Durable-competitive-advantage businesses are better able to retain earnings and are freer to utilize them in a manner that results in an increase in net earnings, thus increasing their stock price and making their stockholders richer.
9. *Does the company repurchase shares?* Companies that benefit from some kind of durable competitive advantage have a surplus of cash, which lets them implement share repurchase programs. The magic of share repurchase programs is that they increase shareholders' ownership in the business with the company's capital, not their own.

10. *Are the company's share price and book value on the rise?* The share prices and book values of durable-competitive-advantage companies have typically been increasing over ten years. The share prices of price-competitive businesses typically do nothing over ten years, and their book values are occasionally decimated by the struggle of staying competitive in a price-competitive arena.

Once Warren establishes that a company has a durable competitive advantage, he invests in this company only if it makes business sense (a topic we address later). He has found that his best opportunites are presented to him when the shortsighted market overreacts to bad news. After he makes his purchase, he continues to hold the stock, letting the retained earnings increase the underlying value of the business. The market, seeing the underlying increase in the value of the business, then correspondingly drives up the market price of the stock. *This is the method that Warren has used to create his superwealth. The trick is to find the durable competitive advantage and buy when the stock market is pricing it cheap.*

14

How to Determine When a Privately Held Business Can Be a Bonanza

Long ago Warren discovered that some privately owned companies had established a durable competitive advantage by developing a regional monopoly or brand-name product, making their owners rich.

To his amazement he also discovered that he could often buy these businesses at a fraction of what their publicly traded cousins sold for. This meant that he could often purchase them for a mere four to six times pretax earnings, which would give him an immediate 16% to 25% pretax return on his investment. (Obviously most of us are not in the market to buy an entire business. Warren's thinking on this is of interest because he uses the same kind of reasoning when he purchases a fractional interest of a business in the stock market.)

These businesses are all firmly entrenched and have long, successful business histories. The companies that manufacture brand-name products have good growth potential, but the companies with regional monopolies are limited in their ability to grow. This inability to expand operations means that these regional monopolies are of limited value to the vast majority of corporate America. However, to Warren's Berkshire, they offer a way to accumulate businesses that have the capacity to spin off cash that it can invest elsewhere. Think of them as AAA bonds that pay a 16% to 25% pretax return that will increase with inflation—something that the bond market will never serve up.

Many of the privately held businesses that Berkshire buys are wholly owned and managed by one family that has developed a strong attachment to its workers and a unique business culture.

Many of these owner/managers want to continue working in the business and don't want the culture they have created destroyed. Over the years Berkshire, in offering these owner families an opportunity to cash out while preserving the corporate culture that they have spent a lifetime creating, has become the preferred buyer. It's an odd kind of competitive advantage that has created many great investment opportunities for Berkshire. Let's look at a couple of companies Berkshire has acquired to get a better idea of how this strategy works.

NEBRASKA FURNITURE MART

In 1983, Warren went into Nebraska Furniture Mart, an Omaha furniture store that has held a regional monopoly for over forty years. He was looking for its owner, an eighty-nine-year-old Russian immigrant and family matriarch, who had built her business on a reputation of honesty and cheap prices, by the name of Rose Blumkin—affectionately known as Mrs. B. When he found her, he proudly announced that since it was his birthday, he wanted to buy her store. She shot back, in a thick Russian accent, that she would sell it to him for $60 million and not a penny less. Warren said, "Deal," walked out of the store, and came back an hour later with a check. When she inquired if he wanted his accountants to see the store's books before he handed over the check, he replied, "No, I trust you more."

The store's pretax net earnings of $14.5 million, against the selling price of $60 million, equates to an initial pretax return of 24% ($14.5 million ÷ $60 million = .24). Berkshire ended up buying 80% of the store, with Mrs. B and her children keeping the other 20%. Mrs. B and the kids wanted to keep working at the Mart, something that she loved to do, every day of the week. By 1993 the Mart had $21 million in pretax net earnings, which equates to a 35% pretax rate of return against a 1983 selling price of $60 million for the entire company. NFM's pretax net earnings grew at a compounding annual rate of 3.7%, which is about even with the rate of inflation and the population growth for Omaha during that period. When Berkshire bought NFM, it effectively bought a bond that paid a 24% pretax rate of return that would grow on average at 3.7% yearly.

NFM's durable competitive advantage is that it is the low-cost provider of carpet, furniture, electronics, and appliances in the Omaha region. With more than 450,000 square feet of retail space and 1 million square feet of warehouse space, it stomps the competition in merchandise selection and price. The company derives its power from owning its own retail and wholesale space, long since paid for, and from its ability to buy in such large quantities that it commands deep discounts from manufacturers. This equates to lower operational costs and lower merchandise costs, which means that it can offer its customers lower prices. Its customers know that the NFM offers the largest selection at the lowest prices and don't even bother to shop elsewhere. Though its margins are thin, it makes up for them with superhigh inventory turnover. NFM's game is to sell a lot of merchandise.

Any business seeking to compete with NFM faces the formidable cost of building or leasing an equally massive amount of retail and warehouse space, which it then has to stock. This expense would squeeze the competitor's already thin margins to nothing. Warren discovered that in almost every major metropolitan area some furniture retailer has acquired a regional monopoly just like NFM. He has been on a campaign to acquire as many of these businesses as possible. Besides NFM, he has acquired R. C. Willey Furniture of Salt Lake City, Star Furniture of Houston, and Jordan's, which dominates the New Hampshire and Massachusetts markets.

SEE'S CANDY

In 1972, Berkshire purchased See's candy, a California-based, brand-name candy manufacturer and retailer. The company's durable competitive advantage is that it has been in business since the 1920s and has developed a dedicated customer following for its specialty chocolates. When Berkshire paid $25 million for See's, it was reporting $4.2 million a year in pretax net earnings. This equates to Berkshire's earning an initial pretax annual return of 16.8% ($4.2 million ÷ $25 million = .168). By 1999, See's had $74 million in pretax net earnings, which equates to a 296% pretax return against a 1972 purchase price of $25 million. See's managed to grow its pretax earnings at an annual rate of 11.2%

due in part to inflation and an increase in the number of its retail outlets. See's has been a very sweet investment for Warren.

FECHHEIMER BRO.

Berkshire bought 86% of Fechheimer Bro., a uniform manufacturer, in 1986, based on a valuation of $55 million for the entire company against pretax earnings of $13.3 million. That equates to a 24% initial pretax return on the money ($13.3 million ÷ $55 million = .24). By 1996, Fechheimer Bro. had $17 million in pretax net earnings, which equates to a 31% pretax return against the 1986 purchase price of $55 million ($17 million ÷ $55 million = .31). Fechheimer Bro. managed to grow its pretax earnings at an annual rate of 2.4%, which is about in line with inflation. Fechheimer's uniform business is not as good a business as See's candy.

SCOTT FETZER

Berkshire bought Scott Fetzer, a collection of sixteen companies that included brand-name products Kirby Vacuum and World Book, in 1985 for $320 million against pretax earnings of $67.4 million. That equates to a 21% initial pretax return ($67.4 million ÷ $320 million = .21). By 1995, Scott Fetzer had approximately $92 million in pretax earnings, which equates to 29% pretax return against the 1985 purchase price of $320 million ($92 million ÷ $320 million = .29). Scott Fetzer managed to grow its pretax earnings at an annual rate of 3.2%, which also is about in line with inflation.

PUBLIC COMPANIES THAT BERKSHIRE HAS TAKEN PRIVATE

Warren discovered that occasionally even entire publicly traded companies could be bought at prices that offered Berkshire an attractive rate of return. These businesses all have long successful histories that typify businesses with durable competitive advantages, be it a brand name, distribution network, low-cost producer of a product or service, or a monopoly. Let's look at a couple of Berkshire's acquisitions.

JOHNS MANVILLE

In 2000, Berkshire purchased Johns Manville, the nation's largest manufacturer of insulation products, commercial and industrial roofing, filtration systems, and fiber mats. It paid $1.8 billion for the entire company against pretax earnings of $343.75 million. That equates to a 19% initial pretax return on Berkshire's money. From 1990 to 2000, Johns Manville grew its per share earnings at an annual rate of 9.5%, which is better than inflation. Warren could argue that Berkshire bought an initial pretax return of 19% that would grow at an annual rate of 9.5%.

BENJAMIN MOORE

Also in 2000, Berkshire acquired 100% of Benjamin Moore, a leading manufacturer and retailer through authorized dealers of premium paints, stains, and industrial coatings, which was founded in 1883. Berkshire paid $1 billion for the entire company against pretax earnings of $137.7 million. That equates to a 13.8% initial pretax return on Berkshire's money ($137.7 million ÷ $1 billion = .138). From 1990 to 2000, Benjamin Moore grew its per share earnings at an annual rate of 9.7%, beating the average annual inflation. Warren could argue that Berkshire bought an initial pretax return of 13.8% that would grow at an annual rate of 9.7%.

TAX ASPECTS

There is also a tax aspect to these acquisitions. By buying an entire company Berkshire can avoid a level of taxation on the economic growth of the business. To explain this, let's look at the economics of See's candy.

Suppose See's candy was a publicly traded company before Berkshire bought it and that instead of buying the entire company Berkshire bought only 10% of the outstanding shares. Every time See's earns $1 it has to pay a 34% corporate income tax, which reduces it to $.66. This after-tax $.66 either gets retained and added into See's shareholders' equity pot or is paid out as a dividend. If See's pays out to Berkshire the $.66 as a dividend, then Berkshire will have to pay a 14% tax on the dividend income. If See's chooses to retain the $.66 and it is added to the equity pot, it will increase the value of its business and ultimately the price of its shares. If at some time in the future Berkshire wants to unlock the increased value of See's accumulated retained earnings, it would have to sell its See's shares, which means that its profits from the sale would be subject to a capital gains tax of 35% on the difference between what it paid for the stock and what it sold it for. So if Berkshire paid $10 a share for See's and sold it for $25 a share, it would have to pay a capital gains tax on $15 in profits ($25 – $10 = $15).

But since Berkshire bought all of See's, instead of just 10%, then any earnings See's pays out to Berkshire will be exempt from the 14% tax on dividends. If Berkshire decides to sell it, the amount of earnings that See's retained during Berkshire's ownership will for tax purposes be added to Berkshire's purchase price for See's. In this scenario, if Berkshire paid $10 a share for See's and retained $8 a share, its basis for capital gains taxes would increase to $18 a share ($10 + $8 = $18). Thus, if it sold See's for the equivalent of $25 a share, it would have to pay a capital gains tax on only $7 of the $15 in profits ($25 – $18 = $7). Though this may not seem like much per share, if Berkshire really did sell See's, it could equate to a savings of approximately $25 million—the price Berkshire originally paid for the company! Sometimes it's better to eat the whole cake rather than take a few nibbles.

WHAT YOU SHOULD HAVE LEARNED FROM THIS CHAPTER

- By purchasing privately held businesses that have a durable competitive advantage, Berkshire can earn an initial pretax return between 13.7% and 25% that will most certainly increase with inflation and may even do better.
- These privately held companies offer certain tax advantages

over the purchase of minority interests in publicly traded businesses. Any way you look at it, these businesses are cash cows that Berkshire is buying at bargain prices compared to their long-term worth.

15

Warren's Secret Formula for Getting Out at the Market Top

When do you sell? That depends on whether the company has a durable competitive advantage or is a price-competitive business, whether underlying changes are going on in the business, and whether the market is offering you a high enough price.

Warren has bought and sold hundreds of securities over his lifetime, *but his big money has always come from buying companies with a durable competitive advantage and holding them over the long term, in some cases for thirty or more years.* However, he has sold even these companies when the price was high enough or a better opportunity came along or circumstances changed the economics of the business. Let's look at these selling situations and how they have contributed to his wealth.

WARREN'S FORMULA FOR SELLING OUT AT THE TOP

Warren believes that if you are lucky enough to latch on to a company with a durable competitive advantage at a price that makes business sense, you should make it a long-term holding. Even so, in certain situations it makes sense to sell stock in these businesses when their market prices go high enough. Warren has sold large portions of his portfolio of durable-competitive-advantage businesses on two occasions.

The first time was in 1969 after a bull market that had lasted through most of the sixties, bubbled in 1971 and 1972, and subsequently collapsed in 1973 and 1974. Stocks that were trading at P/Es of 50 or better when he sold them had by 1973–74 dropped to single-digit P/Es. When Warren got out of the market, he told his partnership investors that as a value-oriented investor he could no longer find anything to buy so he was leaving the game. (Remember, the market has more than likely bubbled when value-oriented investors leave the game.) The second time Warren sold was in 1998, when many stocks in Berkshire's portfolio had risen to historically high P/Es of 50 or more. He brilliantly sold a huge interest in the company's portfolio for 100% of cash-rich insurance giant General Reinsurance in a tax-free transaction.

Warren sees that when stocks that have historically traded at between ten and twenty-five times earnings begin trading at forty or more times earnings, for no other reason than that the market is going through a period of mass speculation, it's time to get out. He knows that the economics of the companies in which he invests do not warrant P/E ratios of 40 or more. Let's look at an example.

Coca-Cola was earning $1.42 a share in 1998 and had been growing its earnings for the last ten years at an average annual rate of 12%—very healthy numbers. If you bought a share of Coke and held until 2008, you could expect that share to produce $24.88 in total earnings by the end of the tenth year. Regardless of what you paid for the share, $24.88 is approximately what you would earn by owning it. (Please note that we have forgone the effects of taxation to keep things simple.) What would you have been willing to pay for a share of Coke stock back in 1998? If you had paid its 1998 trading value of $88 a share, you would effectively have been paying sixty-two times for Coke's $1.42 per share earnings. Was that a good buy? Let's do a little comparison shopping. If you took that $88 and invested it in a corporate bond that was paying 6%, you would earn $5.28 a year ($88 x .06 = $5.28). If you held the bond for ten years, you would earn a total of $52.80. So what do you want to do—earn $24.88 on your $88 investment, or $52.80? You want to earn $52.80 of course! Your money is better spent by buying the 6% bonds than by paying sixty-two times earnings for Coke.

But what if you paid $28.40 or twenty times earnings for a share of Coke? This is a much better deal. This is because $28.40 worth of 6% bonds would only pay you a total of $17 over ten years ($28.40 x .06 = $1.70 x 10 years = $17). Not as good as the $24.88 that you would earn if you had bought Coke for $28.40 a share. *In fact, the lower Coke's share price goes, the more enticing a buy it becomes.* But for Coke to be worth sixty-two times earnings, it would either have to be growing its per share earnings at an annual rate of 30% to 40% or bond interest rates would have to dip to 2% to 3%. The kinds of companies that benefit from a *durable* competitive advantage that Warren would be interested in seldom, if ever, see that kind of growth. (Microsoft has, but it isn't a Buffett-type company.)

We know that in 1998 Coca-Cola was insanely priced—you shouldn't be paying a P/E of 62 for it. The next question is, if you owned it in 1998, should you have sold it? We know that if you kept it for another ten years, you could expect to earn a total of $24.88. But if you sold it for $88 a share and invested that money in 6% corporate bonds, over the next ten years you would earn a total of $52.80. Now dig this! Warren is famous for averaging a 23% annual return. If he had sold his Coke stock for $88 a share in 1998 and reinvested that money at an annual rate of 23%, the $88 he received would produce a yearly income of $20.24, which after ten years would have produced $202.40 a share in total earnings. Compare $202.40 with the $24.88 he would have earned if he had held the stock and you can see that selling in 1998 would have been the sensible thing to do.

In 1998, Warren did sell part of his holdings in Coca-Cola, but he didn't sell it for 62 times earnings, the market price for Coke's stock. He sold it for 167 times earnings—almost three times the market price. Who paid that much for it? The shareholders of General Reinsurance. Let's look at this transaction and the economics behind it to get a better idea of how Warren worked this magic. (Please note: This kind of transaction is unique to Warren's empire and is not the kind of thing that the average investor can engage in. We discuss it here for its educational value.)

As the stock market rose higher and higher in the late nineties, two things happened to Berkshire that set the stage for the General Reinsurance deal. The first was the fantastic rise in value of the individual stocks that Berkshire held in its portfolio. Several were at all-time highs: Coca-Cola at 62 times earnings, Washington Post at 24 times earnings, American Express at 20 times earnings, Gillette at 40 times earnings, and Freddie Mac at 21 times earnings. The second was the incredible rise in the price of Berkshire shares. Berkshire sold for $80,900 a share in 1998, or approximately 2.7 times its per share book value of $29,743. This means that the stock market was valuing Berkshire's stock portfolio at 2.7 times its portfolio's market value. If you had bought a share of Berkshire in 1998 for $80,900 you were effectively paying 167 times earnings for Coke, 65 times earnings for the Washington Post, 54 times earnings for American Express, 108 times earnings for Gillette, and 57 times earnings for Freddie Mac. At these prices Warren would have sold out in a New York minute. The problem was that to get 167 times earnings for his Coke stock he had to sell his Berkshire stock, and there was no way he could have dumped billions of dollars' worth of Berkshire on the market without sending its share price into the floor.

The solution was to find an insurance company loaded with bonds that would be willing to be acquired by Berkshire in exchange for its shares. Why bonds? Because bonds could easily be turned into cash at a value that was neither overvalued nor undervalued. Think of cashing in a certificate of deposit. General Reinsurance was loaded with $19 billion worth of bonds. So Warren called up the CEO of General Reinsurance and asked if he cared to swap 100% of General Reinsurance and its tasty bond portfolio for $22 billion in Berkshire stock. (Admittedly Warren didn't add that Berkshire's stock portfolio was grossly inflated, nor did he tell the CEO that the market was overvaluing Berkshire's shares.) General Reinsurance's management could only see the face value of the deal, which meant that they could swap their stock, which was trading at $220 a share, for $283 a share in Berkshire stock. It sounded like a great deal. Warren saw that he could swap partial ownership of Berkshire's overpriced stocks for General Reinsurance's liquid bond portfolio. Effectively, Warren sold to the shareholders of General Reinsurance 9 million shares of American Express, 35 million shares of Coke, 10 million shares of Freddie Mac, 17 million shares of Gillette, 309,000 shares of the Washington Post, 11 million shares of Wells Fargo, and a 17.9% interest in the rest of Berkshire. Of the $22 billion in Berkshire stock that was paid to General Reinsurance shareholders, $17.8 billion was for inflated securities that were carried on Berkshire's books at an already historically high market value of $6.6 billion and an actual cost of $1.3 billion. In exchange, Berkshire's shareholders picked up 82.1% of General Reinsurance's business, its $19 billion bond portfolio, and its $5 billion stock portfolio. A sweet deal if ever there was one.

Another fascinating aspect of this transaction was that even though Berkshire acquired General Reinsurance, the transaction was engineered as a tax-free merger. This means that Warren sold the equivalent of $17.8 billion in securities that it carried at a cost of $1.3 billion, and didn't have to pay a single penny in capital gains taxes. It doesn't get any better than that.

Since the General Reinsurance merger was completed, Warren has been peeling off billions from Berkshire's newly acquired bond portfolio to buy interests in or fully acquire H&R Block, Justin Industries, Yum Brands, Mueller Industries, Furniture Brands International, Johns Manville, Shaw Industries, Liz Claiborne, Nike Inc., Dun & Bradstreet Corp., USG Corp., and First Data Corp., to name a few.

Key Point ➢ A good rule of thumb is to add up the expected per share earnings of a company over the next ten years and then compare that sum with what you would earn if you sold the stock and placed the proceeds in bonds instead. If owning the bonds would earn you more, you are better off selling the stock. If owning the business would earn you more, you should keep the stock. The reverse is also true. If you are thinking of buying shares in a company, first consider whether you would earn more money by buying bonds. If so, you should not be buying the stock.

What this method does is keep you focused on the underlying economics of the business. Warren says that the price of a company's shares will, over time, *always* track the underlying economics of the business. Sometimes the shortsighted market will grossly overprice a company's shares in relation to what the business's future earnings are worth relative to what bonds are paying. That is when you want to sell. At other times the shortsighted stock market will grossly underprice a company's shares in relation to what the business's future earnings are worth relative to what bonds are paying. That is when you want to buy. It's that simple and it's very businesslike. That is why Warren calls it investing from a business perspective.

A BETTER OPPORTUNITY PRESENTS ITSELF

Warren has found that it is often advantageous to sell out of an investment when the underlying business hasn't performed well in order to take advantage of a new opportunity. But don't make the mistake of selling flowers to buy weeds. If you are lucky enough to get into a company that has a strong durable competitive advantage and management that knows how to maximize profits, then hold it until you are offered an insanely high price. Don't worry about short-term price fluctuations. With a great business it doesn't matter. Remember that both Warren and Bill Gates made all their big money by holding on to the same stock for more than twenty years.

WHEN THE BUSINESS OR ENVIRONMENT CHANGES

Warren says that when you're holding an investment—even one with a durable competitive advantage—you have to keep your eye on the horizon to make sure that a change in the business or its environment doesn't change a durable-competitive-advantage company into a price-competitive business or, worse yet, render it completely obsolete. He believes that companies that manufacture products or are in the retail business can easily make this shift. Any change will affect sales, which show up on the quarterly income statement. Warren says that it's almost impossible to see a disaster in the making with financial institutions because of their ability to hide problems until they become disasters. Therefore it is better to be on the safe side whenever you invest in financial institutions. Warren sold Freddie Mac for this very reason. When Warren first invested in the company, it was in the relatively safe business of securitizing single-family-home mortgages and selling them to investment institutions like pension funds. In search of bigger profits, it graduated into commercial mortgages, introducing an element of risk with which Warren wasn't comfortable.

THE TARGET PRICE FOR THE SECURITY HAS BEEN MET

Sometimes an investment has a target sale price. All arbitrage situations fall into this category. Warren has also invested in companies converting from corporate form to partnership form. When this happens, a price spread often develops between what a business is worth as a corporation and what it is worth as a partnership that will pay out all its income. Warren buys before the transformation and sells after it has been completed and the market has revalued it. Warren's investment in Tenneco Offshore is one of these types of investments. Let's take a look at it.

In 1981, Tenneco Offshore was planning to convert from corporate form to partnership form to avoid certain taxes. For every $1.21 that Tenneco earned it had to pay $.41 in corporate income tax. This left $.80 that could be paid out as a dividend to shareholders, who then had to pay income tax on it. If Tenneco converted to a partnership, it could skip the corporate tax and pay out the entire dollar. It's a neat trick with only one catch: The partnership must pay out the dollar because the partners/shareholders have to pay income tax on the dollar whether they receive it or not. It's no fun to have to pay tax on money you don't receive. Tenneco owned a large pool of natural gas and was paying out to its shareholders 100% of proceeds from the sale of the gas. The company was paying out annually $0.80 a share as a dividend and since interest rates on treasury bonds were at an all-time high of 14%, the market was valuing the company at $5.71 per share ($0.80 ÷ 14% = $5.71—see discussion of stock value relative to treasury bonds in chapter 18). When the company converted into a partnership, it could skip the corporate tax and pay out $1.21 a share, which means that the market should have valued the partnership at $8.64 a share ($1.21 ÷ 14% = $8.64). The shortsighted stock market ignored the announcement that Tenneco was going to convert to a partnership and continued to trade it at $5.71 a share. Seeing this price discrepancy, Warren started buying his shares. After Tenneco made the conversion, the market revalued it upward to $8 a share. And then Warren sold his interest.

WHAT YOU SHOULD HAVE LEARNED FROM THIS CHAPTER

- Warren made his big money by holding on to durable-competitive-advantage companies for the long term.
- At the height of a bull market, durable-competitive-advantage businesses can reach prices at which it makes business sense to sell.
- A change in the business environment may also dictate a sale.
- A change in a company's business model can dictate a sale.
- Reaching a stock's target price can dictate a sale.

16

Where Warren Buffett Is Investing Now!

You'll find two lists here: The first is made up of companies in which Warren has invested *between* 1998 and 2001, either personally, through his foundation, or through Berkshire Hathaway. The second is made up of investments he has made over the last thirty years, which we believe are of great educational value.

Be aware that simply because Warren has made investments in these companies or they met his selective criteria doesn't mean he would buy them today. He bought when the price was right. Remember: You want to identify the company with a durable competitive advantage and then let the price of its shares determine when you pull the trigger. The right price may come tomorrow or it may come five years from now.

Also keep in mind that at times Mr. Market is wildly enthusiastic about some of these businesses and prices them high. On other days he will be very pessimistic about their prospects and price them low. You are interested in the days that Mr. Market is pessimistic, not the others.

Below we provide you with the Web site addresses and phone numbers of these businesses. Almost all have comprehensive sites; you can also call them to obtain free annual reports. As we noted earlier, you might log on to EDGAR at www.sec.gov/edgar.shtml to get a company's 10-K filing, an informational and financial document filed once a year with the SEC. It's a bit like an annual report but contains more detailed information. Keep in mind that *Value Line* covers a great many of the companies listed below and is a great source for historical numbers. The msn.com financial Web site moneycentral.msn.com also contains a great deal of historical financial information that is useful.

A final bit of advice: *Be patient.* A great selective contrarian buying opportunity doesn't happen every day, but when it does, it's an invitation to make a fortune.

Bon appétit!

RECENT INVESTMENTS

Aegis Realty. ***Trading symbol:*** **AER.** ***Industry:*** **real estate.** ***Phone:*** **212-593-5797.**

Aegis Realty is a real estate investment trust (REIT) that owns and manages three million square feet of shopping-center space. We believe Warren was buying it in 2000 for around $8 to $9 a share. It pays a dividend of $.96 a share and has a book value of $14.81 a share. This is an interest play that pays a 10% return and a Grahamian value play that's selling below book value.

Dun & Bradstreet Corp. ***Trading symbol:*** **DNB.** ***Industry:*** **information.** ***Phone:*** **908-665-5803.** ***Internet:*** **www.dnbcorp.com.**

Dun & Bradstreet sells business information about other businesses. Warren bought this in 1998 because it is a great company and it was about to spin off its lucrative Moody's Investors Services. In spin-offs, the market sometimes fails to fully appreciate the value of the whole divided into separate parts. This is a Berkshire holding, believed to have been purchased in 1999 before the spin-off for approximately $15 a share. As of May 2001, it trades at $27 a share. Moody's Investors Services was spun off on September 30, 2000, at $26 a share, and as of May 2001 it trades at $32 a share. On Warren's original $15 investment in D&B he made $12 on the D&B side and $32 on the Moody's side for a total profit of $44, which equates to a 293% return on his original investment of $15. Where was the rest of Wall Street? Off chasing tech stocks, of course. Oops!

First Data Corp. ***Trading symbol:*** **FDC.** ***Industry:*** **credit card transactions.** ***Phone:*** **201-342-0402.** ***Internet:*** **www.firstdatacorp.com.**

Someone has to process those millions of credit card transactions and the company that does it is First Data Corp. It's a fantastic business with which Warren has long been fascinated. This is a

Berkshire holding. Warren started buying it in 1998 during a fall contraction/panic sell-off that dropped its price down to $20 a share against earnings of $1.56 a share, which equates to an initial return of 7.8%. Its per share earnings had a 15% annual rate of growth. In May 2001 its stock was trading at $66 a share, which equates to a 48% compounding annual rate of return. Nice.

Furniture Brands International. ***Trading symbol:*** **FBN.** ***Industry:*** **furniture.** ***Phone:*** **314-863-5306.** ***Internet:*** **www.furniturebrands.com.**

Warren probably saw this one in *Value Line,* did his scuttlebutt at the Nebraska Furniture Mart, and discovered that Furniture Brands International was the number one manufacturer of residential furniture in America. This is a Berkshire holding. We believe that he started buying it in 2000 for around $14 a share against earnings of $1.92 a share, which equates to an initial return of 13.7%. Its per share earnings have been growing at an annual rate of 28%. This is a great business. Everyone buys furniture at some time or another, and FBI is there to sell it to them. It has been in business since 1921 and has strong earnings and great returns on equity and total capital. Over the years it has come to dominate its field. Warren bought after the 1999 bubble burst. It didn't stay down long. By February 2001 it was trading at $25 a share, giving Warren a quick 79% return on his money.

GPU, Inc. ***Trading symbol:*** **GPU.** ***Industry:*** **utility.** ***Phone:*** **973-455-8377.** ***Internet:*** **www.gpu.com.**

GPU is a utility holding company that distributes electricity to two million people in New Jersey and Pennsylvania. It also serves 1.4 million customers in Australia. This is a Berkshire holding. We believe Warren started buying this stock in February of 2000, for around $25 a share, against a book value of $28.46 a share, dividend payout of $2.18, and 1999 per share earnings of $3.25 a share. Warren's buying opportunity came when the cost of creating energy increased to more than GPU could charge its customers, which caused it to lose $1.74 a share in the second quarter of 2000. To increase rates, the company has to apply to Pennsylvania regulators. If the regulators don't increase rates, GPU will go out of business and the good people of Pennsylvania will go without power. As of May 2001, First Energy, another utility holding company, had made a bid of $36 a share for the company, and the wise regulators of Pennsylvania are considering giving GPU a huge rate increase.

H&R Block. ***Trading symbol:*** **HRB.** ***Industry:*** **financial services.** ***Phone:*** **816-753-6900.** ***Internet:*** **www.hrblock.com.**

H&R Block prepares income tax returns. It is currently expanding its financial services group. We did a case study on this one so we won't belabor the point. Check it out.

HRPT Properties Trust. ***Trading symbol:*** **HRP.** ***Industry:*** **REIT.** ***Phone:*** **617-332-3990.** ***Internet:*** **www.hrpreit.com.**

This is a real estate investment trust (REIT) that focuses on commercial real estate. Its earnings are solid and it pays a dividend every year between $.88 and $1.51 a share. It is presently repurchasing its shares. We believe Warren has been buying this stock at a price rumored to be $7 to $8 a share, where it traded for much of 2000. At that price he is getting an initial return of between 12.5% and 20%. We might add that at that price it was considerably below its book value of $11.60 a share—a Grahamian value play? As of May 2001 you could still buy it at $8.90 a share.

JDN Realty. ***Trading symbol:*** **JDN.** ***Industry:*** **REIT.** ***Phone:*** **404-262-3252.** ***Internet:*** **www.jdrealty.com.**

JDN Realty is a real estate investment trust (REIT) that develops, acquires, leases, and manages shopping centers in eighteen states. It has a book value of $14.80 a share and pays a dividend of $1.20 a share. We believe Warren started buying its stock at around $9 a share. The book value represents real estate that has been depreciated and is worth far more than it is carried on JDN's books. Warren bought the stock at an initial return of 13% ($1.20 ÷ $9 = 13%) and as an asset play.

Johns Manville. Acquired by Berkshire in 2000.

Johns Manville was a great company in great financial shape until it sold a ton of products loaded with asbestos that made people deathly ill. These people sued Johns Manville by the tens of thousands, pushing it into bankruptcy. The bankruptcy court put 78% of the ownership of the company into a trust in settlement of the lawsuits. Even though the company was making a great deal of money selling nonasbestos products and the stock was publicly traded, investors weren't very interested. Tech stocks were the ticket of the day, not stodgy old insulation companies.

In 2000, Berkshire purchased Johns Manville, the nation's largest manufacturer of insulation products, commercial and industrial roofing, filtration systems, and fiber mats. It paid $1.8 billion for the entire company against pretax earnings of $343.75 million. That equates to a 19% initial pretax return on Berkshire's money. From 1990 to 2000, Johns Manville grew its per share earnings at an annual rate of 9.5%, which is better than inflation. Warren could argue that Berkshire bought a bond with an initial pretax return of 19% that would grow at an annual rate of 9.5%.

Justin Industries. Acquired by Berkshire in 2000.

Justin Industries makes Acme Bricks and brand-name western boots like Tony Lama. Warren bought the entire company for $570 million against pretax earnings of approximately $51 million, which equates to a pretax return of approximately 8.9%. Earnings have been growing at 16% a year for the last ten years. Warren could argue that he just bought a bond that paid a pretax return of 8.9% that would increase at 16% a year. It beats the static 6% pretax return that treasuries were paying.

La-Z-Boy Inc. ***Trading symbol:*** **LZB.** ***Industry:*** **furniture.** ***Phone:*** **201-295-7550.** ***Internet:*** **www.lazyboy.com.**

La-Z-Boy is the number one manufacturer of upholstered furniture in the United States and the number one seller of recliners in the world. This is a Berkshire holding. We believe Warren started buying La-Z-Boy after the market crashed in February 2000 for $14 a share, on earnings of $1.46 a share. As of June, 2001, it trades at $19 a share. It has been growing per share earnings at 15.7% a year. Expect Warren to continue buying if he can get it cheap.

Liz Claiborne. ***Trading symbol:*** **LIZ.** ***Industry:*** **apparel.** ***Phone:*** **201-295-7550.** ***Internet:*** **www.lizclaiborne.com.**

Liz Claiborne is America's number one seller of clothes and accessories for the career woman. Its clothes are sold in department stores and in its 275 retail outlets. It also makes Donna Karan jeans and Lucky Brand dungarees. It's been in business for more than twenty years. The durable competitive advantage is its brand name, which it stitches to clothing made cheaply in another part of the world.

In 1998, as momentum investors fled low-tech businesses for high-tech businesses, Liz Claiborne saw its stock tumble from a high of $53 a share to a low of $27. Warren stepped into the market, buying nearly 9% of the company. In 1998, Liz Claiborne earned $2.57 a share against an asking price of $27, which equates to an initial return of 9.5%. By 2000 it was earning $3.43 a share, which equates to a 12.7% return on his initial investment. The longer you stay, the better it gets.

Mueller Industries. ***Trading symbol:*** **MLI.** ***Industry:*** **copper plumbing.** ***Phone:*** **901-753-3200.** ***Internet:*** **www.muellerindustries.com.**

This is a Berkshire holding. Warren is believed to have started buying Mueller Industries, the leading low-cost producer of copper plumbing fittings, tubes, and related products, during the October 2000 sell-off that knocked Mueller down from $32 a share to $21 against solid earnings of $2.16 a share. The company has been in business since 1917 (talk about durable) and has a low-cost infrastructure that allows it to stomp the competition. As of May 2001, Mueller is trading at $34 a share, giving Warren a superfast 62% return on Berkshire's money. Warren loves those fall sell-offs.

Nike Inc. ***Trading symbol:*** **NKE.** ***Industry:*** **shoes.** ***Phone:*** **503-671-6453.** ***Internet:*** **www.nike.com.**

Nike is the world's number one shoe company and has more than 40% of the U.S. sports shoe market. This shows up in Berkshire's portfolio, but we don't have any hard information on Warren's purchase price. We believe he was buying Nike in 1998 and 2000 when it traded below $30 a share. Buying opportunities include a recession in the shoe business, a general recession, and a correction or panic sell-off.

USG Corp. ***Trading symbol:*** **USG.** ***Industry:*** **wallboard.** ***Phone:*** **312-606-5725.** ***Internet:*** **www.usg.com.**

USG is the *low-cost producer* of wallboard and the number one maker of gypsum wallboard in the world. This is a classic bad-news play. As we write, the price of wallboard is falling and the company is facing asbestos litigation, which has dropped the stock's price from $45 a share to $10. Warren is buying like crazy. So far he has acquired a 15% stake in the company. In June 2001 the company filed for bankruptcy, but many analysts thought this filing would actually help stabilize current operations. The verdict is still out on this one.

Yum Brands. ***Trading symbol:*** **YUM.** ***Industry:*** **fast food.** ***Phone:*** **502-874-8300.** ***Internet:*** **www.yum.com.**

Yum Brands owns three major fast-food brand names: KFC, Pizza Hut, Taco Bell. This is a Berkshire holding. We believe Berkshire began its purchases in 2000 after the market crash at approximately $24 a share against earnings of $3.65 a share, which equates to an initial return of 15%. As of March 2002 the stock traded at $55 a share.

HISTORICAL INVESTMENTS

Amerada Hess. ***Trading symbol:*** **AHC.** ***Industry:*** **oil.** ***Phone:*** **212-536-8396.** ***Internet:*** **www.hess.com.**

Amerada Hess is an oil company. Warren made this investment based on asset evaluation. He multiplied the price of oil by the number of barrels it had in the ground and found that it was selling at a significant discount. He paid $26 a share and we believe he sold it a year later at approximately $50 a share. Not too shabby.

American Broadcasting Companies, Inc. Merged with Capital Cities, which merged with Disney.

ABC is a television network that in the early seventies had one of the most durable competitive advantages around. We believe

Warren started buying it during an advertising recession in 1978 for approximately $24 a share and sold it in 1980 for approximately $40 a share. After it merged with Capital Cities in 1984, it merged with Disney.

American Express. ***Trading symbol:*** **AXP.** ***Industry:*** **financial.** ***Phone:*** **212-619-6974.** ***Internet:*** **www.americanexpress.com.**

American Express is a major financial services company that just about does it all. But its strength is travel-industry-related services for businesses, and at this, it's king. Its credit card business is a kind of toll bridge that makes money every time someone uses an American Express card. As discussed, Warren first invested in the company in the sixties during the salad-oil scandal that destroyed its equity base but not its core business. Warren sold out after the company recovered.

In the early nineties AmEx started to have problems. From September 1991 to September 1994 the company lost approximately 2.2 million individual card users and saw its share of the total credit card market drop from 22.5% in 1990 to 16.3% in 1995. This was caused in part by AmEx's push to become a one-stop shop for all your financial needs. In diversifying into different financial products, it lost focus on its credit card operations—the bread and butter of its business. Keep in mind that businesses with a durable competitive advantage are sometimes managed by teams that ignore the wonderful underlying parts of the business that made the company great in the first place. In AmEx's case, Harvey Golub rode to the rescue as the company's new CEO. Warren jumped on Golub's wagon and began buying the stock. Remember, you invest not only in the company, but also in the people who run it. Warren made his 1994 purchase right before the spin-off of Lehman Brothers (an investment bank). AmEx gave its shareholders one-fifth of a share in Lehman for every share of AmEx they owned. The one-fifth Lehman was worth approximately $4. Warren paid $26 a share for the AmEx and then got $4 a share in Lehman stock via the spin-off. This equates to an immediate 15% return on his investment. Today his AmEx stock is worth approximately $166 a share, which equates to a 30%

compounded annual rate of return. When it comes to the American Express card, Warren is happy that people don't leave home without it.

Anheuser-Busch. ***Trading symbol:*** **BUD.** ***Industry:*** **beer.** ***Phone:*** **314-577-2000.** ***Internet:*** **www.anheuser-busch.com.**

Anheuser-Busch is the world's largest brewing company. It has what Warren calls a durable competitive advantage: You order your beer by brand name, and brand names it has aplenty: Budweiser, Bud Light, Busch, Michelob, Red Wolf lager, ZiegenBock Amber, and O'Doul's. It gets great returns on equity and total capital and has strong earnings growth. You need a recession or panic sell-off to get a buying opportunity on this one. Anheuser-Busch is a Buffett Foundation holding.

Bristol-Myers Squibb. ***Trading symbol:*** **BMY.** ***Industry:*** **drugs.** ***Phone:*** **212-546-4000.** ***Internet:*** **www.bms.com.**

Bristol-Myers Squibb sold about $22 billion in proprietary medical products, ethical pharmaceuticals, and health and beauty products in 2000. It has been in business since 1887, and unless people are going to stop getting sick, it is going to be in business for a long time to come. We believe Warren was buying it in 1993, on the threat of government regulation, for around $13 a share, with earnings of $1.10 a share and historical returns on equity and capital of over 30%. So far Warren has earned a 23% average annual return on this investment.

Campbell Soup. ***Trading symbol:*** **CPB.** ***Industry:*** **food.** ***Phone:*** **856-342-4800.** ***Internet:*** **www.campbellsoups.com.**

Campbell's has 70% of the condensed-soup market. It also owns Franco-American, V8, Swanson, Pepperidge Farm, Vlasic, Mrs. Paul's, Prego ("you're welcome" in Italian), and dozens of other brand names that you might find in your grocery basket. The durability of this company's competitive advantage is amazing. Winter comes along and people start buying soups. Look for recessions, panic sell-offs, a warm winter, which can hurt soup sales, or just a business screwup to make the stock attractively priced. This company shows up in the Buffett Foundation holdings. Soup is good food and so is the stock at the right price.

Capital Cities Communications. Acquired ABC, which was then acquired by Disney.

Warren loves owning television stations because they make a lot of money and are cheap to run—you buy a transmitter, put up an antenna, plug it into the wall, and you're in business. Network affiliated TV stations make money because they are key advertising bridges that businesses have to use to reach potential consumers. Capital Cities owned a bunch of television stations and cable TV networks and was incredibly well run. Warren owned the company in the late seventies and then sold it in the early eighties, which he admitted was a mistake. When it acquired ABC, back in 1986, it needed an equity infusion, so the CEO asked Warren whether he wanted in. Warren made an offer and the company said yes. He bought $515 million worth, paying $17.25 a share and then sold out (in a cash-and-stock deal) when Disney acquired Capital Cities in 1995 for $127 a share. That equates to a 24% compounded annual return on his 1986 investment. Another lesson in the long-term-hold department.

Cleveland-Cliffs Iron Company. ***Trading symbol:*** **CLF.** ***Industry:*** **mining.** ***Phone:*** **216-694-4880.** ***Internet:*** **www.cleveland-cliffs.com.**

Cleveland-Cliffs is the largest supplier of iron ore products to North American steel companies. It owns and operates five iron ore mines with several large steelmakers. The company has been around since 1840. What makes it interesting is that during a recession in the steel business it simply closes down the mines until demand returns. Warren first bought shares in this company during the 1984 steel industry recession and sold it after the industry recovered. The most recent buying opportunity with this company occurred in 2001 when an overabundance of iron ore met a recession in the steel industry, which killed iron ore prices and sent the stock tumbling from a high of $50 to a low of $14. The company's durable competitive advantage is that it is tied in with the steel companies and can stop production and cut expenses without damaging its competitive advantage. You buy this one in a recession and sell when it's over.

Coca-Cola Co. ***Trading symbol:*** **KO.** ***Industry:*** **beverage.** ***Phone:*** **404-676-2121.** ***Internet:*** **www.cocacola.com.**

Coca-Cola has the mother lode of durable competitive advantages. Coke is the world's top soft-drink company. It sells more than 230 brands of beverages, including coffees, juices, and teas. It commands 50% of the global soft-drink market and 2% of the world's daily fluid consumption. This is one of the biggest bets that Warren ever made, and it's also one of his most profitable. Buy this one during a recession and panic sell-off. Under no circumstances should you ever pay more than thirty times earnings for it. Expect Warren to be buying more anytime it drops to a P/E below 25.

Cox Communications. ***Trading symbol:*** **COX.** ***Industry:*** **cable TV.** ***Phone:*** **404-843-5975.** ***Internet:*** **www.cox.com.**

Provides cable TV service to 6 million customers and digital TV to 350,000 subscribers. Media conglomerate Cox Enterprises controls 68% of Cox Communications' stock. It also offers Internet access and local and long-distance phone service. It is the monopoly cable TV provider in most of the markets it services. Think of it as 6.3 million people who are addicted to channel surfing sending it checks each month. Cox's net profit margin was 23% in 2000. Compare that to Ford Motor's net profit margin of 1% and you can see why Warren loves the cable TV business and abhors the automobile business. This is a Buffett Foundation holding.

The Walt Disney Company. ***Trading symbol:*** **DIS.** ***Industry:*** **entertainment.** ***Phone:*** **818-560-1930.** ***Internet:*** **www.disney.com.**

Warren first bought into Walt Disney Company in 1966, when it was selling for $53 a share, which meant that the market was valuing the entire business for $80 million, less than *Snow White* and the other cartoons were worth. Included in the deal you also got Disneyland. Warren bought $5 million worth and sold it a year later for $6 million. He says that if he had kept that 5% stake it would now be worth more than $1 billion (which equates to a 19%

compounding annual rate of return for the thirty-year period). Lessons like this taught Warren that holding companies with a durable competitive advantage for the long term was the easiest way to become superrich. He later acquired 21.5 million shares of Disney when it acquired Capital Cities in 1995. At the top of the bull market between 1998 and 2000, he was rumored to be selling Disney directly in the market, and as we noted earlier, he sold it indirectly in the General Reinsurance deal.

Disney is the second-largest media conglomerate in the world. It owns the ABC television network, TV stations, radio stations, theme parks, movie studios, and of course, the monarch of the Magic Kingdom—Mickey Mouse. Wait for a recession to buy this one and then hold on for the ride of your life.

Exxon Corporation. ***Trading symbol:*** **XOM.** ***Industry:*** **oil.** ***Phone:*** **972-444-1000.** ***Internet:*** **www.exxonmobil.com.**

In the early eighties the Fed jacked up interest rates to kill inflation. It also killed the economy and the stock market. Lots of stocks were selling cheap but Warren placed his bet on Exxon, the largest and best run of the oil companies, on the theory that no matter what happened to the economy, individuals and businesses would keep guzzling oil. The high interest rates kept Exxon's stock down to $44 a share, against earnings of $6.77, which equates to an initial return of 15.2%. It had been growing its per share earnings at an annual rate of 6.7% and had been buying back its own shares. Warren paid approximately 6.5 times earnings. By 1987 it was trading at $87 a share, which would have given him an annual compounding rate of return of approximately 25%.

Freddie Mac. ***Trading symbol:*** **FRE.** ***Industry:*** **mortgages.** ***Phone:*** **703-903-2239.** ***Internet:*** **www.freddiemac.com.**

Freddie Mac is a wonderful company that buys residential mortgages from banks and mortgage brokers and securitizes them before selling them to investors. At one time, Warren owned a ton of this stock, but now he is selling it because the nature of the company changed. It got more risky and Warren hates risk.

F. W. Woolworth Company

F. W. Woolworth was once one of the largest retail chains in America. Warren bought it in 1979 for $20 a share against earnings of $6.02 a share, which equates to an initial return of 30%. It had a book value of $41 a share. By 1985 it was at $50 a share, which equates to an annual rate of return of 20%.

Gallaher Group Plc. ***Trading symbol:*** **GLH.** ***Industry:*** **tobacco.** ***Phone:*** **1932-859-777.** ***Internet:*** **www.gallaher-group.com.**

This company owns Gallaher Tobacco Limited, the market leader in the United Kingdom. It makes Benson & Hedges cigarettes. Gallaher Tobacco sold its American tobacco operations in 1994 and said good-bye to all that bad press and possible expense associated with cancer lawsuits. Cigarette products have great profit margins, which mean big bucks. Gallaher owns other things as well, but it is tobacco that reaps the bountiful harvest. The tobacco operations are a classic durable-competitive-advantage business. English tobacco companies don't face the kind of lawsuits American ones do, so the downside risk is smaller. This stock shows up as a Buffett Foundation holding, though when it was purchased and for how much we can't say.

Gannett Company. ***Trading symbol:*** **GCI.** ***Industry:*** **newspaper.** ***Phone:*** **703-558-4634.** ***Internet:*** **www.gannett.com.**

Warren Buffett's 1994 purchase of shares in Gannett, the largest newspaper publisher in the United States with ninety-nine other newspapers, was made during an advertising recession for $24 a share, or fifteen times earnings. During the 1999 bubble it traded at twenty-four times earnings. He could have sold it in 2002 for $76 a share, which would have given him an annual rate of return of 15.2%. Not too shabby.

Geico. Acquired by Berkshire.

Warren's initial big investment was made as the company was on the verge of insolvency. Warren decided to ride to the rescue, believing that the company's durable competitive advantage was still intact. He was right and watched his $45 million investment grow over the next fifteen years to more than $2.3 billion. That equates to a compounding annual rate of return of 29.9%—the stuff investment legends are made of.

General Electric. ***Trading symbol:*** **GE.** ***Industry:*** **diversified industrial.** ***Phone:*** **203-373-2211.** ***Internet:*** **www.ge.com.**

Originally GE had a lockdown on the electrification of the planet. For most people electricity is a fact of life, but a mere one hundred years ago it wasn't. One company provided the knowledge and equipment to wire the planet, and that company was GE. And it made a fortune. Today GE is one of the largest and most diversified industrial giants on earth. With this position it has the financial power to play in any game it wants.

Warren has long admired this company—it is a Buffett Foundation holding—but has never been able to buy a big piece at a price he thinks is attractive. The return on equity for the last ten years has fluctuated between 18% and 23% (which is great) and return on total capital between 16% and 25%. The per share earnings have been growing at an annual compounding rate of 11.8%, which is also electrifying. GE carries only $400 million in long-term debt against $10 billion in earnings. You need a real good recession to buy this one at a fair price. During the 1999 bubble it traded at a P/E of 36, which is no bargain. Take a strong look anytime the P/E drops below 15, where it traded in the eighties and early nineties.

General Foods Corp. Acquired by Philip Morris.

In 1979, Warren began buying up the stock of a food company called General Foods, paying an average price of $37 a share for approximately 4 million shares. Warren saw strong earnings, $5.12 a share, which had been growing at an average annual rate of 8.7%.

This gave him an initial return of 13.8%, which he could argue was going to grow at 8.7% a year. Then, in 1985, the Philip Morris Company saw the value of General Foods' many brand-name products, which created a strong and expanding earnings base, and bought all of Warren's General Foods stock for $120 a share in a tender offer for the entire company. This gave Warren a pretax annual compounding return on his investment of approximately 21%. That's right, a pretax annual compounding return of 21%. A nice number in anybody's book.

Gillette. ***Trading symbol:*** **G.** ***Industry:*** **grooming and batteries.** ***Phone:*** **617-463-3000.** ***Internet:*** **www.gillette.com.**

Razor blades and batteries wear out quickly, and people have to buy more of them if they want to be clean shaven or to keep their portable electrical devices humming. Gillette knows how to make money. This is a Berkshire holding. For the last ten years the return on equity has been above 30% and the return on total capital above 20%. Per share earnings over the last ten years have grown at an annual rate of 14%. During the 1999 bubble it traded at a P/E of 40, which is way too high for this company. If you can get it at a P/E below 15, you can make some money.

Hershey Foods. ***Trading symbol:*** **HSY.** ***Industry:*** **food.** ***Phone:*** **717-534-6799.** ***Internet:*** **www.hersheys.com.**

Warren is rumored to have purchased Hershey Foods on several occasions, but we have no confirmed purchase to sink our teeth into. He has used it as an example in discussing the concept of a durable competitive advantage. Its been making chocolate forever and is the largest producer in America. The majority of the voting stock of the company is held in trust for the benefit of the Milton Hershey School for Orphans. The company's founder, Milton Hershey, left the majority of his wealth to benefit the children who had made him rich. What this means to you the investor is that there is one large shareholder—the trust for the orphanage—which can wield an incredible amount of weight. The company gets high returns on shareholders' equity and total capital. Its per share earnings have been growing at an annual rate of 9.9% for the last ten years. It traded at a P/E of 33 during the bubble, which is too steep for this business. Try to get it at a P/E below 15, which you could have done up until 1996. Even if you have a sweet tooth, wait for a recession or panic sell-off to take a bite.

Interpublic Group of Companies. ***Trading symbol:*** **IPG.** ***Industry:*** **advertising.** ***Phone:*** **212-399-8000.** ***Internet:*** **www.interpublic.com.**

In 1974, Interpublic was the largest company in the international advertising business. Now it is number three. Advertising agencies, according to Warren, earn a royalty on the growth of other businesses. When manufacturers want to take their products to market, they have to advertise, so they use an agency. Agencies produce and place ads in the media and are paid a percentage of what the advertiser spends for these services. Agencies are almost inflation-proof. Inflation causes advertisers to spend more for the same amount of work, and the more advertisers spend, the more the agencies make. Agencies are service businesses so they spend only modestly on capital equipment, which means that profits don't go toward replacing worn-out plant and equipment. Plus, only 4% of U.S. advertisers change agencies every year! In other words, those big accounts stay in place. Many of the large agencies that dominated the marketplace years ago still dominate it today. Seven of the top ten are in their fifth or sixth generation of management. The key here is that there is no limit on how big they can grow. As long as businesses grow and the media continue to be where manufacturers take their products to market, advertising agencies will continue to grow as well.

The numbers on Interpublic are great. For the last ten years it has earned an annual return on equity of 16% or better, with the last three years at over 20%. Per share earnings for the last ten years have been growing at an annual rate of 13.8%. Warren used the 1973–74 recession to buy 17% of Interpublic, which traded as low as $3 a share, against earnings of $.81. He paid a total $4,531,000 for 592,650 shares, for an average price of $7.65 per share. We don't know when he sold his interest in this company. We do know that if he had held his position, he would have 74.6 million shares, adjusted for stock splits, worth approximately $2.8 billion. This equates to a compounding annual rate of return of approximately 27% for the twenty-seven-year period. If you're patient, you can get a great price on this one. During the 1999 bubble it traded at a P/E of 33—too high for even this wonderful business. In the midnineties you could have bought it for fourteen times earnings. Check it out.

Kaiser Aluminum & Chemical Corp. ***Trading symbol:*** **KLUCQ.** ***Industry:*** **aluminum.** ***Phone:*** **713-267-3777.** ***Internet:*** **www.kaiseral.com.**

This is one of the few investment mistakes that Warren made in his early days. He bought based on earnings in good "businesslike" fashion, but the earnings soon vanished as they often do in a price-competitive business. He lost money on this one.

McDonald's Corp. ***Trading symbol:*** **MCD.** ***Industry:*** **fast food.** ***Phone:*** **630-623-3000.** ***Internet:*** **www.mcdonalds.com.**

McDonald's made the hamburger into a brand-name product with some twenty-eight thousand restaurants—no easy feat. Over the last ten years the company has had a yearly return on equity between 16% and 20%, which is delicious. And its per share earnings have been growing at an annual rate of 12%. It's a great company, and at the right price it is a great investment. Warren acquired 60 million shares in 1994 and 1995 for $1.2 billion, which equates to $20 a share. He was then rumored to be selling them in 1997 to 1999 for between $30 and $45 a share as he sold into the bubble. This turned out to be a wise decision. At the right price Warren will once again be buying McDonald's shares, and so should you.

Media General Inc. ***Trading symbol:*** **MEG.** ***Industry:*** **television.** ***Phone:*** **804-649-6000.** ***Internet:*** **www.mediageneral.com.**

Media General is a major newspaper publisher and owner of TV and cable systems. Warren was buying it in 1978 and 1979 for $16 a share, with per share earnings of $3.42 a share, which equates to an initial return of 21%. Again, the Fed's raising interest rates helped make this low price possible. No hard information on when he sold it, but we believe it was 1985, for around $70 a share.

Mercury General Corp. ***Trading symbol:*** **MCY.** ***Industry:*** **insurance.** ***Phone:*** **213-937-1060.** ***Internet:*** **www.mercuryinsurance.com.**

Mercury is the largest agency writer of passenger auto insurance in California, and California has a lot of cars. It gets great returns on equity. Buy this one when it is trading close to or below book value, which you could have done in 1988, 1990, 1991, 1992, and 2000. This is a Buffett Foundation holding.

New York Times. ***Trading symbol:*** **NYT.** ***Industry:*** **newspaper.** ***Phone:*** **212-556-1234.** ***Internet:*** **www.nytco.com.**

This company owns the *New York Times, Boston Globe,* fifteen smaller dailies, and half the *International Herald Tribune.* It also owns eight TV and two radio stations. This is a Buffett Foundation holding. In the early nineties the numbers were lousy, but they are starting to look better.

Ogilvy & Mather Int'l. Inc. No longer publicly traded.

Warren bought 31% of Ogilvy, the fifth-largest ad agency in America, after the 1973–74 stock market crash for approximately $4 a share against earnings of $.76 a share. No record of when he sold it. By 1978 it was trading at $14 a share, which would have given him an annual compounding rate of return of 30%. By 1985 it was trading at $46 a share, which equates to an annual compounding rate of return of 24%.

Pepsico, Inc. ***Trading symbol:*** **PEP.** ***Industry:*** **beverage.** ***Phone:*** **914-253-2000.** ***Internet:*** **www.pepsico.com.**

Before Warren started drinking three or four Cherry Cokes a day, he was a Pepsi man. PepsiCo is a fantastic company with an annual return on equity for the last ten years of over 20% and per share earnings growing annually at 8%. This is a Buffett Foundation holding. Look to buy it in a recession or during a panic sell-off.

Times Mirror. ***Trading symbol:*** **TMC.** ***Industry:*** **newspaper.** ***Phone:*** **213-237-3700.** ***Internet:*** **www.tm.com.**

In 1980 the Fed pushed interest rates up to the 14% level, which killed stock prices. Warren put on his selective contrarian hat and went shopping. One of his purchases was Times Mirror, owner of the *Los Angeles Times,* for an amazing $14 a share against per share earnings of $2.04, which equates to a P/E of 6.8 and an initial return of 15%. By 1985 it was trading at $53 a share, giving Warren a 30% compounding annual rate of return. During the

1999 bubble it traded at twenty-one times earnings. You can't trade this one anymore—in March 2000 Tribune Company saw the great opportunity here and bought the company.

Torchmark Corp. ***Trading symbol:*** **TMK.** ***Industry:*** **insurance.** ***Phone:*** **205-325-4200.** ***Internet:*** **www.torchmark.com.**

This is an insurance and financial services company. It consistently earns a return on equity in excess of 19%. Its per share earnings have been growing at an annual rate of 10.9% for the last ten years. Warren has been buying this one for years, most recently in February 2000 right after the 1999 bubble. You could have bought it then at $20 a share with earnings of $2.82 a share, which equates to an initial return of 14%. As of May 2001, it trades at $37.50 a share.

Wal-Mart Stores. ***Trading symbol:*** **WMT.** ***Industry:*** **merchandising.** ***Phone:*** **501-273-4000.** ***Internet:*** **www.wal-mart.com.**

With over twenty-four hundred stores, Wal-Mart has the power to outbuy the competition. This means it can give its customers a better buy on just about anything. Thus every price-conscious consumer shops there. More shoppers mean more volume, which means more money. How much? Wal-Mart's annual return on equity for the last ten years has always been over 20%. Its per share earnings have been growing at an annual rate of 24%. It is, after all, the world's largest retailer. It got that way by going into small towns and driving the competition out of business, thus establishing a monopoly. Its distribution network is so sophisticated that it has created a barrier to entry that protects the company from competition. Berkshire reported that it owned 4.39 million shares of Wal-Mart as of 1997.

Warner-Lambert Company. ***Trading symbol:*** **WLA.** ***Industry:*** **pharmaceutical.** ***Phone:*** **973-540-2000.** ***Internet:*** **www.warner-lambert.com.**

This is a pharmaceutical, consumer health care, and gum and mint company. It has such brand-name products as Listerine, Bromo-Seltzer, Halls cough tablets, Rolaids antacids, Schick and Wilkinson Sword razors and blades. Its gums and mints division owns Dentyne, Trident, Freshen-up, Bubblicious, Mondo, Cinn-a-Burst, Clorets, and Certs. Its over-the-counter drugs are protected by patents. The return on equity is consistently above 30% and per share earnings have been growing at 11% annually for the last ten years. During the 1999 bubble it traded at a P/E of between 30 and 45. If you can get it for a P/E of below 17, the economics really work. In the early nineties, when it looked as if the federal government was going to start regulating drug prices, rumor had it that Warren was buying into this company at a P/E of 13. He then sold out because he couldn't establish the large positions that would give him greater weight in dealing with management. In 2000 the company merged into Pfizer, so there's not point in adding this one to your list.

Washington Post. ***Trading symbol:*** **WPO.** ***Industry:*** **newspaper.** ***Phone:*** **202-334-6000.** ***Internet:*** **www.washpostco.com.**

The *Washington Post* was Warren's first taste of owning a monopoly newspaper and the incredible profits that it can earn. This one had a majority owner who kept a close eye on things, namely Katharine Graham. She and Warren hit it off big after he bought into the paper in 1973. He coached her on the virtues of share repurchases and how not to venture into areas of business outside the company's circle of confidence. A quick learner, she caused the stock to rise from the $5.69 a share Warren paid for it in 1973 to more than $500 a share today. The return on equity for this company fluctuates between 13% and 19%. Its per share earnings have been growing at approximately 9% annually. In addition to the newspaper, the Washington Post Company owns *Newsweek* magazine, six TV stations, and numerous cable TV systems in eighteen states. It is doubtful that the company will do anything stupid that would create a buying opportunity, so you are going to have to wait for a recession in advertising rates or a general stock market decline to buy. Since the long-term picture of the company looks sound, any price under $400 a share should be a good buy, and any price under $300 a share is a screaming bargain. Warren bought the Washington Post during the 1973–74 crash for $5.69 a share against earnings of $.76 a share, which equates to a

P/E of 7.5. During the 1972 and 1999 bubbles it traded at a P/E of 24. Katharine has passed on, but her life's work, the *Post,* remains a fantastic business.

Wells Fargo. *Trading symbol:* WFC. *Industry:* banking. *Phone:* 415-396-3606. *Internet:* www.wellsfargo.com.

This is the bank of banks and it is growing by leaps and bounds. Warren bought into it during a banking recession in which just about every major bank in the nation took a bath over bad real estate loans. The stock market, being shortsighted, exited stage right and drove the bank's stock down to $15.75 a share. Warren, exploiter of short-term folly that he is, jumped on this one with $497.8 million to buy 28.8 million shares at an average price of approximately $17. It has recently traded at $49 a share. In 1999, at the top of the real estate boom, Warren exited stage left and started selling his shares. Here we have Warren buying in during a recession and selling out during a boom. Banks go through this boom-and-bust real estate cycle every ten to fifteen years. The shortsighted stock market panics when things go bust and sends bank stocks into the ground. When things boom again, the shortsighted stock market sends bank stocks skyward. Anyway you look at it, it's a nice ride. You can do what Buffett does and buy the strongest of the litter.

Wyeth. *Trading symbol:* WYE. *Industry:* drugs. *Phone:* 973-660-5000. *Internet:* www.ahp.com.

This drug company is a leading manufacturer of patented prescription drugs, but it also owns some wonderful over-the-counter brand names such as Advil, Anacin, Robitussin, and Chap Stick. The return on equity for the last ten years has always been over 30%. Per share earnings growth has been at 7.9%. At the right price, it's a great buy, and worth holding on to for the long term. People have a habit of getting sick, and that's not going to change anytime soon. Your big buying opportunities will be bear markets and panic sell-offs during bull markets.

17

Stock Arbitrage: Warren's Best-Kept Secret for Building Wealth

Stock arbitrage—investing in corporate sellouts, reorganizations, mergers, spin-offs, and hostile takeovers—is one of Warren's greatest secrets for making millions. It is probably the least understood of his investment operations. During Warren's early employment with Graham's New York investment firm, he studied its arbitrage operations. He found out that over the thirty years that the firm had been conducting arbitrage operations it had produced a low-risk average annual return of 20%. Needless to say, Warren was an instant convert and immediately immersed himself in the study of managing an arbitrage portfolio.

Five years ago, learning the ins and outs of stock arbitrage would only have been useful to institutional investors, like Warren, who could wrangle cheap institutional rates out of stock brokerage firms. Small guys and gals were kept out of the game by the high commission rates individual clients were charged by the major brokerage firms. Additionally, finding out and keeping track of arbitrage investment opportunities required access to a wealth of information. In the old days Warren would read through the business sections of five or six major newspapers every day looking for newly announced arbitrage opportunities in which to invest. Once he spotted an opportunity, he would carefully track it to make sure that nothing went wrong—such as the buyer backing out of the deal—to ensure that he wasn't blindsided by events that could turn potential profits into real losses. Back in the old days (i.e., before the Internet) arbitrage was a full-time job.

Since the advent of on-line trading, the days of individual investors paying exorbitant transaction fees are over. In fact, on-line trading companies often charge less than one cent a share. Some, like American Express, offer free trading for anyone who keeps a minimum balance of $100,000 or more. That's right—free trades! Not even the big boys like Warren got them for free in the old days.

Spotting and keeping track of arbitrage opportunities is now as simple as flipping on your computer and surfing the Internet. It's all there. You can keep track of any and all arbitrage opportunities with just a few clicks of a mouse. What once took Warren hours to do you can now do in minutes. It's truly a revolution, and it's a revolution that can make you rich!

These arbitrage opportunities—what Warren calls "workouts"—arise from corporate sellouts, reorganizations, mergers, spin-offs, and hostile takeovers. Warren prefers to commit capital to investment for the long term, but when no opportunity for long-term investment presents itself, he has found that arbitrage or workout opportunities offer him a vastly more profitable venue for utilizing cash than do other short-term investments. In fact, over the thirty-odd years during which Warren has been actively investing in arbitrage, he estimates that his average annual pretax return has been approximately 25%. That's a healthy rate of return in anybody's book.

In the early days of the Buffett Partnership, up to 40% of its total funds in any given year were invested in arbitrage or workout situations. In dark years like 1962, when the entire market was headed south, the profits from workouts saved the day. They allowed the partnership to be up 13.9% compared to the Dow's miserable performance—down 7.6%. (Note: The Buffett Partnership's investments in normal operations in 1962 actually lost money, but the arbitrage/workout profits turned a disaster into the stuff of which financial legends are made.)

Although there are many types of arbitrage/workouts or "special situations," as Graham called them, Warren has come to be comfortable with what Graham called "cash payments on sale or liquidation." In this type of arbitrage, a company sells out its business operations to another company or decides to liquidate its operations and distribute the proceeds to its security holders.

In 1988, Warren bought 3,342,000 shares of RJR Nabisco stock for $281.8 million after the announcement by RJR's management that they were going to try to buy the company from the shareholders. Management's buyout offer brought other potential buyers out of the woodwork, the biggest being the buyout firm KKR. KKR eventually won the bidding war, making Warren an even richer man.

An investment opportunity arises for the arbitrageur when a price spread develops between the announced sale or liquidation price and the market price for the company's stock before the sale or liquidation.

Say, for example, that Company X announces that it will sell all its stock to Company Y for $120 a share at some future date. Let's also say that the arbitrageur is able to buy the stock for $100 a share before the close of the transaction, which the arbitrageur intends to sell at some future date to Company Y for $120 a share. In this situation the arbitrageur will make a profit of $20 a share—the difference between the market price paid, $100, and the sale price of $120. The question becomes, when will the transaction close so that the arbitrageur can cash out at $120 a share and make the $20-a-share profit?

Thus, the big question is one of time. The longer the time from the purchase date to the date the transaction closes, the smaller your annual rate of return. Let us show you.

If you pay $100 a share and the company is selling out in twelve months at $120, your profit would be $20 a share and your pretax annual return would be 20%. But what would happen if, because of some complication, the transaction didn't close for, say, two years? Your pretax annual return would drop to 10%.

Likewise, if you got lucky and the transaction closed in six months instead of twelve, then your pretax annual rate of return would jump to 40%.

The arbitrage/workout situation is essentially an investment with a fixed profit and hopefully an established termination date. The amount that you are going to earn is fixed—in our example, $20 a share. The length of time that the security is held will determine the pretax annual rate of return. The shorter the length of time, the larger the pretax annual rate. The longer the length of time, the smaller the pretax annual rate. It goes without saying that an open-ended time can lead to disaster and should be avoided.

Other risks accompany these situations. The transaction might not be open-ended, but it could take longer than expected. If the transaction fails to occur, the stock price will drop back to the price at which it was previously trading. That's no way to get rich.

Hundreds of factors can cause these transactions to take longer than expected or not occur at all. Sometimes the shareholders reject the offer; other times government antitrust people kill the party; and at times the IRS takes an eternity issuing a tax ruling (taxes play an important part in this sort of transaction). Anything and everything can go wrong.

Warren protects himself from some of the risk by investing only in situations that have been announced. That sounds like the normal, intelligent thing to do. What kind of fool would invest in a transaction that hasn't been announced? Care to take a guess? You got it. Wall Street! Yes, the Wall Street wizards have worked their brains overtime and figured out that they can make a lot of money by investing in companies that are *rumored* to be takeover candidates. Trading on rumors can mean huge profits, but it also exposes investors to much greater risk.

Warren has found, after having invested in hundreds of arbitrage/workout situations, that an almost certain annual rate of return of 25% is usually more profitable than a 100% rate that is a big maybe. The gnomes of Wall Street can trade on rumors, but Warren will only invest after the sale or merger has been announced.

During the Buffett Partnership years, from 1957 to 1969, Warren believed that the arbitrage/workout investments would produce, year to year, the most steady and absolute profits for the partnership, and that in years of market decline they would give the partnership a big competitive edge.

You should understand that when the stock market is going down, shareholders and management start to worry about the sinking price of the company's stock and are therefore more willing to consider selling out, liquidation, or some form of reorganization. Also, falling stock prices mean more attractive prices, which draws more interest from potential buyers. Thus, when the market starts to sink, the opportunities in the field of arbitrage start to rise.

GETTING STARTED

Getting started is easy. You have two great choices for finding arbitrage opportunities on-line: mergerstat.com, and msn.com's www.moneycentral.msn.com, both of which list daily all the major mergers and acquisitions. Mergerstat.com is devoted exclusively to listing and tracking daily all major merger and acquisition activity around the world. Go to the home page of mergerstat.com and you will find, for free, a list of all the deals over $100 million that were announced on that day. You can do a significant amount of research before having to pay a fee for more information.

With msn.com's www.moneycentral.msn.com just click on "Markets," then "News by Category," and then "Topics." Go to the "Topics" bar and choose "Mergers and Acquisitions." This will give you a list of all the news stories that have reported recent merger and acquisition activity.

Now find a transaction in which one company is acquiring a publicly traded company for cash. (There will be quite a few in which one company is acquiring such a company for stock, or a combination of both cash and stock. Stay away from these situations. The stock component adds a variable that can complicate the transaction. It's easier to work with the cash deals until you become experienced in the arbitrage game.) Write down the name of the company being acquired and its stock symbol. Read any and all news stories on coming mergers or acquisitions, figure out the per share buyout figure, when the transaction is expected to close, and the current trading price for the company's shares. If it looks as if the transaction will more than likely be completed and a profitable price spread has developed between the buyout price and the current market price, call the company and confirm whether the acquisition is still on and when they expect it to close. Getting information straight from the horse's mouth is always better than reading a report in some financial newspaper. If you subscribe to a news service like Nexus, you will be able to track the acquisition up until the time it closes. If all looks good, make your buy and keep track of the transaction by keeping your eye on your news sources.

Let's run through an example to see how it all works.

Say that on June 1, 2001, you check mergerstat.com and discover that Y Corp. has just announced that it will buy Z Corp. for $25 a share and that the transaction should be completed by January 1, 2002.

You check the current trading price for Z Corp., which is $24 a share. (Understand that because of the time value of money and the risk that the transaction might not occur, Z Corp.'s share price will probably never trade at exactly $25 a share between the date that the purchase is announced and the date the transaction closes.)

If you buy Z Corp.'s stock on August 1, 2001, for $24 a share and tender it on January 2, 2002, to Y Corp. for $25 a share, what is your annual rate of return for this transaction? With a few adjustments you can use a Texas Instruments BA-35 Solar financial calculator to run a fast calculation to determine your approximate annual rate of return. (Please note: Any financial calculator that will perform future and present value calculations will suffice.)

The first thing you need to know is when the deal will close. If the transaction was expected to take exactly one year to complete, we can figure our annual rate of return by punching into the Texas Instruments calculator 1 as the number of years (N), $24 for the present value (PV), and $25 for the future value. Now hit the compute key (CPT) and then the interest key (%i). You get an annual rate of return of 4.2%. But since the transaction is going to take a shorter time, five months, to close, the annual rate of return actually increases because your money is only tied up for five months. Let's see how this works.

Since most transactions won't take longer than a year to close, you adjust the time period on your calculator to represent a fractional year, in this case five months. To make this adjustment, you divide 1 by 12, the number of months in a year, which will give you .083333, then multiply .083333 by the number of months between the date of your purchase and the time that the transaction is scheduled to close. In our example the transaction is expected to close within five months. So 5 times .083333 is .41666. You then punch in .41666 for the number of years (N), $24 for your present value (PV), and $25 for your future value (FV). Then hit the compute key (CPT) and then the interest key (%i), and you will get an equivalent annual rate of 10.29%.

This method is faster than the Graham method discussed in the original edition of *Buffettology*, but it doesn't calculate in the risk factor that the transaction might not take place at all. Warren believes that you should only invest in situations that you are certain will be completed. To guard against the odd transaction that fails to close and creates a loss, Warren likes to invest in a large number of arbitrage plays, believing that the wins of many will more than compensate for the losses of a few.

A WORD OF WARNING!

A ton of money can be made from stock arbitrage, and you should seriously consider investigating this area of investing. Always remember, as we said earlier, that Warren only takes arbitrage positions *after the buyout or liquidation has been announced.* If you do it before the announcement, based on rumor, then you are engaging in the highly lucrative, but highly dangerous, game of speculative stock arbitrage, a pursuit that has sunk many a big-time player.

WHAT YOU SHOULD HAVE LEARNED FROM THIS CHAPTER

- ✦ With arbitrage, Warren was able to produce positive results for his investment partnership even in down years.
- ✦ The Internet trading companies have brought down commission prices to the point that arbitrage is even profitable for individual investors working with small sums of money.
- ✦ Warren will only take arbitrage positions in deals that have been publicly announced.
- ✦ Mergerstat.com and www.moneycentral.msn.com list daily merger activity and are excellent sources of information about publicly announced mergers.

18

For the Hard-Core Buffettologist: Warren Buffett's Mathematical Equations for Uncovering Great Businesses

You should understand by now that investing the Buffett way means finding a company with durable competitive advantage, then waiting for a buying opportunity (such as a recession, an October correction or a panic sell-off, or a onetime solvable problem) to deliver a stock price that makes business sense. Understanding what does and what does not make business sense is what separates billionaires from millionaires. What you buy and the price you pay will determine how much money you make. You already know what kind of company you should be buying—one with a durable competitive advantage. From there it is just a matter of paying the lowest possible price.

How important is it to purchase for as low a price as possible? Incredibly important. Many investment analysts and writers who study Buffett believe that if you are buying an excellent business and you anticipate holding it for a number of years, you needn't be all that concerned about the price you pay. *Nothing could be more wrong.* Consider this. In 1991, H&R Block traded between $19 and $38 a share. Ten years later, in 2001, it traded at $80 a share. If you paid $19 for a share back in 1991, and sold it for $80 a share in 2001, then your pretax annual compounding rate of return would be approximately 15.4%. If you paid $38 a share in 1991 and sold it for $80 a share in 2001, then your pretax annual compounding rate of return would be approximately 7.7%. Had you invested $100,000 in H&R Block at $19 a share, in 1991, it would have compounded annually at 15.4% and grown to be worth approximately $418,849 by 2001. If you had invested $100,000 in H&R Block at $38 a share back in 1991, it would have compounded annually at 7.7% and grown to be worth approximately $209,969 by 2001 That's a difference of $208,880! Pay more, earn less. Pay less, earn more.

To assist you in making the above calculations the wonderful folks at Texas Instruments have programmed the equation into an inexpensive financial calculator, the Texas Instruments BA-35 Solar. You and I only have to learn how to punch buttons to come up with the future value. We suggest that you purchase one because it makes things so much easier.

To perform the above equation on your Texas Instruments BA-35 Solar financial calculator: Make sure that the calculator is in its financial mode (hit the Mode key until you see a small FIN on the screen). Then punch in H&R Block's 1991 per share market price of $19 as the present value (the PV key), then punch in the number of years, 10 (the N key). Punch in the per share price at which you sold the stock in 2001, $80, as the future value (the FV key). Then hit the calculation key (CPT), then the interest key (%i). Then the calculator will tell you that your compounding annual rate of return for the ten-year period on your original investment of $19 a share is 15.4%.

Warren's rule for price is simple: You want to pay the lowest price possible because ultimately it is going to determine your compounding rate of return and whether you are going to get rich.

GETTING STARTED

Once you have focused on a company that looks interesting and have assembled the following information:

- current income statement
- current balance sheet

- per share earnings for ten years
- return-on-equity figures for ten years

you can get out your financial calculator and start running the intrinsic-value equations that Warren uses to determine the earning power of a company. You do this to determine two things: first, whether the company has a durable competitive advantage, and if it does, just how powerful it is; and second, whether the company is selling at a price that makes business sense, which usually happens when either the stock market or the company is experiencing some kind of calamity.

FINANCIAL EQUATION #1

PREDICTING EARNINGS AT A GLANCE

Warren has found that without some predictability about a company's future earnings it is impossible to tell whether the company will have the strength to survive the bad news that gives rise to a buying situation. The simplest test you can perform is also the most basic. It gives you an instant perspective on whether the company has predictable earnings. Although every security analyst performs this calculation the first time his or her eyes scan an investment survey like *Standard & Poor's* or *Value Line,* few will acknowledge that it is an actual calculation. But it is, because it is where you must start statistical analysis. Simply put, you merely look at and compare the company's reported earning per share for a number of years. Are they consistent or inconsistent? Do earnings trend upward or do they rocket up and plunge down like a roller coaster? Are they strong? Do they indicate a loss or earnings weakness in the current year?

The investment survey services, such as *Standard & Poor's* and *Value Line,* make this comparison of yearly figures easy by providing you with a list of earnings dating back a number of years. So does the MSN Web site www.moneycentral.msn.com, the Yahoo! financial Web site, and about a dozen others. We are an investing nation awash in financial figures.

THE FOUR TYPES OF EARNINGS SITUATIONS THAT YOU WILL CONFRONT

You will be confronted with four types of earnings situations, three that interest us and one that does not. In a perfect situation, a company's per share earnings are consistently strong and show an upward trend, as shown in Exhibit A as Company I. A company that we are definitely not interested in has wildly erratic earnings as shown in Exhibit A as Company II.

EXHIBIT A

Company I		Company II	
Durable-Competitive-Advantage Business		Commodity Business	
Year	*Per Share Earnings*	*Year*	*Per Share Earnings*
91	$1.07	91	$1.57
92	1.16	92	.16
93	1.28	93	(1.28) loss
94	1.42	94	.42
95	1.64	95	(.23) loss
96	1.60	96	.60
97	1.90	97	1.90
98	2.39	98	2.39
99	2.43	99	(.43) loss
00	2.69	00	.69

Company I has more predictable earnings than Company II. You don't need to be a genius to see that. The earnings of Company I have increased every year but 1996, in which they dropped from $1.64 to $1.60 a share. Company II's earnings are all over the place, with no apparent trend.

Quick question. For which company would you be willing to predict future earnings? You should have picked Company I. Even though all you know about the company is its ten years of earnings, you know that they are (1) strong and (2) have an upward trend. Your next question should be, "What were the economic dynamics that created this situation?"

Company II might have some investment merit, but from a Buffett point of view, the lack of strong earnings indicates that Company II's future earnings would be impossible to predict. Warren would at first glance only have considered Company I.

Warren's mentor, Benjamin Graham, was fond of saying that you didn't need to know someone's weight to know that he was fat. The same holds true in reviewing the earnings history of a company. First, gather the per share earnings figures for the last seven to ten years to see whether they present a stable or unstable picture. There will be a lot of black-and-white examples, but also quite a few in a gray area. If something seems fishy, don't be afraid to move on. If it smells interesting, don't be afraid to dig a little deeper.

APPLICATION OF EARNINGS PREDICTABILITY TO A NEGATIVE EARNINGS SITUATION AT A GLANCE

In some bad-news situations, the per share earnings will have suffered a setback in the current year. This may be as simple as a weak performance compared to the year before or may be serious enough to produce an actual loss.

Company III is a perfect example of a company that has produced a substantially weaker performance in 2000 than in 1999; Company IV shows an actual loss *(see page 204)*.

Both Company III and Company IV have earnings that are strong, consistent, and growing until year 2000. The question is whether this is an aberration or the way of things to come. The only way to find out is by putting on your analyst's hat and delving into the recent history of the company. If the companies have competitive advantages, you have to figure out whether they are strong enough to overcome the obstacles that have hurt these earnings. Is the condition permanent or is it something that management or the economic environment can correct over time?

WHAT YOU SHOULD HAVE LEARNED

- ✦ Merely looking at a ten-year summary of a company's per share earnings will tell you a great deal about a company.

- ✦ Warren is looking for a company that has shown a strong upward trend in per share earnings over the last ten years.
- ✦ He is not interested in companies that have wildly gyrating earnings.
- ✦ He is interested in companies with histories of strong per share earnings that have suffered temporary setbacks in the most recent year.

Company III		Company IV	
Probable Durable Competitive Advantage in Trouble		Probable Durable Competitive Advantage in Trouble	
Year	*Per Share Earnings*	*Year*	*Per Share Earnings*
91	$1.07	91	$1.07
92	1.16	92	1.16
93	1.28	93	1.28
94	1.42	94	1.42
95	1.64	95	1.64
96	1.60	96	1.60
97	1.90	97	1.90
98	2.39	98	2.39
99	2.43	99	2.43
00	.48 → Sharp decline	00	(1.69) → Actual loss

FINANCIAL EQUATION #2

A TEST TO DETERMINE YOUR INITIAL RATE OF RETURN

Before we go any further, understand that Warren invests from what he calls a "business perspective." This means that he views the earnings of a company in which he has invested in proportion to his ownership in the company. So if a company earns $5 a share and Warren owns 100 shares of the company, he figures that he has just earned $500 ($5 x 100 = $500).

Warren also believes that this company has the choice of either paying that $500 out to him via a dividend or retaining those earnings and reinvesting them for him, thus increasing the underlying value of the company. Warren believes that the stock market will, over time, acknowledge this increase in the company's underlying value and cause the stock's price to increase.

This differs from the view that most Wall Street professionals hold. They don't consider earnings their own until they are paid out via dividends. In the early eighties the stock of Warren's holding company, Berkshire Hathaway, traded at $450 a share. Today it trades at around $75,000 a share and has yet to pay a dividend. The increase in the market price of the stock came from an increase in the underlying value of the company brought about by Warren's profitable reinvestment of Berkshire's retained earnings.

Since Warren considers the earnings to be his in proportion to the number of shares that he owns, it is possible to determine the *initial* rate of return you can expect to get at a particular trading price.

In 2000, H&R Block was trading at $30 a share against estimated earnings for the year of $2.57 a share. This means that if you paid $30 for a share of H&R Block stock in 2000, your initial rate of return would be 8.6% ($2.57 ÷ $30 = 8.6%).

With Warren's 2000 purchase of Yum Brands at $24 a share, against 2000 earnings of $2.77 a share, he could calculate his initial rate of return as 11.5% ($2.77 ÷ $24 = 11.5%).

Warren couples this initial rate of return with the estimated-earnings growth figure to determine that he is buying an H&R Block equity/bond that pays a 8.5% initial rate of return that will expand as H&R Block's per share earnings grow at an estimated rate of 7.6%. Think of it as a bond that pays 8.5% the first year, 9.1% the second year, 9.8% the third, 10.5% the fourth, and so on until the investment is sold. (With the Washington Post, an investment that Warren has held for twenty-eight years, the annual rate of return on his initial investment by the year 2000 had grown to 116%. The longer he holds it, the better it gets!)

This is where Warren and Graham initially derive the theory that the price you pay will determine your rate of return. The higher the price, the lower the rate. The lower the price, the higher the rate. You want the highest possible rate of return, which is obtained by paying the lowest possible price.

WHAT YOU SHOULD HAVE LEARNED

- Warren has an unorthodox view of a company's earnings. He considers them in proportion to the number of shares he owns. If the company earns \$5 a share and he owns 100 shares, then, as he sees it, he has earned \$500.
- Warren believes that if you paid \$25 a share for a stock that was earning \$5 a share, you would be getting an initial rate of return of 20% (\$5 ÷ \$25 = 20%).
- The price you pay determines your rate of return.

FINANCIAL EQUATION #3

A TEST FOR DETERMINING THE PER SHARE GROWTH RATE

Management's ability to grow the *per share earnings* of a company is key to the growth of the shareholder's investment. To get per share earnings to grow, the company must employ its retained earnings in a manner that will generate more earnings per share. The increase in per share earnings will, over time, increase the market valuation of the company's stock.

A really fast and easy mathematical method of checking the company's ability to increase per share earnings is to figure the annual compounded rate of growth of the company's per share earnings for the last ten years and the last five years. This will show you the annual compounding rate of earnings growth over the long and the short run. We use the two numbers to allow us to see the true long-term nature of the company and to determine whether management's near-term performance has been in line with the long-term.

Let's look at some examples and then do some in-depth analysis.

First, we'll examine the yearly per share earnings of newspaper giant Gannett Company:

Earnings for Gannett from 1990 to 2000

Year	*Per Share Earnings*	*Year*	*Per Share Earnings*
90	$1.18 → Present value	96	$1.89
91	1.00	97	2.50
92	1.20	98	2.86
93	1.36	99	3.30
94	1.62	00	3.70 → Future value
95	1.71		

Get out your TI BA-35 Solar financial calculator. To calculate the company's per share earnings annual compounding growth rate, treat the first year as your present value, in this case 1990's earnings of $1.18. Then use 2000's earnings of $3.70 as the future value. The number of years is ten (you count 1990 as the base year, 1991 as the first year, and 2000 as the tenth year). While your TI calculator is in financial mode, punch in $1.18 and press the present value key (PV); punch in $3.70 as the future value and press the future value key (FV); now punch 10 as the number of years, press the number of years key (N), and hit the CPT key followed by the %i key. You will get the annual compounding rate of growth for the ten years, which is 12.1%.

Do the same for the five-year period from 1995 to 2000 using as the present value 1995's earnings of $1.71. The future value will be the earnings for 2000, $3.70. Five is the number of years. Punch the CPT key followed by the %i key and the calculator will tell you that your annual compounding rate of growth was 16.6% for 1995 to 2000.

These two numbers tell you several different things. The first is that the company has had a higher rate of earnings growth in the last five years than it did in the ten-year period from 1990 to 2000. The question you need to ask is, what were the business economics that caused this change? Was Gannett buying up its stock? Finding new business ventures to be profitably involved in? Or was it simply seeing an increase in advertising revenue with a corresponding increase in profits?

ADAPTING THE PER SHARE GROWTH RATE TO NEGATIVE EARNINGS

You are going to confront situations in which a company has had strong earnings growth for a number of years, but whose per share earnings in the most recent years show either a sharp decline or are negative, as shown below in Company I and Company II.

Company I		Company II	
Possible Durable Competitive Advantage in Trouble		Possible Durable Competitive Advantage in Trouble	
Year	*Per Share Earnings*	*Year*	*Per Share Earnings*
89	$0.95→Present value	89	$0.95→Present value
90	1.07	90	1.07
91	1.16	91	1.16
92	1.28	92	1.28
93	1.42	93	1.42
94	1.64	94	1.64
95	1.60	95	1.60
96	1.90	96	1.90
97	2.39	97	2.39
98	2.43	98	2.43
99	2.70→Future value	99	2.70→Future value
00	.48→Exclude this year	00	(1.43) loss→Exclude this year

How do you determine the per share growth rate? It all depends on your analysis of the situation. If you find that the current condition will most certainly pass, then you can safely eliminate the negative year from your calculations. Simply start back one additional year. Thus, with Companies I and II, use 1989's earnings of $.95 per share as the present value and 1999's earnings of $2.70 as the future value. The number of years would be ten. This would equate to an annual compounding growth rate of approximately 11%. Canceling out the most recent year can only be done if one is sure that the present situation is treatable and not life-threatening to the business. (Note: Alternatively you could use eight or nine as the number of years but you should never use fewer than seven.)

EXERCISE TO DETERMINE PER SHARE EARNINGS CONSISTENCY AND GROWTH RATE

Pick a company that you believe has a durable competitive advantage and calculate its per share earnings growth rate using the following exercise *(see page 210).*

If you want to calculate the earnings growth rate for last five years, use 1995 as the base year, 2000 as the future value, and 5 as the number of years (N).

WHAT YOU SHOULD HAVE LEARNED

- Management's ability to grow per share earnings is key to growth in share price.
- To get per share earnings to grow, the company must employ its retained earnings in a manner that will generate more earnings per share.
- The increase in per share earnings will, over time, increase the market valuation of the company's stock.

FINANCIAL EQUATION #4

A STOCK'S VALUE RELATIVE TO TREASURY BONDS

Warren believes that all investments compete with one another and that the return on treasury bonds is the benchmark that all investments must ultimately compete with. To establish the value of the company relative to treasury bonds, divide the current per share earnings by the current return on treasury bonds.

In the case of Warren's investment in H&R Block in 2000, the

YEAR		PER SHARE EARNINGS	
90		______	→Present value (base year)
91	one	______	
92	two	______	
93	three	______	
94	four	______	
95	five	______	
96	six	______	
97	seven	______	
98	eight	______	
99	nine	______	
00	ten	______	→Future value

↑ Number of years out from base year

Financial equation for use with TI BA-35 Solar calculator: *earnings per share growth rate.* Use 1990 per share earnings as your present value (PV); 2000 as your future value (FV); and 10 (N) as the number of years. Hit the compute key (CPT) and then the interest key (%i) and your annual compounding growth rate per share will be calculated ______.

per share earnings were $2.77 a share. Divide $2.77 by the return on treasury bonds, which was approximately 6% in 2000, and you get a relative value of $46.16 a share ($2.77 ÷ .06 = $46.16). This means that if you paid $46.16 for a share of H&R Block, you would be getting a return equal to that of the treasury bonds—6%. This means that H&R Block has a value relative to treasury bonds of $46.16 a share.

In 2000, Warren bought H&R Block stock for $24 a share, a price that was below the stock's relative value to treasury bonds. His initial rate of return was 11.5% compared to the 6% being paid on treasury bonds. Which investment would you want? Remember that from 1990 to 2000 H&R Block had been growing its per share earnings at 7.6% annually.

Thus, ask yourself, what would I rather own—$24 worth of a treasury bond with a static return of 6%, or a H&R Block equity/bond with a return of 11.5%, whose per share earnings are growing at an annual rate of 7.6%? In fact you may not want to own either, but given a choice between the two, the H&R Block equity/bond is certainly more enticing.

If the H&R Block purchase doesn't get you excited, consider Warren's purchase of Furniture Brands International, the number one manufacturer of residential furniture in America. He bought it in 2000 for $14 a share against earnings of $1.92 a share, which equates to an initial rate of return of 13.7%. Its per share earnings have an annual growth rate of 28%. Care for a 13.7% rate of return that is growing at 28% a year? Sure you do.

Many analysts believe that if you divide the per share earnings by the current rate of return on treasury bonds, you end up with the intrinsic value of the company. But all you end up with is the value of the company relative to the return on treasury bonds.

The same thing applies to the theory that the intrinsic value of a business is its future earnings discounted to present value. If you use the return on treasury bonds to determine the discount rate, you end up with a discounted present value relative to the return on treasury bonds.

Also, remember that the return on treasury bonds is a pre-income-tax return, and the net earnings figure of a corporation is an after-corporate-tax return. So comparing the two without taking this into account is wrought with folly. Still, it is a method that has a place in our box of tools.

WHAT YOU SHOULD HAVE LEARNED

- ✦ All investments compete with one another for investors' capital.
- ✦ Ultimately the safest investment is a U.S. treasury bond.

- The yield on a treasury bond competes with the return paid on other investments.
- One can obtain a business perspective by comparing the value of a prospective investment to that of a treasury bond.

Relative Value Work Sheet

Name of Company	Per Share Earnings		Return on Treasury Bonds		Relative Value	Current Market Price
1.____________	________	÷	________	=	________	________
2.____________	________	÷	________	=	________	________
3.____________	________	÷	________	=	________	________
4.____________	________	÷	________	=	________	________
5.____________	________	÷	________	=	________	________

FINANCIAL EQUATION #5

USING THE PER SHARE EARNINGS ANNUAL GROWTH RATE TO PROJECT A STOCK'S FUTURE VALUE

It is possible to project the future price of a company's stock by using the company's per share earnings historical annual growth rate. Let's look at an example.

Gannett Corporation, the newspaper giant, had consistent per share earnings growth from 1980 to 1990. From that decade's performance we will project per share earnings from 1990 to 2000. Then we will project a price range that Gannett stock will be trading at in 2000. We will then project the annual compounding rate of return you would have earned if you had bought a share of Gannett in 1990 and sold it in 2000.

TO PROJECT GANNETT'S FUTURE PER SHARE EARNINGS FOR 2000

From 1980 to 1990, Gannett's per share net income grew from $.47 to $1.18 or at an annual compounding rate of approximately 9.6%. Projecting the per share earnings of Gannett forward ten years from 1990 to 2000, using a 9.6% rate of growth, we get projected per share earnings of $2.95 for 2000. The equation for this is PV = $1.18, N = 10, %i = 9.6%, punch the CPT button, then the future value (FV) button, and you get $2.95. So, in 2000, Gannett will have per share earnings of $2.95.

TO PROJECT THE MARKET PRICE OF GANNETT STOCK IN 2000

A review of the price/earnings ratio for Gannett for 1980 to 1990 shows that the stock traded from 11.5 to 23 times earnings. Averaging the two P/Es, we come up with a P/E of 17.5. Valuing Gannett's 2000 projected per share earnings of $2.95 at a P/E of 17.5 equates to a projected 2000 stock price of $51.62 ($2.95 x 17.5 = $51.62).

TO PROJECT THE ANNUAL COMPOUNDING RATE OF RETURN YOU WOULD HAVE EARNED IF YOU HAD BOUGHT A SHARE OF GANNETT IN 1990 AND SOLD IT IN 2000

By looking in the *Wall Street Journal* one could see that Gannett stock could be bought in 1990 for $14.80 a share. Get out your Texas Instruments BA-35 Solar calculator and punch in PV = $14.80, FV = $51.62, N = 10, and hit the CPT key. Then hit the interest key, %i, and you get an annual compounding return of 13.3%. This means that if you spent $14.80 a share for Gannett stock in 1990, you could have projected an annual compounding rate of return of 13.3% for the next ten years.

Since we are using past data for this Gannett example, let's look and see what really happened to the $14.80-a-share investment we made in 1990. In 2000 the company had earnings of $3.63 a share compared to our estimate of $2.95 a share. (Okay, it's not an exact science.) The stock in 2000 traded between $53 and $70 a share compared to our estimate of $51.62. Let's say you sold your stock at $53 a share in 2000. Your pretax annual compounding rate of return on the $14.80 investment you made in 1990 would be (PV = $14.80, FV = $53, N = 10, hit the CPT key and %i key) 13.6%. If you had sold the stock in 2000 for the high price of $70 a share, your pretax annual compounding rate of return would have been 16.8% for 1990 to 2000.

Thus, in the case of Gannett, the stock market revalued the stock to a higher price multiple than projected and increased our fortunes beyond our expectations.

(In case you are wondering, if you had invested $100,000 in Gannett at $14.80 a share in 1990, compounding at an annual rate of 16.8%, it would've grown to approximately $472,528 by 2000.)

You should understand that Warren is not calculating a specific value for the stock, as many who watch and write about Warren believe. Nor is Warren saying that Gannett is worth X per share and I can buy it for half of X, as Graham used to do. Warren is instead asking, if I pay X per share for Gannett stock, given the economic realities for the company, what is my expected annual compounding rate of return going to be at the end of ten years? After determining the expected annual compounding rate of return, Warren then compares it to other investments and the annual compounding rate of return that he needs to stay ahead of inflation.

By functioning in this manner he can buy a stock and forget about tracking its price week by week or month by month. Warren knows approximately what his long-term annual compounding rate of return is going to be. He also knows that over the long-term the market will value the company to reflect this increase in the company's net worth. Which is why he is famous for being cavalier about day-to-day market fluctuations.

WHAT YOU SHOULD HAVE LEARNED

- If the company has a durable competitive advantage, it is possible to project the future price of the company's stock by using the company's per share annual growth rate.
- Warren is not calculating a specific value for a stock.
- Warren asks himself this question: If I pay X for a share of stock,

given the economic realities of the business, what is my expected annual compounding rate of return going to be in ten years?

- ✦ Warren compares his projections to what other investments are paying.
- ✦ By functioning in this manner Warren can buy a stock and forget about how Wall Street values it on any given day.

FINANCIAL EQUATION #6

UNDERSTANDING WARREN'S PREFERENCE FOR COMPANIES THAT EARN HIGH RATES OF RETURN ON EQUITY

To Warren Buffett's way of thinking, companies with a durable competitive advantage have such consistent earnings that their stocks become a sort of bond. He calls the stock an equity/bond, and it pays an interest rate equal to the yearly return on equity that the business is earning. The earnings-per-share figure is the equity/bond's yield. If the company has a shareholders' equity value (book value) of $10 a share and net earnings of $2.50 a share, Warren would say that the company is getting a return on its equity/bond of 25% ($2.50 ÷ $10 = 25%).

But since a business's earnings fluctuate, the return on the equity/bond is not a fixed figure as it is with other bonds. Warren believes that with an equity/bond, one is buying a variable rate of return, which can be positive for the investor if earnings increase, or negative if earnings decrease. The return on the equity/bond will fluctuate as the relationship of equity (book value) to net earnings changes.

To fully understand why Warren is so interested in high returns on shareholders' equity, let us work deeper into a hypothetical example we presented earlier in the book.

In case you don't remember, shareholders' equity is defined as a company's total assets *less the company's total liabilities.* This is comparable to the equity you have in your house. Let's say that you bought a house to rent and you paid $200,000 for it. To close the deal you invested $50,000 of your own money and borrowed $150,000 from a bank. The $50,000 you invested in the house is your equity in the property ($200,000 sales price – $150,000 mortgage = $50,000).

When you rent your house out, the amount of money that you earn from the rent, after paying your expenses and mortgage, would be your return on equity. If you rented your house for $15,000 a year and had $10,000 in expenses, mortgage payments, and taxes, then your net earnings would be $5,000 a year. Then the return on your $50,000 in equity would be the $5,000 you earned. This equates to an annual 10% return on equity ($5,000 ÷ $50,000 = 10%).

Likewise, if you owned a business, we'll call it Company A, and it had $10 million in assets and $4 million liabilities, the business would have shareholders' equity of $6 million. If the company earned, after taxes, $1,980,000, we could calculate the business's return on shareholders' equity as 33% ($1,980,000 ÷ $6,000,000 = 33%). So the $6 million of shareholders' equity is earning a 33% rate of return. (Warren's Company A's equity/bond would also be earning a 33% return on equity.)

Imagine that you owned another business. Call it Company B. Imagine that it too has $10 million in assets and $4 million in liabilities, which, like Company A, gives it $6 million in shareholders' equity. But imagine that instead of making $1,980,000 on an equity base of $6 million, it only makes $480,000. This means that Company B would be producing a return on equity of 8% ($480,000 ÷ $6,000,000 = 8%).

	Company A	Company B
Assets	$10 million	$10 million
Liabilities	$4 million	$4 million
Shareholders' Equity	$6 million	$6 million
After Tax Earnings	$1,980,000	$480,000
Return on Shareholders' Equity	33%	8%

Both companies have exactly the same capital structure, yet Company A is four times as profitable as Company B. Of course the better company is Company A.

Let's say that the management at both Company A and Company B are really good at what they do. Company A's management is really good at getting a 33% return on equity and Company B's is really good at getting an 8% return on equity.

What company would you rather invest more money in—Company A, whose management will earn you a 33% return, or Company B, whose management will only earn you an 8% return? You, of course, choose Company A.

As the owner of Company A, you have the choice of either getting a $1,980,000 dividend from Company A at the end of the year or you can let Company A retain your earnings and let its management earn you a 33% return. What do you do? Is earning a 33% rate of return sufficient? Of course it is. Company A is making you very rich. So you let it keep the money.

As the owner of Company B, you have the choice of getting either a $480,000 dividend at the end of the year or you can let Company B retain your earnings and let the management earn you an 8% return. Is an 8% return sufficient for you? The picture is not nearly as clear as it is with Company A. Let me ask you this: If I told you that you could take Company B's dividend and invest it in Company A, will that help you make up your mind? Of course it would. You would take your money out of Company B where it was only earning 8% and invest it in Company A, where it would earn 33%.

By now you can start to see why companies that earn high returns on shareholders' equity are big on Warren's list. But there are a few more twists to the wealth-creating power that high returns on equity will produce. Let's look deeper.

Pretend that you don't own either Company A or Company B but you are in the market to buy a business. So you approach the owners of Company A and Company B and tell them you are interested in buying their business and ask them if they are interested in selling.

As we discussed a few pages ago, Warren believes that all rates of return ultimately compete with the return that is paid on treasury bonds. He believes that the government's power to tax ensures the bonds' safety and that investors are very aware of that. This competition of rates, according to Warren, is one of the main reasons that the *stock market goes down when interest rates go up* and *why the stock market goes up when interest rates go down.* A stock investment that offers a 10% return is far more enticing than a government bond offering a 5% return. But jack up interest rates to the point that the government bond is offering you a 12% return and the stock's return of 10% suddenly loses its appeal.

Keeping this in mind, the owners of Companies A and B compare what they could earn by selling their businesses and putting their capital into treasury bonds. They might be able to forget about the hassles of owning a business and still earn the same amount of money. Let's say that at the time you made your offer to buy, you could buy government bonds and earn an 8% return.

In the case of Company A, which is earning $1.98 million a year, it would take $24.75 million worth of government bonds to generate $1.98 million in interest. So the owner of Company A tells you that he will sell you the company for $24.75 million. If you pay $24.75 million for Company A, you would be paying roughly four times shareholders' equity of $6 million or 12.5 times its current earnings of $1.98 million.

In the case of Company B, which is earning $480,000 a year, it would take $6 million worth of government bonds to generate $480,000 in interest. So the owner of Company B says that he will sell you his company for $6 million. This means that if you pay $6 million for Company B, you will be paying one times shareholders' equity of $6 million or 12.5 times Company B's current earnings of $480,000.

Two companies, A and B, both with the same capital structure, but A is worth, relative to the return on government bonds, $24.75 million, and B is worth $6 million. If you paid $24.75 million for Company A, you could expect a return of 8% in your first year of ownership. If you paid $6 million for Company B, you could also expect an 8% return in your first year of ownership.

One of the keys to understanding Warren is realizing that he is not very interested in what a company will be earning next year. *He is interested in what the company will be earning in ten years.* While shortsighted Wall Street focuses on the current situation, Warren realizes that to let powers of the durable competitive advantage and compounding rate of return work their wonders he has to focus on the long term. This is why companies that have durable competitive advantages and earn high rates of return on shareholders' equity are so important to him.

Let's look at how Warren might view this situation.

Warren would find Company A far more enticing than Company B. The economics of Company A are such that it can earn a 33% return on shareholders' equity. If management can keep this up, the retained earnings will earn 33% as well. Every year the shareholders' equity pot is going to grow. *It is the growing equity pot and the earnings that go with it that interest Warren.* Let us show you.

Year	*Equity Base**	*ROE***	*Earnings (added to the next year's equity base)*
1	$6,000,000	33%	$1,980,000
2	7,980,000	33	2,633,400
3	10,613,400	33	3,502,422
4	14,115,822	33	4,658,221
5	18,774,043	33	6,195,434
6	24,960,478	33	8,239,927
7	33,209,405	33	10,959,104
8	44,168,509	33	14,575,608
9	58,744,117	33	19,385,559
10	78,129,675	33	25,782,793
11	103,912,470	33	34,291,115

*Beginning year equity base **Return on equity

What you are seeing is the shareholders' equity base compounding at a 33% rate of return. (Remember, Warren is after the highest-compounding rate of return possible.)

By the beginning of year eleven, Company A will have an equity base of $103,912,470 and expected year eleven earnings of $34,291,115. If treasury bonds are still at 8%, it would take $429 million in government bonds to produce $34,291,115.

If you paid $24.75 million for Company A at the beginning of year one and sold it for its equity value of $103,912,470 at the beginning of the eleventh year, effectively holding the investment for a full ten years, your annual compounding rate of return would be 15.4%. If you sold it for $428 million, the amount of treasury bonds that it would take to earn the $34,291,115 that Company A is projected to earn in year eleven, your annual compounding rate of return would be 33%—a much nicer number to put in the bank.

The economics of Company B are such that it can only earn an 8% return on shareholders' equity. This means that if management keeps this up, the retained earnings will only earn 8% as well. Which means that every year the shareholders' equity pot is going to grow by 8%.

Year	*Equity Base*	*ROE*	*Earnings (added to the next year's equity base)*
1	$6,000,000	8%	$480,000
2	6,480,000	8	518,000
3	6,998,400	8	559,872
4	7,558,272	8	604,662
5	8,162,934	8	635,035
6	8,815,969	8	705,278
7	9,521,247	8	761,700
8	10,282,947	8	822,636
9	11,105,582	8	888,447
10	11,994,028	8	959,522
11	12,953,550	8	1,036,284

By the beginning of year eleven, Company B will have an equity base of $12,953,550 and expected year eleven earnings of $1,036,284. If government bonds are still paying 8%, it would take $12.95 million in government bonds to produce $1,036,284.

If you paid $6 million for Company B at the beginning of year one and sold it for its equity value of $12.95 million at the beginning of the eleventh year, effectively holding your investment for a full ten years, your annual compounding rate of return would be 8%. If you sold it for $12.95 million, the amount of government bonds that it would take to earn the $1,036,284 that Company B is projected to earn in year eleven, your annual compounding rate of return would still be 8%.

Suppose you only have $6,187,500 and you think to yourself, wouldn't it be better to spend it buying all of Company B instead of spending it to buy 25% of Company A? Warren has figured out that even 25% of Company A is a better investment than owning 100% of Company B. If you paid $6,187,500 to buy 25% of Company A and you sold it for 25% of the company's equity value, $25,978,000, in the beginning of the eleventh year, then your annual compounding rate of return would still be 15.4%. If you sold it for 25% of the company's treasury bond value, $107 million, your annual compounding rate of return would remain 33%.

You may have realized by now that paying $24.75 million, or 12.5 times earnings, for Company A is a fantastic deal if you expect to be earning a 33% annual compounding rate of return for ten years. In fact, Company A may be worth a lot more. The question that Warren must address is how much more? Let's figure it out.

Say that instead of paying $24.75 million or 12.5 times earnings for Company A, you paid $59.4 million, or thirty times Company A's year-one earnings of $1.98 million. And let's say you sold it at the beginning of year eleven for 12.5 times year eleven's projected earnings of $34,291,115, which equates to $428,638,937. If you paid $59.4 million or thirty times earnings for Company A in year one and sold it in ten years for $428,638,937, then your annual compounding rate of return would be 21.8%.

If you paid forty times Company A's year-one earnings, $79.2 million, and then sold Company A in ten years for $428,638,937, your annual compounding rate of return would be 18.3%. An annual compounding rate of return of 18.3% for ten years is something most investment managers can only dream about.

Very Important Point: *Warren knows a secret: Excellent businesses that benefit from a durable competitive advantage and can consistently* *earn high rates of return on retained earnings (shareholders' equity) are often bargain buys at what seem to be high price-to-earnings ratios.*

We know what some of you are thinking, that this is just a hypothetical scenario and never happens in real life. The market, you're thinking, is efficient and things are priced at what they are worth.

Well consider this:

In 1993, Bristol-Myers Squibb had shown a consistent capacity for earning high rates of return on shareholders' equity—in the neighborhood of 35% annually. If you had invested $100,000 in Bristol-Myers Squibb stock in 1993 and held it for eight years, to 2001, your $100,000 investment would have grown to approximately $538,000 in stock market value. This equates to a pretax annual compounding rate of return of approximately 23%. Add the dividends that you would have received—approximately $37,000—and your pretax annual compounding rate of return goes to 24%. Think about earning a pretax annual compounding rate of return of 24% for eight years with an investment in a company that has been in the same line of business since 1887. Talk about durability.

Warren saw Bristol-Myers Squibb's durable competitive advantage at that time, and the high rates of return that it was earning on shareholders' equity, and bought 957,200 shares. The rest is the stuff investment legends, and billionaires, are made of.

WHAT YOU SHOULD HAVE LEARNED

- Warren thinks of a share of stock as a kind of equity/bond in which the per share earnings equate to the equity/bond's yield.
- Since the earnings of a business vary from year to year, the rate of return paid on Warren's equity/bond is not fixed as it is with a normal bond.
- This variable rate of return, if it is increasing, can be a positive for investors. If it is decreasing, then it becomes a negative for investors.
- The growing equity pot and the earnings that go with it are what interest Warren.

FINANCIAL EQUATION #7

DETERMINING THE PROJECTED ANNUAL COMPOUNDING RATE OF RETURN: PART I

Warren has figured out a way to project the annual compounding rate of return that a potential investment in one of these durable-competitive-advantage businesses might produce. When the stock price drops to a point that makes the projected annual compounding rate of return attractive, Warren buys shares. The bad-news phenomenon creates the buying opportunity. Too high a stock price, which creates a low projected annual compounding rate of return, and Warren lets the purchase pass. A really low stock price, which creates a high projected annual compounding rate of return, and Warren whips out the checkbook and starts buying like crazy!

In Warren's world the projected annual compounding rate of return rules supreme. Before we delve into this formula, however, you should understand that all these mathematical equations merely serve to give you a better picture of the economic nature of the beast. Each of these calculations will tell you a little something different. Each gives you another perspective on the business's earning power. Earning power is the key to predictability, and predicting future results is the key to becoming wealthy.

Warren has defined the intrinsic value of a business as the sum of all the business's future earnings discounted to present value, using treasury bonds as the appropriate discount rate. Warren cites *The Theory of Investment Value* by John Burr Williams (Harvard University Press, 1938) as his source for this definition. Williams, in turn, cites Robert F. Wiese, "Investing for Future Values" (*Barron's,* September 8, 1930, p. 5). Wiese stated that "the proper price of any security, whether stock or bond, is the sum of all future income payments discounted at the current rate of interest in order to arrive at the present value." (It is interesting to note that both Williams and Wiese were referring to future dividends paid out and not the future earnings of the company. Warren uses future earnings as the discounted value, regardless of whether they are paid out.)

We all know that projecting what a business might earn over the next one hundred years is next to impossible. Sure, you could try, but the realities of the world dictate that some change will occur and destroy or change the economics of the business in question. Just look at the broadcast television industry. It was hardly a bump on the economic landscape in the 1940s. In the sixties and seventies it was a fantastic business for anyone involved. After all, there were only three channels. So great was their monopoly position that Warren said in the early eighties that if he had to invest in just one company and then go away to a deserted island for ten years, it would be Capital Cities. Quite a vote of confidence!

But by 2000, Warren thought that the television business was not what it used to be. Today, dozens of channels compete for ad revenue, all of which compete with the Internet for the viewer's eye. Absolutely unsinkable businesses are hard to find.

History tells us that whether your name is Medici, Krupp, Rothschild, Winchester, or Rockefeller, the wheels of commerce may not always turn in your favor. The competitive advantage that once was enjoyed, like that held by the early television networks, can vanish almost overnight due to a change in technology or at the hands of government regulators. The Medici family of Venice have spent the last five hundred years trying to get over that the Dutch sailed around the southern tip of Africa and destroyed Venice's monopoly on trade with the Orient. Things change, and though history does sometimes repeat itself, fortune favors the brave who constantly test the fertile waters of commerce, looking for new ways of making a buck.

Keeping this in mind, you would invite sheer folly by thinking that you had a chance in a million of projecting a company's earnings for fifty to one hundred years and then discounting them back to present value. There are just too many variables.

It is of interest that Benjamin Graham also noted the insane valuations that discounting a company's future stream of earnings often created, especially when earnings growth was kept constant. Graham stated, "There is no clear-cut arithmetic which sets a limit to the present value of a constantly increasing earning power" (Graham, *Security Analysis,* 1951, p. 389).

Some analysts try to solve this problem by dividing the future earnings into two different periods. The first is assigned a high growth rate and the second is assigned a lower rate. The problem here, as Williams discussed, is that anytime you have a rate of earnings growth that is less than the rate of interest used in the discounting equation, the stock will end up having a finite value, even though growth continues on without limits (see Williams, *The Theory of Investment Value,* p. 89).

An additional problem is the discount rate chosen. If you choose treasury bonds, you are in effect discounting the business's future earnings at a rate that makes them relative to the return on treasuries. Thus, if the rate of interest changes, your valuation changes as well. The higher the interest rate, the lower the valuation. The lower the interest rate, the higher the valuation.

One other problem with using treasury bonds as a discount rate is that their yield is quoted in pretax terms. So a treasury bond that is paying a return of 8% will only earn the individual investor an after-tax return of 5.52%. The future earnings of the company that are being discounted are quoted in after-corporate-income-tax terms, which means that an 8% return will remain an 8% return unless it is paid out as a dividend.

Warren projects the per share equity value of the company forward for ten years. This is done by using historical trends for the return on equity less the dividend payout rate.

Warren determines the approximate equity value of the company in ten years, then multiplies the per share equity value by the projected future rate of return on equity ten years out. This gives him the projected future per share earnings of the company. Using this figure, he is then able to project a future trading value for the company's stock. Using the price he paid for the stock as the present value, he can calculate his estimated annual compounding rate of return. He then compares this projected annual compounding rate of return to what other investments, of comparable risk, are projected to pay, and to what his needs are to keep ahead of inflation.

Look at Berkshire Hathaway. In 1986, Berkshire had stockholders' equity of $2,073 a share. From 1964 to 1986, Berkshire's return on stockholders' equity was 23.3% compounded annually. Back in 1986, if you had wanted to project the company's equity-per-share figure for 2000, all you had to do was get out the old and trusted Texas Instruments BA-35 Solar financial calculator and switch to the financial mode to perform a future value calculation. Let's do it.

First you punch in 1986's per share equity value of $2,073 as the present value (PV key), then the rate of growth for the interest rate, 23.3% (%i key), then the number of years, 14 (the N key). Hit the calculation key (CPT), then the future value key (the FV key), and the calculator tells you that, in 2000, Berkshire should have a per share equity value of $38,911.

You should be asking yourself, how much money am I willing to pay in 1986 for the right to own $38,911 in shareholders' equity in 2000? First of all, you need to determine your desired rate of return. If you are like Warren, then 15% is the minimum return you are willing to take. So all you have to do is discount $38,911 to present value using 15% as the appropriate discount rate.

First, clear your calculator of the last calculation. Punch in $38,911 as the future value (FV), then the discount rate, 15% (%i), then the number of years, 14 (N), then hit the compute button (CPT) and the present value button (PV). The calculator will tell you that in 1986 the most money you can spend on a share and expect to get a 15% annual return over the next fourteen years is $5,499 a share.

A check of the local newspaper in 1986 would tell you that the market was then selling a share of Berkshire's stock for around $2,700. You think, wow, I might be able to get a better return than even the 15% I'm looking for. To check it out, punch in $2,700 for the present value (PV) and $38,911 for the future value (FV) and 14 for the number of years (N). Then hit the compute button (CPT) and the interest button (%i) and the calculator will tell you that you can expect an annual compounding rate of return of 20.9%.

By 2000, Berkshire had in reality ended up growing its per

share equity value at a compounding annual rate of approximately 23.6%, to $40,442.

But get this. While you were patiently waiting for the value of Berkshire to grow, the market decided it really liked Berkshire and bid the stock to a high of $71,300 and a low of $40,800 a share by 2000. If you paid $2,700 for a share of Berkshire in 1986 and sold it in 2000 for $71,300 a share, this would equate to a pretax annual compounding return of 26.39% for the fourteen years. (To get the rate of return, you would assign $2,700 as the present value, PV, and $71,300 as the future value, FV, and 14 as the number of years, N. Then you would punch the compute key, CPT, and then the interest key, %i, which equals 26.39%.) If you sold the stock for $40,800 a share in 2000, you would have earned a pretax annual compounding return of approximately 21.4%.

Let's say that you paid $71,300 for a share of Berkshire Hathaway in 2000. What would your projected pretax annual compounding return be if you held the stock for ten years?

We know that Berkshire has a per share equity value in 2000 of approximately $40,442 and that it has grown at an average annual compounding rate of approximately 23.6% a year for the last twenty-five years. Assuming this, we can project that in ten years—in the year 2010—the per share equity value of Berkshire Hathaway will be $336,524.

If you paid $71,300 in 2000 for a share of Berkshire that will have a per share equity value of $336,524 in 2010, what is your annual compounding rate of return? Punch in $336,524 for the future value (FV) and $71,300 for the present value (PV) and 10 for the number of years (N). Hit the CPT key followed by the interest key (%i) and presto—your annual compounding rate of return is 16.7%. Interesting, but not that interesting. Berkshire at $71,300 a share in 2000 is an iffy bargain from a business perspective.

Yes, the stock market may go mad by 2010 and value Berkshire considerably higher than its per share equity value. In which case today's buyers would be in luck. Then again it may value it considerably lower. But the economic reality is that if you pay $71,300 for a share of Berkshire, your annual compounding rate of return is going to be approximately 16.7%. Regardless of where the market price for the stock is short-term, the long-term economics of a business will eventually dictate the stock's market price.

Remember the part of Warren's philosophy that says the price you pay determines your rate of return. Well, if you bought Berkshire at its low of $40,800 a share in 2000 and sold it for its equity value of $336,524 in 2010, your pretax annual compounding return for the ten years would be 23.4%. That's far more interesting than the 16.7% you would have gotten had you paid $71,300 a share.

With Berkshire the lower the price you pay, the higher your rate of return is going to be. The higher the price you pay, the lower the rate of return you are going to earn. Pay more, get less. Pay less, get more. It's that easy.

If you think that Warren can't keep earning a 23.6% return on his capital, then you might adjust the growth rate down to a more pedestrian 15%. With a per share equity value of approximately $40,442 in 2000, we can project that at an annual growth rate of 15% it will have increased to approximately $163,610 by 2010. If you paid $40,800 for a share of Berkshire in 2000 and sold it for $163,610 in the year 2010, then your annual compounding rate of return would be approximately 14.8%. Pay the high price of $71,300 a share and your annual return drops to a measly 8.6%, which is neither very interesting nor very profitable.

You can make a stock market price adjustment to this calculation by figuring that over the last twenty-five years Berkshire has traded in the market for anywhere from approximately one to two times its per share equity value. If it trades at double its projected per share equity value in 2010, you are naturally going to do a lot better.

So let's say that you managed to pay $40,800 in 2000 for a share of Berkshire and sold it for $673,048 or two times its projected 23.6% annual compounding equity growth per share value in 2010 of $336,524. Your projected annual pretax compounding rate of return for the ten years would be approximately 32.3%. This is absolutely the best-case scenario, provided you pay the cheap price of $40,800 a share, Warren keeps hitting those 23.6% home runs, and the stock market is lusting for Berkshire in 2010. Any hope of doing better is pie in the sky.

WORKSHEET FOR PROJECTING BERKSHIRE'S FUTURE TRADING VALUE

Just for fun, let's calculate Berkshire's future trading price using a growth rate of 15%, with the stock trading at 1.5 times book value in 2010.

Year		Per Share Book Value
00		$40,442→Present value (base year)
01	one	_____
02	two	_____
03	three	_____
04	four	_____
05	five	_____
06	six	_____
07	seven	_____
08	eight	_____
09	nine	_____
10	ten ↑	$163,610→Future value multiplied by 1.5 equals Berkshire's stock price in 2010: $245,415

Number of years out from base year

Financial equation for use with TI BA-35 Solar calculator: *future trading price of Berkshire.* Use 2000 book value—$40,442—as your present value (PV) and 15% as your interest rate (%i) and 10 as your number of years. Hit the compute key (CPT) and then the future value key (FV). This computes the future book value for Berkshire in 2010. To calculate its future trading price multiply the future book value by 1.5.

If you paid $40,800 for a share of Berkshire in 2000 and then sold it for $245,415 in 2010, your projected annual rate of return would be 19.7%. If you paid $71,300, your annual rate of return would drop to 13.2%. (Note: If you feel inspired, run the future book value for all the projected years and then calculate the future trading price for those years as well.)

WHAT YOU SHOULD HAVE LEARNED

- ✦ It is impossible to discount the future income stream of a company that has ever-increasing net earnings.
- ✦ It is also impossible to determine what a company will earn over the next fifty years.
- ✦ It is possible to determine approximately what a company will be earning ten years from now.

FINANCIAL EQUATION #7

DETERMINING THE PROJECTED ANNUAL COMPOUNDING RATE OF RETURN: PART II

In the preceding section we learned how to calculate the future value of Berkshire Hathaway by projecting its future per share equity value. We also saw that once a future value is determined, it is possible to project the annual compounding rate of return the investment will earn.

In this lesson we will project the future per share earnings of a company and then determine its future market price. We will then use the results of these calculations to project the annual compounding rate of return an investment in the company will produce.

It would be instructive if we explored a real-life example of Warren's decision making, the one that led him to take his initial position in Bristol-Myers Squibb.

THE BRISTOL-MYERS SQUIBB COMPANY—1993

In 1993, Warren, using his equity-as-a-bond rationale, had his holding company, Berkshire Hathaway, buy 957,200 Bristol-Myers

Squibb equity/bonds (shares) at approximately $13 a share, for a total investment of approximately $12,443,600. At the time Bristol-Myers Squibb had shareholders' equity of $2.90 a share and net earnings of $1.10 a share. From Warren's point of view, each Bristol-Myers Squibb equity/bond that he had bought had a coupon attached to it that paid $1.10. This means that each of Warren's equity/bond shares was yielding a 37.9% return on equity ($1.10 ÷ $2.90 = 37.9%) of which approximately 35% was retained by the company and 65% was paid out as a dividend to the shareholders. (All the historical figures given for Bristol-Myers Squibb have been adjusted to reflect stock splits through 2001.)

Thus, in theory, when Warren bought his Bristol-Myers Squibb equity/bond share with a per share equity value of $2.90, he calculated that his $2.90 equity/bond would effectively earn a 37.9% return. He also figured that this 37.9% return was divided into two different types of yields.

One yield would represent 35% of the 37.9% return on equity and would be retained by the company. This amount is equal to $.38 of the $1.10 in per share earnings. This portion of the yield is the after-corporate-tax portion and is subject to no more state or federal taxes.

The other yield is the remaining 65% of the 37.9% return on equity, which is paid out as a dividend. This amount is equal to $.72 of the $1.10 per share earnings. This portion of the return is subject to personal or corporate taxes for dividends.

So our 37.9% return on equity is two different yields. One is a 13.25% (.35 x 37.9% = 13.25) return on equity equal to $.38, which is retained by the Bristol-Myers Squibb Company and added to Bristol-Myers Squibb's equity base.

The other is a 24.65% (.65 x 37.9% = 24.65%) return on equity equal to $.72, which is paid out to the shareholders of Bristol-Myers Squibb as a dividend.

If we assume that Bristol-Myers Squibb can maintain this 37.9% return on equity for the next ten years and continues to retain 35% of this return and pay out as a dividend the other 65%, then it is possible to project the company's future per share equity value and its per share earnings.

This is done by taking 35% of the 37.9% return on equity, or 13.25%, and adding it to the per share equity base each year.

So, if in 1993, Bristol-Myers Squibb had a per share equity value of $2.90, we would increase the $2.90 by 13.25% to give us a projected per share equity value for 1994 of $3.28 ($2.90 ÷ 1.1325 = $3.28).

You can calculate this with your Texas Instruments BA-35 Solar calculator by punching in $2.90 as the present value (PV) and 13.25 as the compounding rate of interest (%i) and 1 for the number of years (N). Then hit the CPT key and punch the future value key (FV).

If you want to know what the per share equity value will be in 2003, punch in $2.90 for the present value (PV) and 13.25 as the compounding rate of growth (%i) and 10 for the number of years (N). Then hit the CPT key and push the future value key (FV), and this will give you a projected per share equity value of $10.06 for 2003.

If you want to project the per share earnings, all you have to do is multiply the per share equity value by 37.9%. In the case of 1993 we would multiply per share equity value of $2.90 by 37.9% and get projected per share earnings of $1.10. For the year 2003 we would multiply the projected per share equity of $10.06 by 37.9% and get projected per share earnings of $3.81.

Let's do the calculations and project out the per share equity value and per share earnings of Bristol-Myers Squibb for ten years beginning in 1993 and ending in 2003 *(see page 233)*.

Projections usually aren't worth the paper they're written on. Most financial analysts are only willing to project earnings for a year or two, and then they give you an overview of the company and pronounce it a buy. But Graham felt that the real role of the analyst was to ascertain the earning power of the business and make a long-term projection of what the company was capable of earning.

In the table on page 233 we have projected per share earnings for ten years. In most situations this would be insanity. However, as Warren has found, if a company earns high rates of return on shareholder equity, created by some kind of durable competitive

Projections for 1993 to 2003				
YEAR	EQUITY VALUE	PER SHARE EARNINGS	DIVIDENDS PAID OUT	RETAINED EARNINGS*
93	$2.90	$1.10	$.72	$.38
94	3.28	1.24	.81	.43
95	3.71	1.41	.92	.49
96	4.21	1.59	1.03	.56
97	4.77	1.80	1.17	.63
98	5.40	2.04	1.33	.71
99	6.11	2.32	1.51	.81
00	6.92	2.62	1.70	.92
01	7.84	2.97	1.93	1.04
02	8.88	3.37	2.19	1.18
03	10.06	3.81	2.48	1.33
*Added to next year's equity value			Total: $15.79	$8.48

advantage, fairly accurate long-term projections of earnings can be made.

From a 1993 perspective, if Bristol-Myers Squibb can maintain an annual 37.9% return on shareholders' equity in the ten years from 1993 to 2003, we can project that the company will be earning approximately $3.81 a share in 2003. By 2003, Warren will also have earned an after-tax pool of dividend payouts equal to $15.114 million (dividend pool of $15.79 x 957,200 shares = $15.114 million).

So Warren can also project that by 2003 his investment in Bristol-Myers Squibb will have paid back his original investment of $12.443 million and he still gets to keep the 957,200 shares of Bristol-Myers Squibb stock as profit. If the company is trading at a historically conservative rate of eighteen times our projected earnings of $3.81 a share, then the 957,200 shares of the Bristol-Myers Squibb stock should be worth $68.58 a share (18 x $3.81 = $68.58) or $65.645 million ($68.58 x 957,200 shares = $65.645 million). This means that if Warren sold his Bristol-Myers Squibb shares in 2003, he would have grossed $65.645 million on the sale of the stock and $15.114 million in dividends, for a total of $80.76 million. Not too shabby.

Please note: *When you are choosing a price-to-earnings ratio (P/E) by which to multiply your projected per share earnings, you get the best perspective by running your calculations with the average annual P/E ratio for the last ten years. You should also run your equations with the high and the low P/E ratio for the last ten years, just to give you a better perspective of how well you might or might not do. But be warned: Stocks* don't always *trade at their historically high P/E. Relying on a historically high P/E ratio to create projections can lead to disaster. Stick with the average annual P/E ratio for the last ten years, especially if there has been a huge spread between the high and the low. When in doubt, choose the middle road. (Note:* Value Line Investment Survey *lists the average annual P/E for ten to fifteen years back.)*

To determine the annual compounding rate of return for 1993 to 2003, take out a Texas Instruments calculator and punch in 10 for the number of years (N) and the initial investment of $12.443 million for the present value (PV) and $80.76 million for the future value (FV). Then hit the CPT key and the interest key (%i). This will give you the annual compounding rate of return of 20.5% *(see page 235).*

What creates all this wealth is Bristol-Myers Squibb's ability to take its retained earnings and earn a 37.9% rate of return on shareholders' equity. It retains 35% of that 37.9%, free of personal income taxes, which is added to the shareholders' equity base in the company. This effectively compounds the retained earnings by adding them to the base sum from which they were created.

Now that we have projected Bristol-Myers Squibb's per share earnings from 1993 to 2003, we can find out whether our analysis has any validity. To do this, we can compare the projected per share earnings for 1993 to 2003 against the actual results reported by Bristol-Myers Squibb for 1993 to 2001 *(see page 236).*

We can see that our margin for error is running between 8% and 32% on projections running from 1993 forward for eight years. Not too bad. It is a bumpy road, but notice that seven years out we are only running an 9% margin of error.

Though we can explore the validity of our 1993 projections by

YEAR		STOCK PRICE
93		$12.443 million→Present value (base year)
94	one	_____
95	two	_____
96	three	_____
97	four	_____
98	five	_____
99	six	_____
00	seven	_____
01	eight	_____
02	nine	_____
03	ten	$80.76 million→Future value
	↑ Number of years out from base year	

Computing the projected annual compounding rate of return for Warren's investment in Bristol-Myers Squibb. Use the initial investment of $12.443 million for the present value (PV); 2003 projected gross proceeds of $80.76 million as the future value (FV); 10 for the number of years (N). Hit the CPT key and then the interest key (%i) and the projected annual compounding rate of return will be calculated: 20.5%.

comparing them to actual figures to 2001, it would not be prudent to base a buy decision on those numbers this late in the game. If you are thinking of buying Bristol-Myers Squibb stock in 2001, you need to run new numbers and make new projections to determine if Bristol-Myers Squibb is trading at a price that makes business sense for you to buy.

**Bristol-Myers Squibb
Comparison of Per Share Earnings Projections
to Actual Results**

Year	Projected Earnings	Actual Earnings	Margin of Error
93	$1.10	$1.10	0%
94	1.24	1.15	8
95	1.41	1.28	10
96	1.59	1.42	12
97	1.80	1.61	12
98	2.04	1.55	32
99	2.32	2.05	13
00	2.62	2.40	9
01	2.97	2.55	16

Our 1993 projections predicted that Bristol-Myers Squibb in 2001 would be trading at approximately $53 a share. In fact, during 2001, Bristol-Myers Squibb traded between a low of $50 a share and a high of $70. This makes the 957,200 shares that Warren bought in 1993 worth between $47.8 million and $67 million, which equates to a pretax annual compounding return of between 18.3% and 23% for the eight years between 1993 and 2001. Add approximately $6.04 million in dividends and Warren's pretax annual compounding return increases to between 20% and 24.8%. What happened here is that the stock market became aware of the long-term power of the Bristol-Myers Squibb economic engine and bid the stock price up to a P/E ratio between 20 and 27. Things don't always work exactly the way one plans, but if you have a durable competitive advantage as strong as Bristol-Myers Squibb has, the surprise is usually on the upside. In Warren's case the upside surprise was worth between $41.44 million and $60.64 million in profit on his original investment of $12.4 million.

Bristol-Myers Squibb may be suffering a few bumps, but in the end the power of its economic engine will continue to make its shareholders rich. The trick is to make certain that you don't buy in at too high a price. Remember, pay the right price and you end up rich; pay the wrong price and you end up in a ditch.

WHAT YOU SHOULD HAVE LEARNED FROM THIS CHAPTER

- It is possible to predict with a fair degree of accuracy the future earnings of some companies and, in so doing, to draw a fairly accurate picture of what the stock price will be ten years out.
- When projecting a future stock price based on an earnings projection, always use the average P/E ratio for the last ten years.
- Because of unforeseen variables, you must be careful not to rely on earnings projections pushed out past ten years.

19

Thinking the Way Warren Does: The Case Studies of His Most Recent Investments

The following case studies use Warren's techniques to value companies in which he has made investments. These case studies include Warren's 2000 purchases of H&R Block and La-Z-Boy. We have also included two case studies that appeared in the original edition of *Buffettology*, Gannett Corporation and Freddie Mac. These original case studies are of interest because it is now possible to see whether Warren's original projections as presented in *Buffettology* were accurate. Both of these companies have since split their stock. For the sake of clarity and comparison of projections with actual results, we've adjusted the historical numbers to reflect these splits.

The format for each case study is the same, with slight variations in the mathematical portions of the price analysis and the projection of the expected annual compounding rate of return. We do this to bring some diversity to the analysis process and to show you some of the different applications of the financial equations.

CASE STUDY ONE

H&R BLOCK, 2000

H&R Block is the king of the income tax preparers. That's a service that it has been selling for more than fifty years. Warren first saw the numbers on this one in *Value Line* and has been following it for years. After the 1999 bubble burst he began buying the stock. During 2000 he purchased 8% of H&R Block for approximately $29 a share. It's a fantastic business.

DOING YOUR DETECTIVE WORK

Warren first became aware of the company through its advertising. (He doesn't use an accountant to prepare his personal income tax return. He does it himself.) *Value Line* follows the company so it is easy to keep an eye on its numbers. It has recently been expanding into the financial services end of the game with the acquisition of Option One Mortgage Corp., McGladrey & Pullen, and Olde Financial. After you have gathered the necessary financial information by visiting its Web site (www.hrblock.com), by calling the company for an annual report (816-753-6900), and by checking out *Value Line,* you can begin your analysis.

1. ***Does the company sell any brand-name products or services that might have a durable competitive advantage or does it sell a price-competitive product or service?***

   When you think of tax preparers, you think of H&R Block. It has done an excellent job of letting the world know that it is America's largest tax service and has been in business for more than forty-five years. Started in a Kansas City office in 1955 by two brothers, Henry and Richard Bloch, it has grown to more than ten thousand offices throughout the United States, Canada, thirteen overseas countries, and two U.S. possessions, serving more than 19 million taxpayers worldwide. The basic service it sells, tax preparation, hasn't changed since the company first opened its doors, nor will it change anytime in the future. If you want to compete with it, you would have to spend billions of dollars to bridge its protective moat. That is something that makes Warren smile. Tough barriers to entry mean that H&R Block will more than likely be ruling the world of tax preparation forty-five years from now.

2. ***Do you understand how the product or service works?***

   You wake up on April 1, realizing that if you don't get your tax return filed, you are going to jail. You run down to the post office and get a bunch of tax forms, take one look at them, and conclude that it will be summer before you figure out where to put what. In desperation you grab everything and run to H&R Block. In no time at all its tax specialists will have prepared your tax return. You get peace of mind and possibly a refund check and H&R Block gets $61.95 of your money.

3. Is the company conservatively financed?

In 2000, H&R Block had a total long-term debt of $872 million and strong earnings of $251 million. It could easily pay off its entire debt in only 3.5 years.

4. Are the earnings of the company strong and do they show an upward trend?

H&R Block's tax year ends June 1. This means that its 1999 fiscal year ended on June 1, 2000. Warren's analysis would've been based on 1999's earnings, which were $2.56 a share. The company's earnings, which grew at an annual compounding rate of 8.2% from 1989 to 1999, have been strong and consistent *(right)*:

YEAR	EARNINGS PER SHARE
89	$1.16
90	1.30
91	1.49
92	1.68
93	1.78
94	1.80
95	1.18
96	1.36
97	1.62
98	2.36
99	2.56

The earnings show an upward trend with the exception of 1995, when they dropped after the sale of a subsidiary.

5. Does the company allocate capital only to businesses within its realm of expertise?

H&R Block has been investing in its operations, developing home-computer tax software, and buying financial service companies. We can answer yes to this question.

6. Has the company been buying back its shares?

It has bought back 9 million of its outstanding shares from 1989 through 2000. This indicates that management uses capital to increase shareholder value when it is possible.

7. ***Does management's investment of retained earnings appear to have increased per share earnings and therefore shareholder value?***

In 1989, H&R Block earned $1.16 a share. This meant that all the capital the business had accumulated until the end of 1989 produced for its owners that year $1.16 a share. Between the end of 1989 and the end of 1999, H&R Block's total earnings were $17.14 a share. Of that $17.14 H&R Block paid out in dividends a total of $9.34 a share and had retained earnings of $7.80 a share ($17.14 – $9.34 = $7.80).

The company's per share earnings increased during this time from $1.16 a share to $2.56 a share. We can attribute the 1989 earnings of $1.18 a share to all the capital invested and retained in H&R Block up to the end of 1989. We can argue that this increase in earnings from $1.16 a share in 1989 to $2.56 a share in 2000 was caused by H&R Block's durable competitive advantage and management's doing an excellent job of investing the $7.80 a share in earnings that the company retained between 1989 and 1999.

Subtracting 1989 per share earnings of $1.16 from 1999's $2.56, the difference is $1.40. We can argue that the $7.80 a share retained between 1989 and 1999 produced $1.40 a share in additional income for 1999, for a return of 17.9% ($1.40 ÷ $7.80 = 17.9%).

Thus we can argue that H&R Block earned a 17.9% return in 1999 on the $7.80 a share in earnings that H&R Block retained from 1989 to 1999.

8. ***Is the company's return on equity above average?***

As we know, Warren considers it a good sign when a business can earn above-average returns on equity. The average return on equity for American corporations during the last thirty years is approximately 12%. To the right is H&R Block's return on equity for the last ten years.

YEAR	ROE
89	24%
90	25
91	26
92	27
93	26
94	27
95	12
96	30
97	13
98	22
99	23

H&R Block had an average annual return on equity for the last ten years of approximately 22%. But more important, the company has earned consistently high returns on equity, which is a strong indication of a durable competitive advantage. (Note: In the years that show a low rate of return, 1995 and 1997, the company sold businesses.)

9. ***Does the company show a consistently high rate of return on total capital?***

A check of *Value Line* shows H&R Block's return on total capital *(right)*:

YEAR	ROTC
89	24%
90	25.1
91	26
92	27
93	26
94	27
95	12
96	30
97	11
98	18
99	15

Over the last ten years the company averaged an annual return on total capital of approximately 20%. But more important, the company has earned consistently high returns on total capital, which is a strong indication of a durable competitive advantage.

10. ***Is the company free to adjust prices to inflation?***

H&R Block has increased its prices right along with inflation.

11. ***Are large capital expenditures required to constantly update the company's plant and equipment?***

There's no big capital expense for manufacturing or for research and development. The company has a lot of offices and a lot of seasonal employment. When H&R Block earns money, it can go out and open more offices, look for other profitable businesses to be in, or buy back its stock, which it does.

SUMMARY OF DATA

Since Warren gets positive responses to the above key questions, he concludes that he can understand H&R Block and that it has a durable competitive advantage. The next question, and it's a big one, is whether H&R Block's stock can be purchased at a price that makes business sense.

PRICE ANALYSIS

As we have said and will say again, identify a company with a durable competitive advantage and then let the market price determine the buy decision.

INITIAL RATE OF RETURN AND RELATIVE VALUE TO GOVERNMENT BONDS

In the case of H&R Block, the per share earnings in 1999 were $2.56. Divide $2.56 by the long-term government-bond interest rate for 1999, approximately 6%, and you get a relative value of $42.67 a share. This means that if you paid $42.67 for a share of H&R Block, you would be getting a return equal to that of the government bonds. In the summer of 1999 you could have bought H&R Block stock for as little as $28 a share. As we said, Warren paid an average price of approximately $29 a share.

With 1999 earnings coming in at $2.56 a share, if you had paid, say, $28 a share, you would be getting an initial rate of return of approximately 9%. A review of H&R Block's per share earnings growth rate for the last ten years indicates that it has been growing at an annual compounding rate of 8.2%. Thus, you can ask yourself this question: What would I rather own—$29 worth of a government bond with a static return of 6% or a H&R Block equity/bond with an initial rate of return of 9%, which has a coupon that is projected to grow at 8.2% a year?

H&R BLOCK'S STOCK AS AN EQUITY/BOND

At the beginning of 1999, H&R Block had a per share equity value of $12.88. If the company can maintain its average annual return on equity of 22% over the next ten years, and we project that it will retain approximately 40% of that return (Note: In projecting what the company will retain, use a historical average for the last seven to ten years), then per share equity value should grow at an annual rate of approximately 8.8% (40% of 22% equals 8.8%), to approximately $29.93 a share in year ten, 2009. (On your Texas Instruments BA-35 Solar calculator, punch in $12.88 as the present value, PV; 10 for the number of years, N; 8.8% for the annual rate of interest, %i; hit the CPT button and then the future value button, FV; and $29.93 will appear as your future value.)

If per share equity is $29.93 in 2009, and H&R Block is still earning a 22% return on equity, then H&R Block should report per share earnings of $6.58 a share ($29.93 x .22 = $6.58). If H&R Block is trading at its average P/E for the last ten years, 22, the stock should have a market price of approximately $144.76 a share ($6.58 x 22 = $144.76). You can argue that if you paid $29 a share in 1999 and sold it in 2009 for $144.76, you would be earning a projected pretax annual compounding return of 17.4%. (Note: Your projected pretax compounding annual rate of return will increase if you include any dividends you are paid when you own the stock. To keep things simple, until your feet get wet, we have excluded the dividend component from the first two examples, H&R Block and La-Z-Boy, and have included it in the last two examples, Gannett Corporation and Freddie Mac.)

PROJECTING AN ANNUAL COMPOUNDING RETURN USING THE HISTORICAL ANNUAL PER SHARE EARNINGS GROWTH

Warren can figure that if per share earnings continue to grow at 8.2% annually, then per share earnings should grow to $5.65 by 2009. If H&R Block is trading in 2009 at its average annual P/E ratio of the last ten years, 22, then we can calculate that market price will be $124.30 ($5.65 x 22 = $124.30).

If you were Warren and had spent $29 for a share of H&R Block stock in 1999, using this method, you could project that in ten years it would be worth $124.30 a share. This equates to a pretax annual compounding return of about 15.6%. (You can get these figures by taking out the Texas Instruments BA-35 Solar calculator and punching in $29 for the present value, PV; 10 for the number of years, N; and $124.30 for the future value, FV. Hit the CPT key followed by the interest key, %i, and presto, your annual compounding rate of return will appear, 15.6%).

SUMMARY OF ANALYSIS

In 2000, Berkshire bought approximately 8.43% of H&R Block's outstanding shares. Warren can argue that Berkshire bought an H&R Block equity/bond with a yield of approximately 9% with a coupon projected to grow at approximately 8.2% a year. He could also figure that if he held the stock for ten years, his projected pretax annual compounding return would be between 15.6% and 17.4%. This means that in ten years' time Berkshire's investment of $29 a share would be worth in pretax terms somewhere between $124 and $144 a share. Sounds impossible, doesn't it? Consider this: By June 1, 2001, H&R Block's shares were trading at $60 a share, which gives Warren a one-year return on his investment of 107%. When you invest in a company with a durable competitive advantage, you don't always have to wait ten years to get rich.

CASE STUDY TWO

LA-Z-BOY, 2000

La-Z-Boy is the king of reclining chairs. It also manufactures upholstered chairs and sofas, sleeper sofas, tables, dining-room and bedroom furniture. They have been in business for more than forty years. That's durability. Warren first saw the numbers on this one in *Value Line* and has been following it for years. After the market crashed in February 2000 he began buying the stock at approximately $14 a share. As of December 2001 it was trading at $22.50. It's a fantastic business.

DOING YOUR DETECTIVE WORK

Warren first became aware of the company when he took a load off his feet and sat in a La-Z-Boy. His purchase of the Nebraska Furniture Mart drove home the durability of this product. *Value Line* follows the company so it is easy to keep an eye on its numbers.

1. ***Does the company sell any brand-name products or services that might have a durable competitive advantage or does it sell a price-competitive product or service?***

When you think of reclining chairs, you think of La-Z-Boy. It also owns brand-name furniture manufacturers England/Corsair, Centurian, Sam Moore, and Bauhaus USA.

2. ***Do you understand how the product or service works?***
   You get home from work, exhausted, feet hurting, and you head straight for your La-Z-Boy, flop yourself down, flick on the TV, and relax.

3. ***Is the company conservatively financed?***
   In 2000, La-Z-Boy had a total long-term debt of $100 million, which, given its strong earnings of $92 million, it could easily pay off in 1.2 years.

4. ***Are the earnings of the company strong and do they show an upward trend?***
   La-Z-Boy's earnings for 2000 were $1.61 a share and have been growing at an annual compounding rate of 14.1% from 1990 to 2000 *(right)*. Earnings are strong, consistent, and show an upward trend.

Year	Earnings per Share
90	$ .43
91	.46
92	.50
93	.63
94	.67
95	.71
96	.83
97	.92
98	1.24
99	1.56
00	1.61

5. ***Does the company allocate capital only to businesses within its realm of expertise?***
   Yes. La-Z-Boy has been investing in its operations and acquiring other furniture manufacturers.

6. ***Has the company been buying back its shares?***
   La-Z-Boy bought back 2%, or 1.4 million, of its outstanding shares from 1990 through 2000. This indicates that management uses capital to increase shareholder value when it is possible.

7. ***Does management's investment of retained earnings appear to have increased per share earnings and therefore shareholder value?***
   In 1990, La-Z-Boy earned $.43 a share. This meant that all

the capital the business had accumulated until the end of 1990 produced for its owners $.43 a share that year. Between the end of 1990 and the end of 2000, La-Z-Boy's total earnings were $9.12 a share. Of that $9.12, La-Z-Boy paid out in dividends a total of $2.63, leaving retained earnings of $6.49 a share ($9.12 – $2.63 = $6.49).

Between the end of 1990 and the end of 2000, La-Z-Boy earned a total of $9.12 a share and paid out in dividends a total of $2.63 a share, adding $6.49 a share to its equity base. The company's per share earnings increased during this time from $.43 to $1.61 a share. We can attribute the 1990 earnings of $.43 a share to all the capital invested and retained in La-Z-Boy up to the end of 1990. We can also argue that this increase in 1990 to $1.61 was caused by La-Z-Boy's durable competitive advantage and management's doing an excellent job of investing the $6.49 a share in retained earnings.

Subtracting 1990 per share earnings of $.43 from 2000's $1.61, the difference is $1.18. We can argue that the $6.49 a share retained between 1990 and 2000 produced $1.18 a share in additional income for 2000, for a return of 18.18% ($1.18 ÷ $6.49 = 18.18%).

Thus we can argue that La-Z-Boy earned an 18.18% return in 2000 on the $6.49 a share in earnings that La-Z-Boy retained from 1990 to 2000.

8. ***Is the company's return on equity above average?***

As we know, Warren considers it a good sign when a business can earn above-average returns on equity. An average return on equity for the American Corporations during the last thirty years is approximately 12%. La-Z-Boy's return on equity for the last ten years looks like this *(right)*:

YEAR	ROE
91	10.2%
92	10.4
93	11.9
94	11.2
95	11.4
96	11.4
97	12.6
98	15.9
99	17.0
00	16.5

This gives La-Z-Boy an average annual return on equity for the last ten years of approximately 12.8%, which is slightly above average for American companies. But what is important is that in 1999 and 2000, the company is showing much higher returns on equity.

9. ***Does the company show a consistently high rate of return on total capital?***

Value Line shows La-Z-Boy's return on total capital as follows *(right)*:

YEAR	ROTC
90	9.0%
91	9.1
92	9.0
93	10.5
94	9.5
95	10.2
96	11.3
97	11.1
98	14.3
99	14.5
00	14.5

La-Z-Boy had an average annual return on total capital for the last ten years of approximately 12.3%, which is slightly above average. But more important, in the last three years we see that the company has earned consistently high returns on total capital, which is a strong indication of a durable competitive advantage.

10. ***Is the company free to adjust prices to inflation?***

La-Z-Boy has increased its prices right along with inflation.

11. ***Are large capital expenditures required to constantly update the company's plant and equipment?***

The company has been making the same reclining chair, with slight modifications, for the last forty years. There is no need to constantly retool its manufacturing plant or spend earnings on research and development.

When La-Z-Boy earns money, it can go out and buy other furniture companies or buy back its own stock, which it does.

SUMMARY OF DATA

Since Warren gets positive responses to the above key questions, he concludes that he can understand La-Z-Boy and that it has a durable competitive advantage. The next and most important question is whether La-Z-Boy's stock can be purchased at a price that makes business sense.

PRICE ANALYSIS

Identify a company with a durable competitive advantage, then let the market price determine the buy decision.

INITIAL RATE OF RETURN AND RELATIVE VALUE TO GOVERNMENT BONDS

In the case of La-Z-Boy, the per share earnings in 2000 were $1.61 a share. Divide $1.61 by the long-term government-bond interest rate for 2000, approximately 6%, and you get a relative value of $26.83 a share. This means that if you paid $26.83 for a share of La-Z-Boy, you would be getting a return equal to that of the government bonds. In 2000 you could have bought La-Z-Boy stock for as little as $14 a share, which was the average price Warren paid.

With 2000 earnings coming in at $1.61 a share, if you had paid, say, $14 a share, you would be getting an initial rate of return of approximately 11.5%. La-Z-Boy's per share earnings growth for the last ten years has averaged an annual compounding rate of 14.1%. What would you rather own—$14 worth of a government bond with a static return of 6% or a La-Z-Boy equity/bond with an initial rate of return of 11.5%, which has a coupon that is projected to grow at 14.1% a year?

LA-Z-BOY'S STOCK AS AN EQUITY/BOND

At the beginning of 2000, La-Z-Boy had a per share equity value of $9.80. If the company can maintain its average annual return on equity of 12.8% over the next ten years, and we project that it will retain approximately 71% of that return (Note: In projecting what the company will retain use a historical average of seven to ten years), then per share equity value should grow annually at approximately 9.1% (71% of 12.8% equals 9.1%), to approximately $23.41 a share in 2010. (On your Texas Instruments BA-35 Solar calculator, punch in $9.80 as the present value, PV; 10 for the number of years, N; 9.1% for the annual rate of interest, %i; hit the CPT button and then the future value button, FV, and $23.41 will appear as your future value.)

If per share equity value is $23.41 in 2010, and La-Z-Boy is still earning a 12.8% return on equity, then La-Z-Boy should report per share earnings of $2.99 a share ($23.41 x .128 = $2.99). If La-Z-Boy is trading at its average P/E for the last ten years, approximately 15, the stock should have a market price of approximately $44.85 a share ($2.99 x 15 = $44.85). You can argue that if you paid $14 a share in 2000 and that you sold it in 2010 for $44.85 a share, you would be earning for the ten years a pretax annual compounding rate of return of 12.34%. (Note: Your pretax annual compounding return will increase if you add in the dividends paid from 2000 to 2010.)

PROJECTING AN ANNUAL COMPOUNDING RETURN USING THE HISTORICAL ANNUAL PER SHARE EARNINGS GROWTH

Warren can figure that if per share earnings continue to grow at 14.1% annually, then per share earnings should grow to $6.02 by 2010. If La-Z-Boy is trading in 2010 at its average annual P/E ratio of the last ten years, 15, then we can calculate that market price will be $90.30 ($6.02 x 15 = $90.30).

If you were Warren and had spent $14 for a share of La-Z-Boy stock in 2000, using this method, you could project that in ten years it would be worth $90.30 a share. This equates to a pretax annual compounding return of approximately 20%. (You can get these figures by taking out the Texas Instruments BA-35 Solar calculator and punching in $14 for the present value, PV; 10 for the number of years, N; and $90.30 for the future value, FV. Hit the CPT key followed by the interest key, %i, and presto, your annual compounding rate of return will appear, 20%.)

SUMMARY OF ANALYSIS

Warren can argue that Berkshire bought a La-Z-Boy equity/bond with a yield of approximately 11.5% with a coupon projected to grow at approximately 14.1% a year. He could also figure that if he held the stock for ten years, his projected pretax annual compounding return would be between 12.34% and 20%.

This means that in ten years' time Berkshire's investment of $14 a share would be worth in pretax terms somewhere between $44.85 a share and $90.30 a share. Doesn't sound possible does it? Consider this: By December 2001, La-Z-Boy's shares were trading at $22 a share, which gives Warren an annual rate of return on his 1.5-year investment of approximately 35%. A company with a durable competitive advantage can often surprise you on the upside.

ORIGINAL BUFFETTOLOGY CASE STUDIES

GANNETT CORPORATION, 1994

Warren's love affair with the newspaper business probably started when he was a boy living in Washington, D.C., where he had a *Washington Post* newspaper route. As you've read here, he later took a sizable position in that company.

In the summer of 1994, during the middle of an advertising recession, Warren began to buy large blocks of the Gannett Corporation, a newspaper holding company. He eventually spent $335,216,000 for 13,709,000 shares of Gannett's common stock. This equates to a split-adjusted purchase price of $24.45 a share. Let's look and see what he found so enticing. (Please note: This analysis of Warren's investment in Gannett Corporation originally appeared in the first edition of *Buffettology,* published in 1996. The stock split two-for-one in 1997. To assist in comparing our earlier projected results with actual results, we have adjusted the historical figures to reflect the two-for-one split.)

DOING YOUR DETECTIVE WORK

The scuttlebutt work on this one is easy. We all know *USA Today,* the newspaper that you can find on any newsstand in America. If you have read this gem of mass circulation, then you may have asked yourself, I wonder who publishes this newspaper and is it publicly traded? Well, Gannett publishes it and it is publicly traded.

A check of the *Value Line Investment Survey* tells us that Gannett publishes 190 newspapers in thirty-eight states and U.S. territories. Its two largest publications are the *Detroit News* (cir: 312,093) and *USA Today* (cir: 2.1 million). Gannett also owns thirteen radio stations and fifteen network-affiliated TV stations.

Once you have assembled the financial information, it's time to work through our questions.

1. ***Does the company have any identifiable consumer monopolies or brand-name products, or do they sell a commodity product?***

   Newspapers and radio and TV stations, we know, are good businesses. Usually a newspaper is a great business if it is the only game in town—less competition means bigger advertising revenue for the owners. The majority of Gannett Corporation's newspapers are, we found, the only game in town! Nice.

2. ***Do you understand how it works?***

   This is, yes, another of those cases where you, the consumer/investor, have intimate knowledge of the product. You're stuck in an out-of-town airport with nothing to do, so you go to the newsstand and buy a newspaper. Which one do you buy? The local paper? No. You haven't any interest in what is going on in local government. But, hey, there's *USA Today*, and it has national news!

3. ***Is the company conservatively financed?***

   In 1994 the company had a total long-term debt of $767 million and a little over $1.8 billion in equity. Given its strong earnings in 1994 of $465 million, Gannett could pay off its entire debt in less than two years.

4. ***Are the earnings of the company strong and do they show an upward trend?***

   Earnings in 1994 were $1.62 a share and had been growing at an annual rate of 8.75% from 1984 to 1994, and at a rate of 5.4% from 1989 to 1994. *(right)*. Earnings were stable, increasing every year from 1984 to 1994 with the exception of 1990 and

YEAR	EARNINGS
84	$ .70
85	.79
86	.86
87	.99
88	1.13
89	1.24
90	1.18
91	1.00
92	1.20
93	1.36
94	1.62

1991, when the entire publishing and media industry was experiencing a recession due to weakening advertising rates. Remember, a general recession in an industry is often a buying opportunity.

The yearly per share earnings figures are strong and show an upward trend. That's what we are looking for.

5. ***Does company allocate capital only to businesses within its realm of experience?***

   Yes. It stays in the media industry.

6. ***Has the company has been buying back its shares?***

   Yes. It bought back 42.4 million of its outstanding shares from 1988 through 1994. This is a sign that management uses capital to increase shareholder value when it is possible.

7. ***Does management's investment of retained earnings appear to have increased per share earnings and therefore shareholder value?***

   From 1984 to 1994 the company had retained earnings of \$5.82 a share. Per share earnings grew by \$.92 a share, from \$.70 a share at the end of 1984 to \$1.62 by the end of 1994. Thus, we can argue that the retained earnings of \$5.82 a share produced in 1994 an increase in after-tax corporate income of \$.92, which equates to a 15.8% rate of return (\$.92 ÷ 5.82 = 15.8%).

8. ***Is the company's return on equity above average?***

   As we know, Warren considers it a good sign when a business can earn above-average returns on equity. An average return on equity for the American Corporations during the last thirty years is approximately 12%. Gannett's return on equity for the eleven years up to 1994 is as follows *(right)*:

YEAR	ROE
84	19.6%
85	19.9
86	19.3
87	19.8
88	20.4
89	19.9
90	18.3
91	19.6
92	21.9
93	20.8
94	25.5

   Gannett had an average

annual return on equity for those eleven years of 20.4%. But more important, the company has consistently earned high returns on equity, which indicates that management is doing an excellent job in profitably allocating retained earnings to new projects.

9. ***Does the company show a consistently high return on total capital?***
   Gannett's return on total capital during this period ranged from a low of 11.2% to a high of 18.8%, with an average of 15.3%—which is what we are looking for.

10. ***Is the company free to adjust prices to inflation?***
    Newspapers used to cost a dime, now they cost fifty cents to a dollar. But newspapers and TV stations make their real money by selling advertising. If you own the only newspaper in town, you can charge high advertising rates because there is not much in the way of alternatives. As noted earlier, classified advertising, supermarkets, auto dealers, and entertainment businesses, such as movie theaters, must advertise in the local newspaper. As a whole, we can assume that Gannett can adjust its prices to inflation without losing sales.

11. ***Are large capital expenditures required to constantly update the company's plant and equipment?***
    All the benefits of earning tons of money can be offset by a company's constantly having to make large capital expenditures to stay competitive. Newspapers and broadcast stations are Gannett's mainstays. So once its initial infrastructure is in place, not a lot is needed down the road for capital equipment or for research and development. Printing presses run for decades before they wear out, and TV and radio stations only need an occasional new transmitter.

This means that when Gannett makes money, it doesn't have to go out and spend it on research and development or major costs for upgrading plant and equipment. Gannett can instead go out and buy more newspapers and radio stations or buy back its stock. This means that Gannett's shareholders get richer and richer.

SUMMARY OF DATA

Since Warren gets positive responses to the above key questions, he concludes that Gannett fits into his "realm of confidence," and that its earnings can be predicted with a fair degree of certainty. But a positive response to these questions *does not* invoke an automatic buy response. We still have to calculate whether the market price for the stock will allow a return equal to or better than on our other options.

PRICE ANALYSIS

Identify a company with a durable competitive advantage, then let the market price determine the buy decision.

INITIAL RATE OF RETURN AND RELATIVE VALUE TO GOVERNMENT BONDS

Gannett's per share earnings in 1994 were $1.62. Divide $1.62 by the long-term government-bond interest rate for 1994, approximately 7%, and you get a relative value of $23.14 a share. This means that if you paid $23.14 for a share of Gannett, you would be getting a return equal to that of the government bonds. In 1994 you could have bought Gannett stock for $23.10 to $29.50 a share. If you had paid what Warren paid, $24.45, you would be getting an estimated initial return of 6.6%.

A review of Gannett's per share earnings growth rate for the last ten years indicates that it has been growing at an annual compounding rate of 8.75%. Thus, what would you rather own—$24.45 worth of a government bond with a static return of 7% or a Gannett equity/bond with an initial rate of return of 6.6%, which has a coupon that is projected to grow at 8.75% a year?

GANNETT'S STOCK AS AN EQUITY/BOND

In 1994, Gannett had a per share equity value of $6.52 (as reported in *Value Line*). If Gannett can maintain its average annual return on equity of 20.4% over the next ten years and continues to retain a historical 60% of that return, then per share equity value should grow at an annual rate of approximately 12.24% (60% of 20.4% equals 12.24%), to approximately $20.68 a share in year 2004. (On your Texas Instruments BA-35 Solar calculator, punch in $6.52 as the present value, PV; 10 for the number of years, N; 12.24 for the annual rate of interest, %i; hit the CPT button and then the future value button, FV; and $20.68 will appear as your future value.)

In 2004, if per share equity value is $20.68, and Gannett is still earning a 20.4% return on equity, then Gannett should report per share earnings of $4.22 a share ($20.68 x .204 = $4.22). If Gannett is trading at its low P/E for the last ten years, 15, the stock should have a market price of approximately $63.30 a share ($4.22 x 15 = $63.30). Multiply by the ten-year high P/E of 23, and you get a per share market price of $97.06 ($4.22 x 23 = $97.06). Add in the projected total dividend pool of $11.92 a share earned from 1994 to 2004 and you get a projected total pretax annual compounding rate of return on your initial investment of $24.45 a share of somewhere between 11.87% and 16.09% for the ten years.

PROJECTING AN ANNUAL COMPOUNDING RETURN USING THE HISTORICAL ANNUAL PER SHARE EARNINGS GROWTH

If per share earnings continue to grow at 8.75% annually, and if Gannett continues to retain 60% of its earnings and pay out as dividends the other 40%, then the following per share earnings and dividend-disbursement picture will develop over the next ten years *(right)*:

YEAR	EARNINGS	DIVIDENDS
95	$1.76	$ .70
96	1.91	.76
97	2.08	.83
98	2.26	.90
99	2.46	.98
00	2.67	1.07
01	2.91	1.16
02	3.16	1.26
03	3.44	1.37
04	3.74	1.49
		$10.52

This means that in 2004 Warren can project that Gannett will have per share earnings of $3.74. If Gannett is trading at the lowest P/E ratio that it has had in the last ten years, 15, then the market price will be $56.10 ($3.74 x 15 = $56.10). Add in the pretax dividend pool of $10.52 and our total pretax return jumps to $66.62 a share.

If Gannett is trading at the highest P/E that it has had in the last ten years, 23, then the market price will be $86.02 a share in 2004 ($3.74 x 23 = $86.02). Add in the pretax dividend pool of $10.52 and our total pretax return becomes $96.54.

If you were Warren and had spent $24.45 a share for your Gannett stock in 1994, using this method, you could project that in ten years it would be worth with dividends somewhere between $66.62 and $96.54 a share. This equates to a pretax annual compounding return of somewhere between 10.55% and 14.72%. (You can get these figures by taking out the Texas Instruments BA-35 Solar calculator and punching in $24.45 for the present value, PV; 10 for the number of years, N; and either $66.62 or $96.54 for the future value, FV. Hit the CPT key followed by the interest key, %i, and presto, your annual compounding rate of return will appear—either 10.55% or 14.72%).

SUMMARY OF ANALYSIS

In the summer and fall of 1994, Warren bought approximately 13,709,000 shares of Gannett common stock for $24.45 a share, for a total purchase price of $335,216,000. When Warren bought the stock, he could argue that he had just bought a Gannett equity/bond with a yield of 6.6% with a coupon projected to grow at approximately 8.75% a year. He could also figure that if he held the stock for ten years, his projected pretax annual compounding return would be between 10.55% and 16.09%.

This means that in ten years' time his investment of $335,216,000 in Gannett would be worth in pretax terms somewhere between $913,226,960 and $1,490,745,000.

HOW ACCURATE WERE WARREN'S GANNETT PROJECTIONS?

When making predictions the ultimate test is time. How good was this one? Well, we have actual figures through 2000 to check against our projections *(see next page)*:

As you can see, Gannett's actual results have surpassed our projections in four of the last six years, with the margin of error rang-

Projected Earnings Compared to Actual Earnings

Year	Projected Earnings	Actual Earnings	Margin of Error
95	$1.76	$1.71	–2.8%
96	1.91	1.89	–1.0
97	2.08	2.50	+20.2
98	2.26	2.86	+26.5
99	2.46	3.30	+34.1
00	2.91	3.63	+25.0

ing from –2.8% to +34.1%. Per share earnings during this period grew at an annual rate of 16.2% as opposed to our projected 8.75%. The stock market, in 2002, seeing this performance has bid up Gannett's shares into the $76 range. Warren paid $24.45 a share in 1994. If he sold it in 2002 for $76 a share, his annual pretax compounding return, excluding dividends, would be approximately 15.2%. Which is right on the money.

FEDERAL HOME LOAN MORTGAGE CORPORATION, 1992

Warren's involvement with the banking industry led him to the doorstep of the Federal Home Loan Mortgage Corporation, popularly known as Freddie Mac. Freddie Mac securitized and guarantees mortgages. When you take out a mortgage with your local bank, the bank sells that loan to Freddie Mac, which in turn packages it (with other mortgages that it has bought) into a large pool of mortgages. Freddie Mac then sells interests in that pool of mortgages to individual investors. When you pay interest on your mortgage, your interest payment ends up in the hands of those investors. On Wall Street these securitized pools of mortgages are called mortgage-backed bonds.

In 1988, when Freddie Mac shifted from being owned by banks to being publicly traded, Berkshire acquired 4% of the company through a Berkshire subsidiary, Wesco Financial. In 1992, with Freddie Mac trading at or near its all-time high, Warren increased

Berkshire's holdings in Freddie Mac by 34,844,400 shares, paying approximately $337 million or $9.67 a share. At the end of 1992 Berkshire owned 9% of Freddie Mac.

Our second case study will be of Berkshire's 1992 increase in its holdings of Freddie Mac. Our focus is on the economics of Freddie Mac that in 1992 compelled Warren to add it to his position. (Please note that Freddie Mac split its stock four-for-one in 1997. All historical figures have been adjusted to reflect this split.)

DOING YOUR DETECTIVE WORK

The scuttlebutt on this one would not be easy. Although it is a visible stock, it is unlikely that you will ever have anything to do with the company in real life.

Value Line and a number of investment houses cover the stock, so you may have discovered it from one of those sources. A check of the business periodicals and a call to the company for annual reports and 10-Ks will supply you with sufficient information to work through our list of questions.

1. ***Does the company have any identifiable consumer monopolies or brand-name products, or does it produce or sell a commodity product?***

   Although mortgages are a commodity product, Freddie Mac, along with a similar company called Fannie Mae, are essentially government-sanctioned entities created by Congress to raise money to help people who want to buy home mortgages. Freddie Mac and Fannie Mae have developed a quasi-monopoly on this segment of the market.

2. ***Do you understand how it works?***

   Most people understand what a mortgage is and how it works. Freddie Mac buys a lot of mortgages from banks and mortgage companies, bundles them together, then sells interests in the bundle to financial institutions, such as insurance companies. This allows banks and mortgage companies to keep making loans.

3. ***Is the company conservatively financed?***

   No. However, Freddie Mac's liabilities are offset by corresponding assets that are highly liquid—mortgages. But since it does enjoy "government agency status," any financial problems would draw the immediate attention of the U.S. Congress, which has a *big* checkbook—the American taxpayer—to help see its little brother through hard times. Still, if there were considerable defaults on the underlying mortgages in the pools, then Freddie Mac could find itself in trouble.

4. ***Are the earnings of the company strong—with an upward trend?***
   The company's earnings grew at 17.6% annually from 1986 to 1992. Earnings are stable, with an upward trend *(see below).*

5. ***Does the company allocate capital only to businesses within its realm of expertise?***
   Yes, the mortgage-backed securities industry.

6. ***Has the company been buying back its shares?***
   No. Nor has it been issuing new shares for acquisitions. (Please note: In 1995, Freddie Mac started a stock buyback program.)

7. ***Does management's investment of retained earnings appear to have increased per share earnings and therefore shareholder value.***

YEAR	EARNINGS PER SHARE
86	$.31
87	.38
88	.48
89	.55
90	.58
91	.77
92	.82

   The company, from the end of 1986 to the end of 1992, had retained earnings of $2.75 a share, while per share earnings grew by $.51 a share. Thus, we can argue that the retained earnings of $2.75 a share produced in 1992 an after-corporate-income-tax return of $.51, which equates to an 18.5% rate of return.

8. ***Is the company's return on equity above average?***
   Warren considers it a good sign when a business can earn above-average returns on equity. An average return on equity for American corporations over the last thirty years is approximately 12%. The return on equity for Freddie Mac is as follows:

YEAR	ROE
86	25.9%
87	25.5
88	24.1
89	22.8
90	19.4
91	21.6
92	17.4

This is an average return on equity for those seven years of 22.3%. But more important, the company has earned consistently high returns on equity, which indicates that management is doing an excellent job of allocating retained earnings and expanding the business.

9. Does the company show a consistently high return on total capital?

Freddie Mac is a finance company, so instead of looking at the return on total capital, we will be looking at the return on total assets, which was averaging 1.3% when Warren was buying the stock. Remember, with a financial institution, anything over 1% is what we are looking for.

10. Is the company free to adjust prices to inflation?

Inflation causes housing prices to rise. Increased housing prices mean bigger mortgages. Bigger mortgages mean that Freddie Mac gets a larger pie to cut from, which means increased profits. If you charge 6% to raise $100 million in mortgage money, you make $6 million. If prices double and the $100 million becomes $200 million and you charge 6%, you make $12 million. The bigger the numbers, the more money Freddie Mac makes.

11. Are large capital expenditures required to constantly update the company's plant and equipment?

Freddie Mac securitizes pooled mortgages, which requires little capital equipment or research and development. It can expand operations at will with nominal plant expansion. Large capital expenditures are not needed to update the company's plant and equipment.

SUMMARY OF DATA

Since Warren gets positive responses to the above key questions, he concludes that Freddie Mac fits into his "realm of confidence" and that its earnings can be predicted with a fair degree of certainty. But a positive response to these questions does not invoke an automatic buy response. We still have to calculate the company's intrinsic value and determine whether the market price for the stock will allow a return equal to or better than on our other options.

PRICE ANALYSIS

Identify a company with a durable competitive advantage, then let the market price determine the buy decision.

INITIAL RATE OF RETURN AND RELATIVE VALUE TO GOVERNMENT BONDS

In 1992, Freddie Mac reported earnings of $.82 a share. Divide $.82 by the long-term interest rate for 1992, which was 7.39%, and you get a relative value of $11.09 a share. That means that if you paid $11.09 for a share of Freddie Mac, you would be getting a return equal to that of government bonds. In 1992 you could have bought Freddie Mac stock for between $8.45 and $12.32 a share. If you paid what Warren was paying, an average of $9.67, you would be getting an initial rate of return of 8.5%.

Freddie Mac's annual per share earnings growth rate for the last seven years was 17.6%. Thus, would you rather own $11.09 worth of a government bond with a static return of 7.39% or a Freddie Mac equity/bond with an initial rate of return of 8.5%, which has a coupon that is projected to increase annually at 17.6%?

FREDDIE MAC'S STOCK AS AN EQUITY/BOND

If Freddie Mac can maintain the average annual return on equity that it earned over the last seven years, 22.3% (as reported in *Value Line*), and if over the next ten years it annually retains its current average of 72% of that return, then per share equity value should grow from $4.92 a share in 1992 to approximately $21.79 a share by 2002.

If per share equity value is $21.79 in 2002 and Freddie Mac is still earning a 22.3% return on equity, then Freddie Mac should report per share earnings of $4.86 a share ($21.79 x .223 = $4.86).

If Freddie Mac is trading at its historical low P/E of 9, this will equate to a market price of $43.74 a share ($4.86 x 9 = $43.74). Multiplied by the historical high P/E of 12.8, you get a per share market price of $62.20. Add the dividend pool of approximately $7.61 and you get a total pretax return of somewhere between $51.35 and $69.81.

This means that Warren's investment of $9.67 a share in 1992 is projected to produce a pretax annual compounding return of between 18.17% and 21.85%. When adjusted for corporate income taxes, this equates to an annual compounding after-tax return of between 14.82% and 17.92%. (One hundred thousand dollars compounding at an annual rate of 17.92% would be worth $519,845 in ten years.)

PROJECTING AN ANNUAL COMPOUNDING RETURN USING THE HISTORICAL ANNUAL PER SHARE EARNINGS GROWTH

If per share earnings continue to grow at 17.6% annually, and if Freddie Mac continues to pay out in dividends 28% of those earnings, then the following per share earnings and dividend disbursement picture will develop over the next ten years *(below)*:

This means that Warren can project that Freddie Mac will have per share earnings of $4.14 in 2002. If Freddie Mac is trading at its lowest P/E ratio ever, 9, then the market price for the stock in 2002 will be $37.26 ($4.14 x 9 = $37.26). If the stock is trading at its highest P/E ever, 12.8, then the market price will be $52.99.

Year	Projected Earnings	Projected Dividends
93	$ .96	$ .27
94	1.13	.31
95	1.33	.37
96	1.56	.43
97	1.84	.51
98	2.16	.60
99	2.55	.71
00	2.99	.83
01	3.52	.98
02	4.14	1.16
		$6.17

If you spent $9.67 for a share of Freddie Mac stock in 1992 and in ten years it was worth somewhere between $37.26 and $52.99 a share, then your pretax annual compounding return will be somewhere between 14.4% and

18.5%. (You can get these figures by taking out the calculator and punching in $9.67 for the present value, PV; and 10 for the number of years, N; and either $37.26 or $52.99 for the future value, FV. Hit the CPT key followed by the interest key, %i, and your rate of return will appear.)

If we add in the dividends, which total $6.17, our projected pretax return jumps to somewhere between $43.43 and $59.16, which equates to a pretax annual compounding return between 16.2% and 19.8%.

IN SUMMARY

In 1992, Warren bought approximately 34,844,400 shares of Freddie Mac common stock at approximately $9.67 a share, for a total purchase price of $337 million. When Warren bought the stock, he could argue that he had just bought a Freddie Mac equity/bond with an initial rate of return of 8.5% that would grow at approximately 17.6% a year. He could also figure that if he held the stock for ten years, his pretax annual compounding return would be between 16.2% and 21.85%.

HOW ACCURATE WERE OUR FREDDIE MAC PROJECTIONS?

Just how accurate were our projections? Let's see:

Year	Projected Earnings	Actual Earnings	Margin of Error
93	$ .96	$1.02	+6.2%
94	1.13	1.27	+12.3
95	1.33	1.42	+6.7
96	1.56	1.65	+5.7
97	1.84	1.90	+3.2
98	2.16	2.13	–1.3
99	2.55	2.96	+16.0
00	2.99	3.39	+13.3

Remember, we are making long-term earnings projections, something unheard of on Wall Street. From the looks of things, our projections were a tad conservative. Freddie Mac turned in a better-than-expected performance in seven out of the last eight years. We can live with that. In 2000 the stock traded from $37 to $66 a share. Warren sold his stock in 2000, which he had bought for $9.67 a share in 1992, giving him a pretax annual compounding rate of return, excluding dividends, somewhere between 18% and 27%. He said that Freddie Mac's business model had changed and that he was no longer comfortable with the risk level of the business. With a highly leveraged business like Freddie Mac it can be an overnight disaster when something goes wrong. The most profitable thing to do over the long run is to play it safe. Warren says that the number one rule for getting and staying rich is not to lose the money, and the number 2 rule is not to forget rule number one.

20

Putting Buffettology to Work for You

At this point you should be ready to start thinking like Warren. After you have assembled the financial information about a company that you have found either on the Internet or from *Value Line,* we suggest that you answer the following questions to help guide you through the Buffett investment thought process.

The questions you need to answer are:

1. ***Does the company have an identifiable durable competitive advantage?***

   If yes, describe it in as simple a manner as you can, as you would to a seven-year-old child. Warren likes to keep things simple. If you can't explain it to a child, then the durable competitive advantage probably doesn't exist. If you can't find a durable competitive advantage, keep your powder dry until you do. Waiting for the perfect pitch never bothered Warren.

   Describe the durable competitive advantage here:

   ____

   ____

   ____

   ____

2. ***Do you understand how the product works?***

   Warren believes that if you don't understand how the product works, you will never be able to determine the chances of its becoming obsolete. Product obsolescence is a real and legitimate fear that Warren keeps close to his belly. Warren ensures that he will never fall victim to this trap by fully understanding the nature of the business in which he is investing. If you can't explain it, forget it and find a business you do understand.

Explain how the product works:

____

____

____

____

3. ***If the company in question does have a durable competitive advantage and you understand how it works, then what is the chance that it will become obsolete in the next twenty years?***
   Warren likes to ask himself, will people more than likely be using this product in twenty years? If the answer is yes, continue on with the analysis. If not, stop, go to a movie, and start again in the morning.

Explain why the product won't be obsolete in twenty years:

____

____

____

____

4. ***Does the company allocate capital exclusively in the realm of its expertise?***

   You want a business that knows its game and stays there. If it is a conglomerate, like GE, you need to know whether it has acquired other businesses that have durable competitive advantages or has diversified into a group of weaker price-competitive businesses. If it looks like a great business or a great collection of good businesses, go fetch yourself a glass of your favorite beverage and settle in for some serious analysis.

   If the company is a conglomerate, list the businesses it owns that have durable competitive advantages and are price competitive. Figure out which direction management is headed. Is management allocating capital to buy more of these wonderful durable-competitive-advantage businesses, or is it fixated on price-competitive-commodity businesses?

Durable Competitive Advantage	*Price Competitive*
______________________	______________________
______________________	______________________
______________________	______________________
______________________	______________________
______________________	______________________

5. ***What is the company's per share earnings history and growth rate?***

   If it is consistently strong, continue the analysis. If there is a weak year or two, you need to ask whether this is a onetime event or something that will become the norm. If it is a onetime event, then continue. (Remember, onetime solvable problems often offer a chance to make fantastic profits.) If weak or erratic earnings are routine, then stop your analysis and save your cash until Mr. Market serves you up something better.

If earnings appear consistently strong, you should gather the company's per share earnings for the last ten years—from *Value Line* or an on-line service such as msn.com—and calculate its annual compounding growth rate for that period using the calculation below.

Year		Per Share Earnings	
02		_____	→Present value (base year)
03	one	_____	
____	two	_____	
____	three	_____	
____	four	_____	
____	five	_____	
____	six	_____	
____	seven	_____	
____	eight	_____	
____	nine	_____	
____	ten_____	→Future value	

↑
Number of years from present value base year

Financial equation for use with TI BA-35 Solar calculator: *earnings per share growth rate.* Use the base year's per share earnings as the present value (PV); year ten as your future value (FV); and 10 as your number of years (N). Hit the compute key (CPT) and then the interest key (%i), and your annual compounding growth rate per share will be calculated.

6. ***Is the company consistently earning a high return on equity?***

A company that doesn't earn a high return on equity will not grow over the long term at a sufficient rate to make you rich. You need a fast and powerful ship if you want to get across the water. This means that you need a return on equity of 15% or better. If the company doesn't get a high return on equity, you should put down your pen and take a walk. If it does, gather together the return-on-equity figures for the last ten years and find their average. (Note: Return-on-equity figures can be found in *Value Line* or at an on-line service like msn.com.)

	YEAR	RETURN ON EQUITY
1.	____	_____
2.	____	_____
3.	____	_____
4.	____	_____
5.	____	_____
6.	____	_____
7.	____	_____
8.	____	_____
9.	____	_____
10.	____	_____

Average return on equity ____

Financial equation for use with TI BA-35 Solar calculator: *average return on equity.* Add up the return-on-equity figures over the last ten years and then divide by ten.

7. ***Does the company earn a high return on total capital?***

The reasoning here echoes what we discussed above about return on equity. Unless management shows that it can get a consistently high return on capital, the company is not worth looking into any further.

	YEAR	RETURN ON TOTAL CAPITAL
1.	____	_____
2.	____	_____
3.	____	_____
4.	____	_____
5.	____	_____
6.	____	_____
7.	____	_____
8.	____	_____
9.	____	_____
10.	____	_____

Average return on total capital ____

Financial equation for use with TI BA-35 Solar calculator: *average return on total capital.* Add up the return-on-capital figures over the last ten years and then divide by ten.

8. ***Is the company conservatively financed?***

For a company to pull out of any business difficulties it may encounter, it needs plenty of financial power. Companies with a durable competitive advantage usually create such great wealth for their owners that they are long-term-debt-free or close to it. Standard debt-to-equity ratios give a poor picture of the business's financial strength in that shareholder's equity is seldom used to extinguish debt. The earning power of a business is the only real measure of a company's ability to service and retire its debt. You need to ask yourself, how many years of current net earnings would be required to pay off all the long-term debt of the business in the current year?

Total long-term debt in the current year ________ divided by total net earnings in the current year ________ equals the number of years needed to pay off long-term debt ________. If long-term debt is more than five times current net earnings, be real careful. Debt can kill.

9. ***Is the company actively buying back its shares?***

The repurchasing of shares is one of Warren's favorite tricks to increase his ownership in a company without having to invest any more of his own money.

Take the number of shares outstanding ten years ago ________, subtract from it the number of shares outstanding in the current year ________, and you get the number of shares the company has purchased over the last ten years ________. A negative number indicates the number of shares that the company has added. Warren is looking for a decrease in the number of shares outstanding.

10. ***Is the company free to raise prices with inflation?***

An interesting question that requires that you do a little investigative work. If the company's product is selling at the same price as twenty years ago, then you are more than likely dealing with a commodity business and should give it a pass. If the price of the product has risen on an average of at least 4% a year over the last twenty years, then you can bet the farm that it's the kind of business that can raise prices along with inflation.

Financial equation for use with TI BA-35 Solar calculator: *company's ability to raise prices with inflation.* Use the price of the product twenty years ago as your present value (PV), the current price of the product as your future value (FV), and 20 as your number of years (N). Hit the compute key (CPT) and then the interest key (%i), and your annual compounding growth rate in price for the product will be calculated. (Note: If you get a negative number, it means that you are probably looking at a price-competitive business and should move on.)

Annual growth rate of product's price ________

11. ***Are large capital expenditures required to update plant and equipment?***

This is a question that you can only answer by reading up on the company. Are they building cars or designing software? Do they have to buy big expensive jets or can they use the same equipment for twenty years without any risk of obsolescence? If you get a yes answer to this question, you better be careful.

PRICE ANALYSIS

12. ***Is the company's stock price suffering from a market panic, a business recession, or an individual calamity that is curable?***

As we discussed, these types of situations usually offer the best prices. If you can't buy during one of these events, then you are probably paying full price for the stock. If you want to get rich, you have to learn how to exploit a bad-news situation and the stock market's shortsightedness.

13. ***What is the initial rate of return on the investment and how does it compare to the return on U.S. treasury bonds?***

Take the company's current per share earnings and divide it by the current price of a single share. This will give you the investment's initial rate of return. Then compare the investment's initial rate of return and expected growth rate per share to the return being paid on U.S. treasury bonds. If the treasuries look juicier, the stock might be overpriced.

Initial rate of return: ________

Growth rate: ________

Rate of return on U.S. treasury bonds: ________

14. *What is the company's projected annual compounding return as an equity/bond?*

Take the company's average per share return on equity for the last ten years ________ and subtract the average percentage that is not retained and is paid out as a dividend ________. Use the resulting difference as the rate of growth that the company's book value will grow ________.

Use the company's book value in the current year ________ as the present value (PV), and use the calculated rate of growth for book value as the rate of interest (%i). Punch in 10 for the number of years out that you want to make your projection (N), then hit the CPT key, followed by the future-value key (FV). This will calculate the per share book value of the company ten years out ________.

To determine the selling price of the company's stock ten years out, take the company's future per share book value ________ and multiple it by the average return on equity ________. This will give you the company's projected per share earnings ________. Then multiply the projected earnings ________ by the company's average annual P/E ratio for the last ten years ________. This will give you the company's per share future trading price ________.

Using the company's current market price as your present value (PV) ________ and the projected future trading price as the future value (FV) ________ and the number of years between the two ________ for the (N) key, you can then hit the CPT key and then the %i key, which calculates the projected annual compounding return that the investment will produce ________.

Average annual growth rate for book value for the last ten years ________.

Average percentage paid out as a dividend _______.
Company's book value in the current year _______.
Company's average annual P/E ratio _______.
Projected growth rate of book value over the next ten years _______.
Projected future trading price of the company's stock _______.
Current trading price for the company's stock _______.

15. What is the projected annual compounding return using the historical annual per share earnings growth?

To calculate the projected annual compounding return on an investment purchased in 2002 and sold during 2012, first determine the annual compounding per share growth from 1992 to 2002 (see calculation above). Then, using the 1992 to 2002 per share growth rate, project forward the company's per share earnings to 2012 and multiply by the average annual P/E ratio for 1992 to 2002. This will give you the projected trading price of the stock in 2012.

Per share earnings in 1992 _______
Per share earnings in 2002 _______

Use the 1992 per share earnings as the present value (PV), 2002 per share earnings as the future value (FV), and 10 for the number of years (N). Then hit the CPT key and the %i key, which will give you the company's per share annual compounding growth rate for that period _______.

Now use the company's per share earnings 2002 for your present value (PV), the company's per share annual compounding growth rate for 1992 to 2002 as the interest rate (%i), and 10 for the number of years. Hit the CPT key and then the future value key (FV), which will give you the projected per share earnings of the company for the year 2012 _______.

Take the projected per share earnings of the company for the year 2012 _______ and multiply it by the average annual

YEAR		STOCK PRICE
02		_____→Present value (base year)
03	one	_____
04	two	_____
05	three	_____
06	four	_____
07	five	_____
08	six	_____
09	seven	_____
10	eight	_____
11	nine	_____
12	ten	_____→Future value

↑

Number of years from present value base year

Financial equation for use with TI BA-35 Solar calculator: *projecting the annual compounding rate of return that the investment will earn.* Take the stock's current trading price and use it as your present value (PV). Use the projected future trading price of the stock as your future value (FV), 10 for your number of years (N), and then hit the CPT key and the interest key (%i). This will give you the projected compounding annual return that the investment will produce.

P/E ratio for 1992 to 2002. This will give you the projected trading price for the company's stock in 2012 _______ *(see above).*

DO YOU MAKE THE BUY?

To buy or not to buy is always the question. If the company you are investigating has a durable competitive advantage and you can buy it at a price that makes business sense, then you should jump on it. If you discover that it has a durable competitive advantage but is selling at too high a price, you should wait for a stock market correction, industry recession, or business calamity to create a more attractive situation. If it doesn't have a durable competitive advantage, then put the company out of your mind, go for a long walk, and then get back to looking for one that has.

One more word of advice: Warren once said that the hardest thing in the world to do is to be patient. So don't rush things! You will find a company with a durable competitive advantage selling at the right price, and it will offer you the opportunity to make a fortune. You might not find this perfect situation overnight. We are looking for diamonds, and occasionally the bad-news situation and the stock market's shortsightedness serves them up to us on a platter of gold. Then you only have to reach out and pick one up.

INDEX